GENDER, POWER AND PRIVILEGE
IN EARLY MODERN EUROPE

WOMEN AND MEN IN HISTORY

This series, published for students, scholars and interested general readers, will tackle themes in gender history from the early medieval period through to the present day. Gender issues are now an integral part of all history courses and yet many traditional texts do not reflect this change. Much exciting work is now being done to redress the gender imbalances of the past, and we hope that these books will make their own substantial contribution to that process. We hope that these will both synthesise and shape future developments in gender studies.

The General Editors of the series are *Patricia Skinner* (University of Southampton) for the medieval period; *Pamela Sharpe* (University of Bristol) for the early modern period; and *Penny Summerfield* (University of Lancaster) for the modern period. *Margaret Walsh* (University of Nottingham) was the Founding Editor of the series.

Published books:

GENDER, POWER AND PRIVILEGE IN EARLY MODERN EUROPE

JESSICA MUNNS AND PENNY RICHARDS

PEARSON
Longman

Pearson Education Limited

Head Office:
Edinburgh Gate
Harlow CM20 2JE
Tel: +44 (0)1279 623623
Fax: +44 (0)1279 431059

London Office:
128 Long Acre
London WC2E 9AN
Tel: +44 (0)20 7447 2000
Fax: +44 (0)20 7447 2170
Website: www.history-minds.com

First published in Great Britain in 2003

© Pearson Education Limited 2003

The right of Jessica Munns and Penny Richards to be identified as
Authors of this Work has been asserted by them in accordance
with the Copyright, Designs and Patents Act 1988.

ISBN 0 582 42329 5

British Library Cataloguing in Publication Data
A CIP catalogue record for this book can be obtained from the British Library

Library of Congress Cataloging in Publication Data
A CIP catalog record for this book can be obtained from the Library of Congress

10   9   8   7   6   5   4   3   2
07   06   05   04   03
Typeset in 11/13pt Baskerville MT by Graphicraft Limited, Hong Kong
Printed and bound in Malaysia

The Publishers' policy is to use paper manufactured from sustainable forests.

CONTENTS

CONTENTS

LIST OF FIGURES AND TABLES

FIGURES

TABLES

ACKNOWLEDGEMENTS

We have had a great deal of help in putting this collection of essays together and are happy to have the occasion of this page to present our thanks. We are grateful to the School of History, University of Gloucestershire, for making printing and copying facilities available, and to Beryl Steel for all her invaluable help – and keeping her head when we had long lost ours. We are grateful for help also from colleagues in Information Technology, particularly Scott Jordan, Peter Maller and Chris Haynes. We send our thanks also to Melissa Root at the University of Denver for help in proofing the original manuscript, and we thank Jean Audouin for help with the English version of Marcello Zane's essay, and Simon Barker for help 'Englishing' the essay by Marc Boone, Thérèse de Hemptinne and Walter Prevenier. We thank Robert Sturges for help along the way. Many thanks also to Pam Sharpe, the series editor, and to Heather McCallum at Longman. We thank, as one truly must, our families, which in this case also means each other as we are sisters, and we are very grateful to our cousin Jessica Shapiro.

LIST OF CONTRIBUTORS

Simon Barker teaches English literature in the School of Humanities at the University of Gloucestershire. He has published widely, in books and journals, on aspects of the representation of militarism in early modern culture. He has recently edited, with Hilary Hinds, *The Routledge Anthology of Renaissance Drama*, and is currently finishing a full-length study of the relationship between warfare and the theatre in Renaissance England.

Marc Boone is Professor of Social and Economic History of the Middle Ages at the University of Ghent and author of many book and journal articles in this field. His books include Marc Boone and Maarten Prak (eds), *Individual, Corporate and Judicial Status in European Cities: late Middle Ages and early modern period* (1996) and, with Thérèse de Hemptinne, Willem P. Blockmans (eds), *Secretum scriptorum. Liber alumnorum Walter Prevenier* (1999).

Joan Curbet is a lecturer and researcher at the Departament de Filologia Anglesa i Germanística, Universitat Autonoma de Barcelona. He has published several articles in international books and journals on the inter-relation between religious discourses and literature from the later Middle Ages to Romanticism. He has edited *Medieval Travel Writing 1096–1492: An Interdisciplinary Introduction* (forthcoming, 2002).

Frances E. Dolan teaches in the English Department, and is a member of the History and Women's Studies Departments at the Miami University, Oxford, Ohio. She has written many book and journal articles on issues of gender and law in the early modern period, edited *As You Like It* (2000) and is the author of *Dangerous Familiars: Representations of Domestic Crime in England* (1994) and, most recently, *Whores of Babylon: Catholicism, Gender and Seventeenth-Century Print Culture* (2000).

Thérèse de Hemptinne is Professor of Medieval History (and auxiliary sciences) at the University of Ghent. She has published widely in the area of gender and Medieval history and her works include, with Marc Boone and Willem P. Blockmans (eds), *Secretum scriptorum. Liber alumnorum Walter Prevenier*, 1999; editor (with Walter Prevenier) of: *Actes du congrès de la Commission* *internationale de diplomatique, La diplomatique urbaine en Europe au moyen âge* (Leuven-Apeldoorn, 1999). With Adriaan Verhulst (m.m.v. Lieve De Mey): *De oorkonden der graven van Vlaanderen (juli 1128–sept. 1191), II Uitgave, band II, Regering van Filips van de Elzas (Eerste deel: 1168–1177)* (2001).

Robert Knecht is Emeritus Professor of French History and a Fellow of the Institute for Advanced Research in the Arts and Social Sciences at the University of Birmingham, a Fellow of the Royal Historical Society, and a member of the Société de l'Histoire de France. He has been chairman of the Society for Renaissance Studies and of the Society for the Study of French History. He is a member of the Advisory Board of the Centre for the Study of Renaissance at the University of Warwick. He has published extensively in the field of French History, and his *Renaissance Warrior and Patron: The Reign of Francis I* (1994), recently appeared in a revised French edition under the title *Un Prince de la Renaissance: François Ier et son royaume* (1998). His other books include, *Richelieu* (1991), *The Rise and Fall of Renaissance France, 1483–1610* (1996), which has been published recently in a second edition (2001); *Catherine de Medici* (1998) and *The French Civil Wars 1562–98* (2000).

Anne McLaren is a senior lecturer in the School of History, University of Liverpool. She is the author of many articles on late sixteenth- and early seventeenth-century political and religious history and her essay 'Reading Sir Thomas Smith's *De Republica Anglorum* as Protestant Apologetic', *The Historical Journal* (1999) was awarded the 2000 Walter D. Love Prize by the North American Council of British Studies. She is the author of *Political Culture in the Reign of Elizabeth I: Queen and Commonwealth* (1999) and is currently working on a book entitled *Embodied Kingship: Regicide and Republicanism in England 1590–1650*.

Jessica Munns teaches in the English Department at the University of Denver. She has published many book and journal articles on Restoration and eighteenth-century literature, co-edited an anthology on cultural studies (1995), written *Restoration Politics and Drama: The Plays of Thomas Otway 1676–85* (1996) and has recently edited his play *Venice Preserv'd* (2001). With Penny Richards she has co-edited *The Clothes that Wear Us: Dressing and Transgressing in Eighteenth-Century Culture* (1995). She has co-edited a collection of eighteenth-century plays based on Aphra Behn's narrative *Oroonoko* (2003).

Walter Prevenier teaches at the University of Ghent and is the author of many book and journal articles, and books, which include: (with Willem P. Blockmans), *The Burgundian Netherlands* (1986); *Marriage and Social Mobility in the Middle Ages* (1992); *Le prince et le peuple. Images de la société du temps des ducs de Bourgogne, 1384–1530* (1998), (with Willem P. Blockmans) *The Promised Lands: the Low Countries under Burgundian rule, 1369–1530* (revised edition, 1999) and, with Martha Howell, *From reliable sources: an introduction to historical methods* (2001).

Penny Richards teaches history in the School of Humanities at the University of Gloucestershire; she has written book and journal articles on early modern French and English history, including articles on Anne D'Este, Duchess of Guise and on Francis I's royal entries. With Jessica Munns she co-edited *The Clothes that Wear Us: Dressing and Transgressing in Eighteenth-Century Culture* (1995) and with Iain Robertson has co-edited *Studying Cultural Landscapes* (2003); she is working on a book on women and patronage in the Guise circle in the sixteenth century.

Robert Sturges teaches in the English Department, University of New Orleans. He has written many book and journal articles on Medieval literature and theories of interpretation and is the author of the SCMLA prize-winning book *Medieval Interpretation: Models of Reading in Literary Narrative 1100–1500* (1991), and is co-editor of the forthcoming *Middle-English Pseudo-Augustinian Soliloquies*. His most recent book is *Chaucer's Pardoner and Gender Theory: Bodies of Discourse* (2000).

Michael B. Young is Professor of History at Illinois Wesleyan University, Bloomington. He is the author of several articles in journals that include *The Historical Journal* and *History*. He has written three books about early Stuart politics, *Servility and Service: The Life and Work of Sir John Coke* (1986), *Charles I* (1997) and *James VI and I and the History of Homosexuality* (1999).

Marcello Zane is a researcher at the Fondazione Luigi Micheletti in Brescia and is on the editorial board of many Italian history journals. He has published books and essays on gender and history in Italian nobility during the early modern period, and on social and political history from the eighteenth to the twentieth centuries. He is currently working on a project about the making of the upper classes in Brescia during the nineteenth century.

Introduction

JESSICA MUNNS AND PENNY RICHARDS

The essays in this collection consider how power and privilege were experienced, distributed and brokered by women and men during the early modern period. In so doing, they also examine the social, political, religious and sexual conflicts that divided families, cities and states. These conflicts were sometimes intractable, sometimes reacted to with violence and occasionally adroitly accommodated. In subject matter the essays range from courts to cities, in time they move from the late Middle Ages to the edge of the eighteenth century, and geographically they discuss England and continental Europe. In their approach, they range from discussions of gender theories to their applications with regard to urban lifestyles, literature, particular families, rulers, warfare, militarism and religion. We do not, however, suggest that these essays offer a coherent 'map' of gender relations in Europe during this period, rather they illuminate particular terrains.

For the moment, at least, the era of grand explanations of an 'age' is over. Particular studies of regions, trades, habits and customs, and microstudies of people, have both complicated and enriched our understanding of this (or any) period. In place of a Burckhardtian vision of the 'Renaissance' as a time of burgeoning humanism, we have a time when some people (mostly elites and those who served them), in some places (Western Europe) and in different time-frames, participated in a 'Renaissance' of art, literature and science.[1] For others, and, as Joan Kelly famously suggested, for most women, that experience passed them by.[2] They were excluded, by their status, by their gender, by the particular time they lived in and by their location. Instead of the 'Renaissance' as a term that can unproblematically characterize a time, we have the less luminous and less loaded term, 'early modern', that has the advantage of inclusiveness. If 'Renaissance' studies tended towards the adumbration and celebration of

1

the emergence of individualism, modern studies have moved, partly due to the influence of Annaliste and structuralist approaches, rather towards the considerations of communities, institutions and the languages/discourses that shaped types of knowledge. As indicated by the reference to Joan Kelly, feminist historical studies have been a major influence in the reshaping of the idea of period and the methods by which topics are selected and discussed. As Frances Dolan's essay in this collection shows, feminist studies have moved from earlier works of excavation towards broader studies of how gender was understood, how women *and* men defined themselves, were defined by others, and by societal institutions, and the role of sexuality in these definitions. Masculinity has ceased to be an unproblematic dominant category defining the 'Other' of femininity. Studies in masculinity have examined ways in which men defined themselves, against each other as well as against women, and in relation to structural and cultural imperatives of status and activity. Gay studies have also been important in discussing ways in which genders were defined and experienced. The work of Alan Bray and Michael Rourke,[3] for instance, has posited the early modern period as one in which homosexuality was not yet significantly associated with effeminacy, not yet defined against a heterosexual norm. Indeed, these studies have demonstrated that gender identities and sexual orientations were not understood in terms of binary oppositions between men and women. Overall, the degree to which gender cannot be understood without reference to status, particular areas, activities and a wide range of social roles and cultural activities has led to reassessments of gender relations in the early modern period and deeply informs all the essays collected here.

The essays in this collection reflect the diversity of styles and approaches currently employed by American, English and continental European scholars in their study of early modern Europe. They are, however, united by their interest in how definitions of sexuality and gender roles operated in a given society, and more particularly, how such definitions – and the activities they generated and reflected – articulated societal concerns inside a given culture. This means that the essays are also intrinsically interdisciplinary, literature as well as history, economics and gender studies, which form the basis of the no longer so new field of 'Cultural History'.[4]

Frances Dolan's essay opens the collection with a discussion of the different approaches taken in the past twenty years to the study of gender and sexuality in early modern England and offers 'an introduction to terms, debates and directions'. For instance, she discusses the ways in which performance theory and gender can help our understanding of the art and practices of the period, and looks at debates, such as that over whether or not the early modern period underwent a 'crisis in gender', or whether to some degree gender is always in crisis. Current new directions are outlined as she describes the many challenges to normative heterosexuality in our reading of the past. As she notes, the shapes these studies take reflect *our* interests and anxieties. However, 'present preoccupations can motivate and invigorate an approach to the past that sees it not as an undistorted mirror of our own concerns but as a vital repository of knowledge, a shifting, fissured, but inescapable foundation of whatever futures we hope to build'.

Many aspects of that which we associate with the Renaissance – the rise of individualism, fostered by capitalistic city-states, and the anxious relationship between such states and powerful princes – first emerged in the Low Countries.[5] The princely courts of Burgundy arguably laid the pattern of court ceremonials, entertainments and festivals for at least two hundred years, while the burghers of the flourishing cities pioneered a wide range of civic rights. Marc Boone, Thérèse de Hemptinne and Walter Prevenier write about the ways in which gender was understood and functioned in terms of the family, the state, the city, the church and the arts in this part of Europe during the late medieval and early modern period. Their essay shows how gender permeated every aspect of life – public and private – from politics, to art, literature, the law courts and marriage customs. As they point out,

> both sons and daughters participated in their parents' strategies for
> safeguarding the family patrimony as a power base. But views on the
> respective economic potential of men and women differed, and so the
> approach and the means varied according to their gender. For girls
> the parents were obsessed by the choice of an eligible husband as early
> as possible, so that continued control of the family inheritance was not
> at risk. . . . For boys this was not an issue, and in any case education
> and apprenticeship took more time, so that there was no risk in
> delaying their marriages.

Different marriage patterns and concerns with regard to sons and daughters are also discussed by Marcello Zane whose onomastic study of name choices and their transmission among an elite – and very militant – Brescian family reveals complex patterns of patrimonal concern and patriarchal domination. His study also reveals the slender, but present, opportunities for wives to transmit their names to posterity, and their, perhaps, more practical ability to transmit their dowries to their daughters. Robert Sturges's essay also takes us from the late medieval to the early modern period with his study of the sexually and politically transgressive figure of Chaucer's Pardoner. The Pardoner, in *The Canterbury Tales*, he argues, is a figure for late medieval anxieties over gender transgression, and two texts from the transitional period between the late Middle Ages and the Renaissance adopt Chaucer's character as a way of representing the relationships among gender, class and power in their own historical circumstances. The Prologue to *The Tale of Beryn* directs its carnivalesque humour against the Pardoner's class pretensions and those of Kit the barmaid, but also signals fifteenth-century anxieties about the class and gender transgressions of single women like Kit. Heywood's *Foure P.P.*, on the other hand is more ambiguous about the possible meanings of sixteenth-century women's power: while the figure of the Pardoner places ultimate power back in the hands of the orthodox Church, Heywood's Catholicism also leads him to imply a measure of support for female political power in the persons of Catherine of Aragon and Princess Mary, in his tale of a female body that 'lay[s] wide open' the castle of patriarchal privilege.

Courtly life constituted an arena of power and privilege for which women and men competed fiercely with each other. Essays by Robert J. Knecht and Michael B. Young look at the roles played by royalty and nobility in the French, English and Scottish courts in the sixteenth and early seventeenth centuries. Knecht examines the views of the nineteenth-century French historian Michelet who wrote that Francis I was dominated by his mother, Louise of Savoy, whom Michelet assesses to have been an evil influence, while his sister, Marguerite of Angoulême is represented as saintly: 'He was completely under their spell. Women made him all that he was, they were also his undoing.' Knecht, however, demonstrates that, while indeed Louise was profoundly influential, shaping the young prince's education and later actively involved in national and court politics, she was not an evil influence on the king or France, and Marguerite, also politically active, was neither as influential nor as 'saintly' as depicted. Nevertheless, his study shows the intricate and multiple ways in which royal and noble women participated as active agents in the political and cultural life. As he concludes, 'the popular notion that high-born ladies in Renaissance France spent all their time weaving tapestries or listening to madrigals needs to be firmly set at rest'.

Michael Young's essay charts the marriage of James VI (of Scotland) and I (of England) to Anna of Denmark. He counters the view that Anna was an unintelligent nullity, pointing out, of the early years, that 'a less adroit woman could easily have been disdained and marginalized, but Anna was "an instant success in Scotland" '. By 1597 it was said that Anna routinely dealt in 'matters of importance to the greatest causes', and in 1598 that 'the Queen knows all'. Her ability to act politically declined after the move to England: James now operated from a greater power base and his increasing reliance on and affection for a series of male favourites, who were also probably lovers, weakened her ability to manipulate the king or create a significant 'Queen's faction'. Nevertheless, he notes, her separate court and her patronage of the arts, especially the masque, gave her oppositional forums from which to critique what she saw as her husband's effeminacy both in terms of sexual preference and dislike of warfare.

4

Anne McLaren's essay also looks at a queen, this time an indubitably powerful one, Queen Elizabeth I. McLaren, however, draws attention to the ideological problems presented to a patriarchal state when a woman inherited the throne. She investigates the political iconography of the image of Elizabeth as Deborah – the wise Judge of Israel – and notes the ways in which this provided the Queen with a distinctly two-edged weapon. If on the one hand such an image was empowering, it also suggested limitations with its insistence on the female monarch as an anomaly whose continued exercise of power rested on her Protestantism, morality and dependence on wise male counsel. As McLaren states, there was a general 'conviction that Elizabeth must govern, and be seen to govern, in immediate conjunction with her godly councillors as a pre-condition of political stability and the establishment of a godly realm'. McLaren also argues that the reconfiguration of monarchy as operating alongside and in collaboration with 'godly councillors' had far-reaching consequences for future monarchs of England.

Gender and politics also dominate Simon Barker's discussion of what was seen as a crisis in masculinity during the age of Elizabeth I. Early modern England, he argues, witnessed the circulation of a mass of prose writing dealing with the relationship between warfare and gender. Harking back to a lost ideal world of masculinity this writing lamented the present confusions over gender identity in the context of military preparedness, discipline and tactics. His chapter contrasts the steady complaining voice of this prose with examples from the more interrogative theatre texts of Shakespeare and his contemporaries in order to explore the artificiality and constructed nature of 'gender' in the context of Renaissance military idealism.

As Barker notes, 'women have always been involved in the business of war', and Penny Richards' essay provides an examination of the ways in which the women of the very powerful Guise family and its affinity were actively engaged in the religious wars of France during the latter years of the sixteenth century. Female militarism does not necessarily involve priming guns and riding into war, but, as with Anna of Denmark, can be a matter of forming militaristically inclined factions. As Richards shows, women were an integral part of the early modern war machine when maintaining a state of military preparedness, and supplying armies with both arms and food was a normal feature of life for great magnate wives in times and places of warfare. However, the women of the Guise family and affinity did all and more than that. Undoubtedly allied to and enmeshed with the political and religious aims of their families, they sought actively to support and, in adversity, revenge their husbands, sons and brothers. To this end, their weapons were the arts of courtly connection, the letter, with which they kept open lines of communication between the aspiring branches of the family and, more directly, propaganda, assassination and, at the last, the defence of Paris. Regarded by contemporaries opposed to the Catholic League as desperate, wicked, inevitably whorish, their activities again remind us that a high-born lady did not merely pass her time in domesticity and leisure but as part of the collaborative entity – the great family – which played a vital and active part in that entity's deployment of privilege and its move into direct conflict with the French monarchy.

Post-Counter Reformation Spain is examined in Joan Curbet's chapter on the treatment meted out to the *Alumbrados* – women who claimed special enlightenment from God – and whose vibrant articulations and very physical experiences of Grace conflicted with the orthodoxy of the Post-Tridentine church. Curbet contrasts their treatment (flagellation and sometimes death) to that experienced by St Teresa. The *Alumbrados* were severely punished, but St Teresa, Curbet argues, through submission to her confessors lived to reform the Discalced Carmelite order. Unlike Elizabeth I, however, whose transgressive position as woman and a ruler was, McLaren argues, integrated into a new concept of the monarch and the realm, St Teresa, Curbet shows, could only be absorbed into the mainstream of Catholic orthodoxy through a type of spiritual regendering, as a contemporary commentator put it:

> this woman ceased to be a woman, restoring herself to the virile state,
> to greater glory than if she had been a man from the beginning. For she
> rectified nature's error with her virtue, transforming herself through virtue

The overall title of this series, 'Women and Men in History', is a sign of the changes in the nature of historical investigation in the past three decades. The essays collected here are part of this ongoing process of rethinking the past and demonstrate that looking at history through the lens of gender opens up a wide variety of avenues and sets us a new series of challenges. That the essays challenge traditional orthodoxies with regard to the dominant role played by men alone in the events of nations and daily lives is obvious. However, they also challenge attempts to generalize from one country or period to another. The solution found by Spanish clerics to a remarkable woman was different to that found by English ideologues. The degree to which activities that conflicted with the desires of dominant groups were punished or tolerated varied and were differently tabulated. Some women surely did weave tapestries and listen to madrigals, but many also led lives more laborious on the one hand, and more dangerously privileged on the other. Patriarchal systems of governance and order were widespread and normative, but masculinity itself was not taken for granted, easily configured or was any less unproblematic than femininity.

CHAPTER ONE

Gender and sexuality in early modern England

FRANCES E. DOLAN

Gender and sexuality have proved highly productive categories of analysis in interdisciplinary studies of early modern England and continue to inspire work that challenges the most fundamental paradigms of historical and cultural understanding, such as progress and decline, inclusion and exclusion, centre and margin, top and bottom. This chapter offers an introduction to terms, debates and directions.

How has gender been defined?

Joan Kelly's highly influential essay 'Did Women Have a Renaissance?' made the question of periodization a foundational concern in women's history.[1] Could women be included in the existing periods and narratives or would their inclusion require revision of our very structures for organizing historical knowledge? While Kelly's question has been rephrased and her conclusion that 'there was no renaissance for women – at least, not during the Renaissance' has been challenged, periodization remains a challenge for scholars of women and gender. 'Early modern' can seem Whiggish and anticipatory, claiming significance for the period only as preparing the way for the 'modern'. Yet the term is also practical because it is so broad, allowing attention to continuity and change across a longer span of time. This is especially helpful when attending to the experience of women and of non-elite men, which often changes more slowly and less dramatically than that of the most privileged men.

In studies of early modern England, gender emerged first as a question focused on women. What about women? What were their experiences, perspectives, values, contributions? At first, the operative assumption was that there were two basic groups of historical actors, men and women; men acted considerably more than women, and therefore dominated accounts of the past. Women simply needed to be included, in whatever limited ways were possible, given how little they had accomplished. This first initiative to discover and include women was often accompanied by the assumption that women in the past were invariably oppressed, excluded and marginalized. If they were not, then they were exceptions who proved the rule of victimization. While it is undeniably true that women suffered from various disadvantages and constraints particular to their gender, it is also important to stress that women found many ways to exercise authority, enact resistance, express themselves and pursue their desires, control money and property, exploit or defend the status quo, or effect change. Some students of the early modern period still think that a feminist approach or an emphasis on gender equals a hunt for victims. As I hope this essay will show, this is not the case. Gender can open many doors on the past. Employing gender as a category of analysis has never determined what one would then see or find.

Investigations of gender soon began to complicate a project of inclusion or addition by destabilizing the narratives and categories of analysis themselves. In the past, how did gender shape who got to do what, and what counted as action? what counted as history? what could be recognized as significant? How might our own ideas about gender inflect what we ourselves can recognize or value? Such questions lead in several different directions: the recognition that gender is not naturally given and constant from one place and time to another, but rather busily inculcated and constantly changing, the discovery that there are many differences (of race, class or status; of religion, region, age or marital status) within that category 'woman' or 'women' that should be attended to, and the awareness that 'man' is also a constructed and internally divided category. If men were not invariably at the centre of early culture and women at the margins, then not only were some women powerful, authoritative figures, but many men were servants and dependants.

Most histories of women and gender in the period start by mapping how it operates as a 'notion', a language, an idea or an ideology.[2] In such an approach, gender does not describe whatever sexual difference can be ascribed to bodies, but rather a complex process of social construction by which an identity is created, conferred, and enacted rather than recognized and named. This does not mean that the social is mapped onto or layered over the biological, but rather that the biological is given cultural meaning through the performance of gender in clothing, grooming, speech and conduct. The performance of gender is understood, then, not as an expression of a gender that is prior and stable, but as constitutive of gender. Gender is the effect of the performance rather than its origin. This process of gender performance changes over time and is uneven, flawed and contradictory.[3]

Given the transvestite stage of the late sixteenth and early seventeenth century in England, at a time when France, Spain and Italy allowed women to take speaking parts in the theatre, sixteenth- and seventeenth-century people themselves might well have understood gender as a performance. In the Induction to *The Taming of the Shrew*, for instance, the Lord explains how Bartholomew the page should play a wife convincingly: proffering duty 'with soft low tongue and lowly courtesy' and enacting affection with 'kind embracements, tempting kisses,/And with declining head into his bosom', as well as tears of joy. If these do not come readily – the 'woman's gift' – 'an onion will do well for such a shift,/Which in a napkin being close conveyed/ Shall in despite enforce a watery eye' (Induction 1, 110, 114–15, 122–4). Here Bartholomew learns to impersonate not only a woman but a gentle-woman and a wife. The Lord expresses his confidence that the page 'will well usurp the grace,/Voice, gait, and action of a gentlewoman' (Induction 1, 127–8).[4] Indeed, when Bartholomew returns 'in Woman's attire' he has become a Lady, and is referred to as one in the speech prefixes.[5] Then, in the play proper, we watch two boys playing two young women, Katharine and Bianca, who also learn how to play *gentle*women and wives.

Cross-dressing on the stage was both the dominant theatrical practice and the source of some controversy. Opposition to theatricality often focused on transvestism and pamphlets attacked the practice on stage and off. When the theatres reopened at the restoration of Charles II, having been closed in 1642 and remaining so during the civil war and interregnum, they employed female actors, offering new sources of scandal and titillation. Controversy now surrounds what we are to make of the early modern transvestite stage: Was it merely a convention that everyone took for granted? Was it deeply disturbing to more people than a few anti-theatrical cranks? How widespread was cross-dressing off the stage? Was the process by which a boy became a woman one not of switching genders but of complexly layering visual signals for gender? How are we to understand the relationship between cross-dressing and status impersonation – on which the stage, in constant and flagrant transgression of sumptuary laws, relied? Were boys who played men as much in drag as those who played women?[6] Few, however, dispute that most who attended the theatre accepted the idea that gender, status and age were identified by attributes that were imitable and transferable.

To say that something is a performance is not to say that it is not real or does not have consequences. If gender was fabricated and reiterated through continuous performance, it still powerfully shaped experience; it also medi-ated between intentions that are often inaccessible to us now and outcomes that may often have been unintended. Thus, while gender constructions imposed limits on the conceptual and practical options available to early modern people, they did not wholly determine them; reconstructing the parameters set by these prescriptions does not exhaust the possibilities that may have been available. Recent scholarship emphasizes the agency of women as well as men, choices as well as constraints, practices as well as prescriptions, and the ways in which persons strategized around and within even the most intractable limits. The contradictions within and among these constructions, as well as how they intersect with or interrupt other categories of social identity, created arenas for agency. Since viewing gender as socially constructed can suggest that some malign and conspiratorial agency – call it 'the patriarchy' perhaps – is inventing gender and imposing it on the unsuspecting and unresisting, theoretical and historical approaches that emphasize the possibilities for agency complicate our understanding of the processes and performances that are gender.

As various theorists have argued, subjects are always simultaneously subjected and active; the process of coming into being as a gendered subject is one of being informed, disciplined and also, in a limited way, enabled.[7] There is no one location of 'power'. As a consequence, no 'one' is doing the constructing. Rather, everyone in a culture participates in the processes by which gender is produced.[8] Increasingly, attention is turning to the locations and technologies of dissemination (the pulpit, the printing press, the court, the school, reading, listening, watching). More than the audiences or consumers, silently absorbing lessons in how to 'be and seem', women also participated actively at all of these sites of production.[9] They were preachers in the dissenting Protestant sects; they were actively involved in printing and publishing and selling print materials; they were queens and ladies in waiting at court; they were teachers, nurses and mothers. Even as consumers, women were actively interpreting what they read or heard. Sometimes they left records of their resistant, critical, or amused responses; often they did not. But various kinds of evidence, such as women's angry critiques to misogynist sermons or texts, suggest that women had a range of reactions to and interactions with attempts to subject them to overly stringent, gendered standards of conduct.

Our best evidence about women's active roles in the production of culture comes from their own writings. Barely available and rarely considered just a few decades ago, these are now readily accessible, and widely taught and studied. Research on women's writings is moving beyond the discovery that women were writers to sustained engagement with women's texts. Women's words do not offer us direct and unmediated access to women's experience any more than men's do. Instead, these texts reveal the complex ways in which women participated in, rather than simply submitted to, the construction, inculcation, interrogation and transformation of gender norms.

Women did not all challenge the status quo. Many of the privileged women who wrote and published benefited from and defended the existing social order; it is these women who, according to Paula McDowell, most often articulate a recognizably modern self, 'gendered, autonomous and unique'. For those women actively involved in various forms of protest and activism, who tended to be of the middling or underclass, 'gender was not necessarily the first category of identity'. Instead, such women 'tended to find empowerment in more dispersed modes of being based in religio-political allegiances, trades or occupations, and other collective social identifications' and 'to envision the self in more traditional ways as social, collective and essentially unsexed'. For McDowell, it was only in the course of the eighteenth century that women 'increasingly came to understand themselves as a group with shared interests and, potentially, shared strengths'.[10] McDowell's fascinating arguments suggest just one of the ways in which women's writings provide a rich, rewarding, unpredictable and heterogeneous body of material of which to ask the questions of how, why, when and to whom gender matters. As always, one answer does not fit all cases and none of the answers is determined by the questions themselves.[11]

If gender was not a fact of life, but rather a practice, then it not only affected the experience of identity, but also provided resources for thinking about and describing the world. David Underdown, for instance, has referred to 'the gendered habit of mind'. As Kim Hall explains this pervasive phenomenon, gender works in many descriptions of difference, verbal and visual, to represent 'the destructive potential of strangeness, disorder, and variety' through 'the familiar, and familiarly threatening, unruliness of gender'. The familiar figure for disorder or inversion is often the 'woman on top', as Natalie Davis argued in a highly influential essay.[12] As Englishness gradually came to be defined through association with masculinity, Protestantism and whiteness, it was also positioned against 'definitional others' who were often allied to the feminine, disorderly women and gender inversion. Gender thus served the complex formation of collective as well as individual identities.[13]

Gender in the early modern period has been described as the focus for 'crisis' or 'panic' by scholars, most notably Susan Amussen and Underdown, who argue that there was widespread anxiety about the gender order from about 1560 to 1660.[14] Others, however, have been challenging this argument as too sweeping or premature. According to David Cressy, for instance: 'Of course there were strains in early modern society, and questions about gender roles and identity, but it is hard to argue that they were more acute than at other times. Nor can it be claimed with confidence that gender mattered more than other social, economic, religious and political problems.' Martin Ingram, too, challenges Underdown's claim that there was a surge in prosecutions of scolds between 1560 and 1640 and questions what this could mean even if there were. Ingram does, however, concede that punishments became more severe in the period. In his view, what singled women out for comment and punishment was not that they were women but that they disturbed the peace; men who spoke or acted in a disorderly way were also disciplined.[15] Cressy and Ingram do not question that scolding and cross-dressing might be found transgressive, but rather question whether it was gender that made them so. They also argue that gender, to a certain extent, is usually in crisis.

Other scholars have also asked whether gender conflicts were really about gender, suggesting that, in a homosocial world, relations between men might have been seen as more valuable, more at risk, and more dangerous than relations between men and women. Thus concerns about conflict, competition or intimacy between men, which were actually more pressing problems, were displaced onto concerns about disorderly women.[16] But how can we be sure which is the real anxiety or the real problem? Gender-as-scapegoat arguments threaten to dismiss gender as a diversionary tactic. They also threaten to redraw the line between the real and the representational, the cause or experience of disorder and the language used to describe it, in too tidy a way. Finally, they sometimes shrink and confine gender into a fixed, separable category and place issues of gender and sexuality into competition. Perhaps, instead, early modern culture was afraid both of secret transactions between men and of those between men and women. Perhaps the threat was intimacy and secrecy as much as anything else.

What's most valuable in the work that argues for a 'gender crisis' is the fact that it does not understand gender as discrete. Attending to analogies between family and commonwealth, the imbrication of private and public, the complicities of gender and class, and the complex social processes by which some women, but not others, became vulnerable to prosecution, Amussen and Underdown argue that gender conflicts were inseparable from other conflicts. They were part of the fabric of social life, as well as a focus of contestation.

Gender and the body

We may experience our own bodies as what is outside of history and of interpretation, the great equalizers, the flatteners of social and historical difference: everyone shits, pisses, bleeds, dies. But work in the last twenty years has made it possible to begin to think about the early modern body as historically constructed, just like the gender identities it wears. We experience our bodies through cultural expectations, vocabularies and practices, which are, in turn, inflected by and constitutive of, not only gender, but also class, status, age, sexuality and race/ethnicity. For instance, Will Fisher argues that, in the Renaissance, beards not only distinguished men from women but men from boys; crucial rather than 'secondary' markers of sexual differ-ence, beards were also disturbingly prosthetic, as the use of false beards on the stage suggests.[17] The body is not then 'nature' as distinct from 'culture', nor is it the raw material of sexual difference that cultural process moulds into 'gender'. Rather, the two – nature and culture, the sexed body and gender identities – are mutually constitutive.

The early modern body was a 'humoral' body. An elaborate analogy between the body and the elements described the body as governed by four 'humours': yellow and black bile, blood and phlegm. Health and happiness depended on maintaining the proper balance of these humours. Thus bleeding and purges were crucial to medical practice. The fluids in the body were also fungible or interchangeable; breast milk, for instance, was viewed as redirected and purified menstrual blood. In addition, the organs might achieve agency, having 'minds of their own' so to speak. In the humoral body, the body and the mind, physical and emotional wellness, were connected. As Gail Paster explains, under a humoral view of the body, 'every subject grew up with a common understanding of his or her body as a semi-permeable, irrigated container in which humors moved sluggishly. People imagined that health consisted of a state of internal solubility to be perilously maintained, often through a variety of evacuations, either self-administered or in consultation with a healer.' For men as well as women, the challenge was to keep the body in balance and, increasingly, to police its boundaries so as to appear 'civilized'. The 'fluidity, openness, porous boundaries' of the humoral body were especially associated with the feminine body. Paster argues that a full understanding of the humoral body works to correct 'a blinkered preoccupation with genitalia' in recent discussions by emphasizing the gendering of other organs, such as the heart, and of body temperature, 'a form of difference thoroughly saturating female flesh and the subject within it'.[18]

Although bodies were not only gendered with regard to genitals, much influential work has focused on reproductive anatomy and function. Thomas Laqueur energized discussion of the early modern body by drawing attention to the persistence of a 'one-sex' (or Aristotelian) model of the body, in which penis and vagina are related homologically, and the clitoris is a morphological penis on the outside of the body. On this model, male and female bodies are only slightly different from one another; they are on a continuum, which begins with the internal genitalia of women and then progresses, through greater warmth and dryness, to the external genitalia of men. Here biological sexual difference is a matter of degree rather than kind. What would the cultural consequences of such a view be? Laqueur himself argues that so subtle a sex difference could not ground a system of gender difference; the burden fell on culture to create and maintain a gender system. Thus sex and gender were not distinct. Some join Laqueur in emphasizing the similarities inherent in this system. Others emphasize that women were viewed as inchoate or failed men, half-baked, in a state of arrested development.[19] The continuum might also make the hermaphrodite – the figure stranded in the middle, the both rather than the either/or – especially disturbing.[20] Still others emphasize that, if the feminine was inferior and unformed, it was also prior. As Laura Levine puts it, femininity was 'the default position, the thing one were always in danger of slipping into'.[21] Such theories push the idea of gender as a constitutive performance, in which behaving or dressing in a certain way can transform who one is, to its logical conclusion; conduct and biology come together. What is over-stated here is the idea that everyone in early modern England had a self-consciously unstable sense of gender identity. Whether ideas about the body that were articulated and debated in medical discourses were broadly disseminated outside them is currently much contested. Yet the two-way traffic between the elite and the popular in this period was so brisk as to cast doubt on the integrity of a boundary between the two.[22]

The one-sex or Aristotelian model was not the only one available. A two-sex or Galenic model became more common after 1600, and eventually so successfully supplanted the earlier one that it was long forgotten. In this view, men and women have distinct anatomies, each perfect in itself, and the two a perfect complement. The two models had rather different consequences for desire and sexual relations. Both assumed cross-sex coupling. Yet the Galenic model fixed sexual difference and provided an anatomical underpinning for cross-sex desire: no continuum here, just the 'natural' symmetry of opposites attracting.

There were two theories of generation as well. In the two-seed (Galenic) model, both parents contributed seeds for conception, yet the father remained the more important because his seed was warmer and more active. In the one-seed (Aristotelian) model, only males contributed seed, so women contributed matter and a location, not spirit, form or intellect. There were arguments about whether the egg or the sperm contained a tiny preformed human; either view emphasized the contribution of one sex over the other. To see the egg as the homunculus was to view the sperm as an animator but not a co-creator; to view the sperm as the homunculus was to reduce the female contribution to incubation. Dispute also surrounded the significance of female orgasm to conception, some arguing that the female's emission of seed through orgasm was essential to conception (hence the argument that a woman who had conceived must have taken pleasure in intercourse and therefore could not have been raped). Mary Fissell argues that the language used to describe reproduction became more freighted by gender in the course of the seventeenth century, as women's bodies were increasingly described as created for men's pleasure and as the ground for men's creativity.[23] Here, too, it is worth wondering how much such disputes might have influenced the experience of embodiment. While this influence must have been indirect and erratic, recent work on the evidence given in prosecutions for infanticide, rape and witchcraft, and on proverbs about fertility and generation, suggest that certain gendered ways of construing the body cut across social and discursive registers.[24] Later, science became the privileged language for articulating sexual difference, but in the sixteenth and seventeenth centuries, this was not yet the case.

Complicating the picture: men, class and sexuality

If crisis attached to or was displaced onto gender, that crisis revolved not only around controlling women, but being men. Challenging the assumption that men are confident, autonomous and self-determining, recent work argues that masculinity in early modern England was not only divided by differences such as religion, status and age, but was also 'anxious': men have 'dilemmas'; masculinity is 'always in question'.[25] As this work reveals, concern focused on controlling women precisely because being able to do so was one of the conditions of 'being a man'. Thus shaming rituals, for instance, focused on men who were unable to control bossy, abusive wives.[26] Obviously, not all men had female dependants they needed to govern. Only some heads of households had wives, daughters and servants to keep in line. Many men would have lived as dependants themselves, rather than as household governors.

How did patriarchies vary and change? How was a patriarchal social, religious and political structure challenged or compromised by having a woman as its ruler? How did the vicissitudes of life limit fathers' power? Some fathers died, leaving their position of authority to be filled by a mother, guardian or oldest son; in the chaotic circumstances of the period, men went into exile because of their political allegiance or their religious beliefs, leaving their families and estates behind them. Taking the disability, death or absence of fathers into account forces us to recognize the vulnerability and adaptability of a patriarchal system.

Manhood was determined not only by patriarchal authority at home, but by the exercise of public duties. In Jaques' famous, highly conventional speech about the 'seven ages of man' in *As You Like It*, manhood emerges in public life. This speech defines adulthood not in terms of marriage or parenthood, but in terms of office. In infancy, the subject of Jaques' speech is undifferentiated by gender: he mewls and pukes in his nurse's arms much as a female baby would do. Yet, for all of Jaques' claim to universalism, his 'man' moves into gender and class as he moves from his nurse's arms and into the world outside the household. Just as 'breeching' distinguished boys from girls by their dress, so this 'schoolboy' distinguishes himself from girls and from less privileged boys when he moves into a series of public spaces and roles. He is a 'whining schoolboy', then a lover, then a soldier, then a justice. Having reached a pinnacle of achievement and influence, sagacity and corpulence, he then begins the decline back into infant dependency, a decline which is explicitly depicted as a loss of manhood: the body shrinks, the 'big, manly voice' turns again 'toward childish treble', and the senses all decline, shutting him off from the world.[27] The speech does not imagine a life course for women; nor does it grant men's relations to women much significance. Women appear here as a nurse, then as the object of youthful adoration, then disappear. In this speech, manhood is both hard earned and short lived.

Of course, not all men became soldiers and justices, or married, property holders. In early modern culture, manhood depended not on having a penis, but on owning property. According to Susan Amussen, 'married, property-owning men' – a very small percentage of the total – were the only ones who were recognized as "real" men'.[28] Were those who did not achieve marriage and property not men? What kinds of masculinity were available to apprentices, servants, students, vagrants, priests? What were the perceived differences between boys and men, and how did one achieve manhood or the recognition of it? While some scholars have shown that men could be 'feminized' by sharing qualities or characteristics, physical or otherwise, usually attributed to women, Richard Rambuss has pointed out that penetrability and leakiness might be viewed as qualities of male as well as female bodies.[29] Other discussions associate 'feminization' not with bodily fluids and functions but with social positions and possibilities. 'Effeminacy' had a different meaning in the early modern period than it does now: it meant not liking men, but being like women – desiring them so much that one came to resemble them, being excessively vain and extravagant in one's dress, choosing or accepting or being forced into a 'feminine' position of dependency or submission. Stephen Orgel argues that 'everyone in this culture is a woman, feminized in relation to someone'.[30] But if at least temporary subordination was so widespread, how meaningful is it to claim that this status was 'feminized' and thereby denigrated? Was one's manhood necessarily at risk in desiring a boy, being ravished by spectacles, finding one's self leaky and penetrable? Or were these part of early modern manhood, but effaced in later constructions?

The law treated sodomy as the most transgressive crime against normative masculinity (if there was such a thing). Sodomy seems to have emerged into scrutiny and regulation depending on who committed it, since there was no clear understanding of the act in itself. This is not to argue that accusations of sodomy were not in any way about sex, but rather that sex became transgressive in association with other concerns. Jonathan Goldberg describes sodomy as a capacious and manipulable category, empty and therefore receptive to multiple, shifting meanings. The confusion and adaptability of the category lies 'precisely in failing to distinguish nonprocreative homo- and heterosexual intercourse'.[31] To be blunt: is it anal sex between men? is it anal sex between men and women? Is it any sexual act other than intercourse between a married man and woman? Is it any sexual act between members of the same sex? According to Goldberg, demonizing this category serves to define and protect both the licensed congress between spouses, and the many interactions between men in a homosocial world. Just as religious intolerance often focused on 'proximate others', whose beliefs and practices were closely related and highly similar to one's own, so anxiety about sexual conduct often focused on behaviours that were 'too close for comfort' to the supposed norm of procreative, cross-sex intercourse, revealing the contradictions and uncertainties that made themselves at home in English culture.[32]

David Halperin's work on ancient Greece has been extremely influential in early modern studies of sexuality because it has helped to give us a vocabulary for understanding how social status and age, as well as gender, figure in evaluations of sexual conduct. For instance, following Halperin, Bruce R. Smith argues that opprobrium attached particularly to the 'passive' partner in homosexual acts, i.e. the one placed in the 'inferior' position associated with women, boys and servants: 'Renaissance Englishmen, like the ancient Greeks and Romans, eroticized the power distinctions that set one male above another in their society.'[33] As has been widely and influentially argued, a sexual act did not translate into an identity in the early modern period, nor did the gender of one's partner in a sex act define a recognizable social identity. Instead, people engaged in a spectrum of practices – autoerotic, homoerotic, heteroerotic.

Not until later were same-sex activities marked off as transgressive; not until later was penetrative intercourse between a man and a woman defined and privileged as the norm.[34] Some claim, however, that the fall into categorization began in this period. For instance, Alan Stewart argues that, when the suppression of the monasteries forced priests out of their all-male communities, sodomy ceased to be seen as synonymous with the clergy, and came to be suspected in all relations between men, especially those relations that were central to humanism involving cohabitation and collaboration.[35] Whenever this process of disarticulation began, hetero- and homosexualities, like masculinities and femininities, were defined in relation and opposition to one another.

Women's sexual transgressions could also become notorious and fatal. I think immediately of the purported sexual transgressions of queens: the charges of adultery and incest against Anne Boleyn; the charge of sexual incontinence against Catherine Howard; the rumours surrounding Mary Stuart's attachment to David Rizzio, a court musician, complicity in the murder of her husband and elopement with (or rape by) the Earl of Bothwell. In all of these cases, sexual charges or rumours had significant consequences. But the charges are all about women's relationships to men. Under what circumstances were women's relations to other women marked out as transgressive? Very rarely. Especially on the continent, when sex between women was criminalized it was imagined as penetration – with the enlarged clitoris of the 'tribade' or with a dildo.[36] But female homoeroticism was rarely construed in this way in England. Some popular texts offer interesting insights into how early modern culture imagined attachment between women, but also failed or refused to visualize its physical expression. In a ballad called 'The Scornful Damsel's Overthrow' (c. 1685), for instance, the damsel of the title spurns every suitor, thinking herself better than they and preferring 'a maiden-life'. As a 'pleasant Frollick', a pretty maid decides to dress as a young man and woo her. They marry; their wedding bed is prepared; then the groom reveals herself to be a woman. As a consequence, 'in this life no comfort could [the scornful damsel] find' and so, disappointed of penetration by her beloved, she instead 'with a Dagger pierc'd her gentle heart'.[37] Similarly, in *As You Like It*, the scornful shepherdess Phebe must settle for Silvius when she learns that Ganymede, the man she prefers, is really a woman (Rosalind). Just as Titania in *A Midsummer Night's Dream* is punished for her pride and disdain by falling for an ass, so these women are disciplined by falling for an equally inappropriate and hopeless love object – another woman. In these texts, the comic plot requires that we join in the assumption that, of course, two women cannot consummate their love, cannot marry, cannot live happily ever after.

In John Lyly's remarkable play *Gallathea* (c. 1585), two girls, Gallathea and Phyllida, separately enter a forest, disguised as boys, for reasons too complicated to go into here. Once there, they fall in love, each thinking the attraction is cross-sex. When it is revealed that they are both girls, they are bitterly disappointed.

NEPTUNE: Do you both, being maidens, love one another?
GALLATHEA: I had thought the habit agreeable with the sex, and so burned in the fire of mine own fancies.
PHYLLIDA: I had thought that in the attire of a boy there could not have lodged the body of a virgin, and so was inflamed with a sweet desire which now I find a sour deceit.
DIANA: Now, things falling out as they do, you must leave these fond, fond affections. Nature will have it so, necessity must.

(V, iii, 141–50)

It seems as if that will be that. Yet even in this exchange, the two heroines' confession that they checked their desires against the outward manifestations of gender 'and so' licensed themselves suggests that the operations of desire are not understood as natural or necessary. Furthermore, neither maiden is able to give up her beloved or promise to move on to a more acceptable attachment. Neptune is cross with them: 'an idle choice, strange and foolish, for one virgin to dote on another and to imagine a constant faith where there can be no cause of affection' (V, iii, 155–7). But Diana sympathizes with them: 'I like well and allow it' (159). Since this is a magical, Ovidian world, Diana offers to transform one of the girls into a boy, providing the penis necessary for a happy ending. Gallathea and Phyllida announce that they do not care who gets transgendered, as long as they will be able to 'embrace' and 'enjoy' one another – which, the play suggests, would not be possible otherwise. Only their fathers care, because of the danger of disinheriting their sons. As the play ends, the characters agree to leave the choice to Diana and head off for the 'church door'.[38]

The inability to imagine or depict what could happen between women might have offered female homoeroticism a survival advantage, since naming, categorizing and regulating sexualities tends to restrict rather than foster them. Valerie Traub argues that when early modern women's relationships with one another coexisted with, rather than replaced, marriage, they were ignored, even tolerated. Yet they were also, through this neglect, eclipsed. They are hard for us to see, document and discuss. Since 'the discourse of law has stood as arbiter of social fact', as Traub points out, it has prevented us from at least speculating about what the law could not see or declined to regulate.[39] Even as we now try to imagine possibilities for intimacy and alliance between women that surviving evidence often only hints at or skirts, we have also been confronting the troubling evidence that women's relations to one another could be antagonistic – when they accused one another of witchcraft or slander, for instance, or when neighbourhood women searched the body or room of a single woman for evidence of childbirth.[40] Like men, women were divided by age, social and economic status, religion and marital status. New research has shown that more women remained single than married in early modern England, and that some women even served as the heads of their own households.[41] Thus marital status – as virgin, wife, widow or spinster – was one of the most important aspects of women's identities and determinants of their options.

Discussions of sexuality in early modern England seem, at last, to be shifting the focus from marriage, challenging the presumption of hetero-sexuality, rethinking the complexities of household membership and taking into consideration the many persons who lived outside marriage. They are also moving away from thinking in terms of authorized cross-sex conduct (marriage), disorderly cross-sex conduct (adultery and fornication), and disorderly same-sex conduct (sodomy) to explore non-transgressive, non-deviant eroticisms in play. If, briefly, those focusing on marriage and the family squared off against those attempting to 'queer the Renaissance', the map of critical positions is now considerably more complicated, and the resulting articulations more supple, less embattled, more mutually informed. Discussions of sexuality are not only both re-evaluating the household and moving outside it. They are also extending to unremarkable behaviours that were both more pervasive and much more difficult to document, such as the erotic investment in the material world and the erotics of religious devotions.

Attention to gender is particularly vulnerable to the charge of presentism, or projecting our own preoccupations onto the past. Certainly, we can foreclose possibilities for fresh insight when we approach the past so heavily armed with preconceptions that we cannot see what is different or unfamiliar or unpredictable. The greater danger is a disregard for the past as altogether irrelevant, unusable or uninteresting. Present preoccupations can motivate and invigorate an approach to the past that sees it not as an undistorted mirror of our own concerns but as a vital repository of knowledge, a shifting, fissured, but inescapable foundation of whatever futures we hope to build.

CHAPTER TWO

Gender and early emancipation in the Low Countries in the late Middle Ages and early modern period

MARC BOONE, THÉRÈSE DE HEMPTINNE
AND WALTER PREVENIER

Introduction

The aim of this chapter is to investigate the role and impact of gender in the public and private life of the Low Countries, from the fourteenth to the sixteenth centuries. The issues under review include social mobility and equality, the economy, violence, emancipation, after emancipation, gender discrimination and segregation. We shall consider whether or not social advancement and social mobility could be considered as realistic goals in those days and, if so, what was the impact of public authorities, urban elites, extended families and parents on these processes? Was social advancement achieved through the institution of marriage, the control of family patrimonies and the regulation of matrimonial and succession legislation? This chapter will also investigate whether or not there were equal opportunities for men and women in economic life. Did education and marriage strategies have any effect on the professional careers of men and women? Were public authorities aware of the importance for economic welfare of a fair gender balance and of an open society?

When studying violence against women, challenges arise in decoding the discourses of lawmakers, lawyers and judges with regard to the prevention and punishment of rapes and abductions. How do we recognize the use of multiple truths in legal rhetoric, and the impact of gender bias in their judgments? There are also problems of interpretation with regard to those regulations designed to protect public morality and institute ethical norms. There may be specific motives that inform legislation aimed at controlling extramarital sexuality. We need also to consider issues of conformity and deviance in terms of religious or moral rules. Moreover, how gender specific were images of men and women in late medieval and early modern art and fiction? Was there any segregation and discrimination between the sexes? How dominant were the signs of emancipation and modernity, and did they appear earlier in the Low Countries than in the rest of Europe, or were they contemporary with their evolution in Northern Italy?

Gender, marriage and social advancment

Social advancement was a realistic goal for ambitious young people in the Low Countries in the Middle Ages. Competitive discourses regarding the goals and means of social advancement ranged from the conservative to the rebellious and the subversive. Economic and social ambition worked in favour of a more open society. How can we otherwise explain the rise and success of so many individuals between *c.* 1000 and 1200? In the thirteenth century, however, this open elite changed into a closed patrician oligarchy, inaccessible to new families. After serious social revolts from 1280 to 1305, workers and the middle classes forced their way into political and economic decision making. This process encouraged aspirations for social promotion. Between the fourteenth and sixteenth centuries one successful option for upward mobility was an advantageous matrimonial alliance.

Marriage and household are institutions with a potential for social regulation by ecclesiastical and civic authorities, and by parents and families. Medieval marriage was a purely religious ceremony without any participation by public authorities. It was a spiritual act and, from the twelfth century onwards, an inviolable sacrament. Its legal procedure was protected solely by canon law. To be fully legal a marriage required the participation of a priest and the free consent of the partners – parental consent was not required.[1] In a clandestine marriage, neither the family nor usually the priest played any role. A clandestine marriage occurred without any of the external formalities required by the Church: nevertheless, such a marriage was valid, although undermining the system of social control.[2] However, if property was involved in a marriage alliance, parents exerted a considerable impact on family life and households. In those cases, parents on both sides intervened in all marriage settlements. They legalized wedding portions and inheritance, formally registering them before the bench of aldermen. Alliances with financially attractive candidates increased not only the nuclear but also the extended family patrimony. Understandably, relatives made heroic efforts to be unofficially involved in the discussions about marriage partners. Should the parents be dead, the relatives functioned as official and legal guardians. In 1540, a Ghent law decreed that any daughter under eighteen, who married without the consent of her parents, could be disinherited.

The triangle of young partners, clergy and patrician families was neither homogeneous, nor immovable. Episcopal courts punished clandestine marriages in which no priest had officiated; which must have suited the wishes of wealthy families. Nevertheless, the clandestine formula was valid until the Council of Trent in 1563. Moreover, innumerable parish priests acted as allies to countless young Romeos and Juliets in the Netherlands who wanted to marry without parental consent and yet to contract a legal alliance in the presence of a priest – a procedure that was legally superior to a clandestine marriage. From the twelfth century onwards, ecclesiastical ideology, and canon law (Council of 1215) accepted that partners could marry legally in church without the consent of parents – so long as the partners freely consented, the marriage was consummated, and the intention to marry published at the church door. Many parish priests obviously did not worry about the elimination of the role of the parents.[3]

Following the late thirteenth- and early fourteenth-century revolts, a much larger group of wealthy families, although still an elite oligarchy, obtained a position of political power. They also wished to influence matrimonial policy. Matrimonial and succession legislation reflected their desire to protect family patrimonies against 'intruders'. In the logic of the elite, this was a key factor in maintaining 'social order'. Wealthy urban elites were attractive political and financial allies for princes, and most of the princes in the Low Countries were eager to support the efforts of town administrators to secure the continuity of economic success and family property, through the enactment of civil and criminal legislation. However, social stability could be secured only if the family worked effectively to protect children, the elderly and handicapped members of the family. This explains two other concepts: the sophisticated urban legislation for the relief of widows and orphans, and the creation of a dense network of safety nets for poor relief, hospitals and old peoples' homes. Ghent, indeed, ran no less than thirty-four of these social facilities, partly public, partly private.[4]

Civic authorities also displayed interest in regulating gender and marriage. Rulers and city boards were aware that households reflect socio-economic conditions and that population issues needed to be controlled. A population census of 1415 in Ypres (Flanders), at that time a town with a declining textile industry, mentions a very high percentage (20.3 per cent), of single-person households, half of them women and most of them located in the impoverished quarters of the city. These people lived predominantly in houses inhabited by more than one family, or rented a room-with-a-kitchen from another family. These people postponed their marriages for economic reasons, considering themselves financially too insecure to found a family.[5] Informal cohabitation, prostitution and the use of contraceptives provided an outlet for their sexual desires. The entire situation suggests the existence *avant la lettre* of a type of Malthusian behaviour. There is no doubt, however, that at least in Flanders, some late medieval observers were aware of the dubious effect of postponed marriages on population and social stability, and considered political measures in response. In 1328 Burghers of Ghent complained that many women found it difficult to marry within their own class. They located this problem in terms of class-consciousness, and from a conservative view of the advantage of socially homogeneous marriages. In 1395 a local notable in the south of Flanders, Yolande de Bar, lady of Cassel, found a progressive if paternalistic solution: she granted the sum of 400 pounds groat (the equivalent of five years' salary for a skilled worker), to a number of poor girls, to make them attractive partners for young labourers.[6]

Gender as a feature of economic life

Gender was undoubtedly central to educational discourses with regard to professions and marriage strategies. Up to the ages of twelve to fourteen, girls' education was treated in exactly the same way as that of their brothers. The avalanche of advice by many European moralists deploring equal education, had little impact in the Low Countries. In the Low Countries girls were sent to school at a young age, as were boys, and with few exceptions they received an identical elementary education which included reading, writing, arithmetic, singing and the catechism. The path of the sexes diverged at the age of twelve to fourteen, when gender began to play a clearer role. For boys, professional education went on for a long while: most of them specialized in a specific craft or trade, as unpaid apprentices to a master. If they were talented, they could become wage-earning journeymen and, after some years, if they were lucky and born to the right family, they became masters. For girls some crafts were open, just as they were for boys; however, in economic reality most women went into professional life and paid work after the age of fourteen. Some women acted as drapers in the lower and middle echelons of the textile industry; however, for most of them the available jobs were in domestic service, and in nursing, sales and prostitution. This sociological difference in the perception of the economic functioning of men and women resulted in the high proportion of women among the unskilled workers. In Leyden between 1498 and 1540, females accounted for 35 per cent of the labour population, but most of them were active as unskilled textile workers; 80 per cent of the servant population was female.[7]

Gender difference in the economic area was rooted in families' different treatment of girls and boys in the marriage market. Both sons and daughters were equally used by parents to safeguard the family patrimony. However, views on the respective economic potential of men and women differed, and so the approach and the means varied according to gender. Parents were very concerned to choose an eligible husband for girls as early as possible so that continued control of the family inheritance was not at risk. One of the main concerns of the family was to prevent the abduction and seduction of their daughters by unwanted candidates. This was not, however, an issue with regard to boys, and in any case education and apprenticeship took more time, so that there was little risk in delaying their marriages. In the case of orphans, late marriages were advantageous to the wider family, as they kept the right (usufruct) to use the inheritance of the boy or girl, and to receive the income (rent, compound) of their goods as if they were the proprietors.[8]

The main motive for giving a high quality education to both sexes lay in the hope that it would assure a safe financial and economic future. The expense of lengthy schooling was considered worthwhile for daughters as well as sons, as it was seen as providing a springboard to solid jobs and a respectable position in society. A variety of evidence shows that women in the late medieval Netherlands were much more literate than traditional historiography has suggested. For example, they often kept the account books and papers of the family business up to date.[9] Wills and deeds of gifts by women show a reasonable level of literacy that was socially crucial for the following reason: statistically the number of widowers was always lower than that of widows in medieval Europe. In Tuscany in 1427, for example, 9.9 per cent of the population were widows but only 4.2 per cent of the population were widowers.[10] The intellectual capacity of these widows was significant in securing the continuity of family trade. In places with developed small business economies, such as Leyden and Douai, the specific local customary law on the smooth transfer of property, when one partner died, secured the survival of this economic unit. However, the factors of personal talent, ambition and the literacy of the widow were equally important in ensuring economic management. These abilities could not have been improvised after the husband's death – they went back to education and to long-standing business experience within the household.[11]

In many parts of Europe as soon as a woman was widowed, a guardian was appointed. In Flanders and Brabant, on the contrary, the widow did not lose the right of disposing of her property herself. She also had the right to make decisions about her business and her children. The background to

25

these rights was based on economic, and not on moral reasoning, but on the 'closed-shop' protectionism of the crafts. This can be deduced from a labour by-law from Hertogenbosch of 1421, that stipulated that if a widow who was actively engaged in a craft remarried she must give up her business, unless she married a man in the same craft. Because of this economic pressure, many widows were careful to keep the employees of their former husband in their service and often married one of them. The 'positive discrimination' in favour of widows (they had more rights than married women) was due to the fact that not only were they considered competent to manage their late husband's business, but that they were indeed successful in this role. The share held by widows in trade and industry was no less important in the Low Countries than it was in Italy.[12]

To move from the individual to the community, concern over collective social and economic welfare was not unknown to the medieval mentality. The desire to safeguard the family patrimony is probably a symptom of individual and group egoism within a family and the notion of a 'collective economic infrastructure' is equally fundamental. As the Low Countries essentially lived from export, their princes created the legal base for international and regional fairs, conferred innumerable tax concessions for trade and concluded trade treaties with cities abroad. The cities in their turn created market buildings, roads, fire departments, social relief institutions and hospitals. Urban aldermen intervened in wage conflicts between industrialists and workers to maintain civic order. Civic authorities understood that they had to adapt matrimonial laws and social systems to the economic specifics of the various cities of the Low Countries. Some towns were very large, others medium or small, some were industrial and others commercial. In each of them the system of matrimonial and commercial legislation reflects this diversity, which itself created considerable variety in the status of men and women. In some senses, the Low Countries presents a dichotomy between two types of cities. On the one hand, there was a model in which small business and family-sized production units prevailed, as in towns such as Leyden and Douai. In these places married men and women functioned equally on the economic level. Here customary law respected the joint property in marriage and guaranteed continuity of the nuclear family's economic life through the smooth transfer of property.[13] However, there were also large industrial centres, such as Ghent and Ypres, engaged in international trade, whose early capitalist style meant that the nuclear family had less impact. Social safety nets were provided by guilds and craft organizations. They defended collective interests by wage claims and threats of strikes. Further protection was secured by the extended family, which took care of poor and sick family members, orphans and was also involved in the choice of marriage partners.

Violence against women:
how to decode the gender factor?

If we try to understand medieval views on and attitudes toward violence against women, we need to decode the terminology and discourse involved. Legal definitions are not always unambiguous. Niermeyer's Lexicon gives for *abductio* the definitions 'forcible withdrawal', and 'allurement' (i.e. without force).[14] Moreover, *raptus* may mean 'abduction' as well as 'rape'. Further confusion arises if we examine legal discourses of bailiffs, lawyers, judges, administrators. Are double moral standards used? Can we see an explicit as well as an implicit reasoning? Why are the decisions of judges so inconsistent and apparently arbitrary? For instance, sometimes they punished the crime of rape with a death sentence or perpetual banishment; at other times they insisted on reconciliation proceedings with financial compensation and sometimes they issued a complete pardon.

One explanation for such inconsistency is that the changing intensity and quality of punishment depended on varying social conditions. Around 1400, in France, the rape and abduction of women was considered as a serious social problem. In a statement in the *Parlement de Paris*, the French king made the point that a recent wave of abductions had destabilized French society, and provoked numerous feuds between families.[15] Harsh punishment was a political option which indicated concern for public order. In 1438 the duke of Burgundy published a decree against the rape and abduction of women in Flanders, justifying his policy with the remark that many of these acts were the means of effecting an advantageous marriage with a wealthier partner.[16] The measures taken by princes to suppress rape and abduction may be considered part of the global suppression of violence in society, and thus as the route to a more civilized and politically controlled society, such as that which Norbert Elias claimed as typical for the 'modern' late medieval state.[17] Most regulations on crime by the princes of the Low Countries, however, were explicitly inspired and carried through in close collaboration with patrician urban elites. The overriding aim was to limit social mobility – part of a static vision of social groups in which patrimonies ought to remain within the control of a limited number of mutually supportive families.[18]

Also at issue in this decoding process is the question of implicit and underlying discourses. For this reading of texts, the use of linguistic and anthropological methods is appropriate. The deconstructionist methods of Jacques Derrida and Noam Chomsky help to illuminate the uncertain and instable relation between signs and significance. The *intertextualité* of Julia

Kristeva shows that any text is the result of its absorption or transformation of another text. The sociologist Pierre Bourdieu has argued that legal discourse is a creative text, which brings into reality that which it expresses. The anthropologist Clifford Geertz's term 'thick description' invites us to interpret the conscious actions of historical actors within the framework of structures and concepts that really exist in a given society and time.

The major handicap for historians looking at legal issues is that they were produced by court notaries and reflect the assumptions of the legal officers and judges who analysed the facts, and decided whether or not to believe the litigants. For example in cases of seduction a variety of perspectives and interpretations come into play.[19] At issue for young lovers is the exercise of free will and marriage without parental consent. For the civil authorities the issue is one of forms of forced marriage, implying coercion, but not violence, as the seduced girl consented to the act. Nevertheless, seduction was an offence and a civil crime. Flemish law defined the parents and the extended families as victims (in their function as controllers of the family inheritance) and as the defending party in civil law.[20] Parents often tried to convince the court that what their daughter called seduction was in fact abduction. The underlying discourse of public authorities and families is not so much care for the protection of the physical and moral integrity of women, but rather a radically conservative and static view of society. The hidden agenda becomes apparent when in the course of the procedure the argument shifts from the initial complaint of the woman to discussions about social order or about encroachments on family inheritance. Often, indeed, the discussion would get bogged down in legalistic procedural devices. Frequently, absurd rumours were taken seriously, while the woman's complaints were not. One more underlying discourse can be surfaced: the anti-feminist prejudice of the judges and the similar predisposition of court officials. The sarcastic tone in the drafts of court secretaries regarding 'false' accusations by abducted women; the assumption that the sexual attack was provoked by the women, and ambiguity over consent to the sexual act, all suggest male chauvinism inspired by the traditions of misogyny reinforced by generations of theologians.

A totally different type of underlying discourse appears in pardon tales, in which grace is sometimes granted to criminals convicted of brutal crimes for which there is no imaginable excuse. The only possible explanation is either that both ruler and offender belonged to one patron–client network, or that the prince hoped to attract the perpetrator into his client network. For instance, in 1447 a minor valet of the squire of Kruiningen in Zeeland, ambitious for social promotion, abducted a rich widow in Hulst and forced her to marry him. The local bailiff arrested him, and the court of the count of Flanders banished him from Flanders for fifty years together with his allies, friends and the squire of Kruiningen. Nevertheless, one year later the valet, the friends and the squire were pardoned by the duke of Burgundy, without any evidence of legal logic. The duke, however, certainly had political motives for such a pardon. The squire was a member of the political party then struggling against the Burgundization of Zeeland and Holland, and was also influential in meetings relating to the granting of regional taxes to the central state. In addition the squire had family ties with important judges in the Court of Flanders. The pardon, therefore, was based on power plays and not on morality. At the same time it signalled the power of the ducal network, and therefore appealed to ambitious members of the nobility and the urban elites.[21]

A further pitfall in reading such texts is the 'plurality' of the notion of 'truth'. In discourses on violence we are confronted with the presence of a number of truths within one single court text, because several individuals may present diverse interpretations of the same event, or because one witness changes his view during the trial. The process of decision-making on crimes happens at successive levels, conducted by several public authorities, each having sharply divided opinions and contradictory information. Those involved are police officers, lawyers, prosecutors and judges, making up the complex hierarchy of the different courts, with the prince as head of state having the power to pardon and annul convictions. We should not forget that in many cases of rape hard evidence was lacking. Most of the acts did not take place in public so that the victim rarely had any way of supplying evidence or witnesses. A decisive piece of evidence was whether or not the woman had cried out loud during the rape. The victim and the witnesses frequently lied about this event before the court, either out of self-interest or due to external pressures. Accusation and defence were often reduced to the word of the victim against that of the accused man, with the judge in the position of listening to conflicting testimonies, many of them going back to unverifiable rumours.

In 1480 Jacob de Pottere was actually executed, after torture, on the basis of rumours about numerous rapes. However, in 1395 Jean de Thuisy was acquitted, even though he confessed after torture to having committed a rape (he later revoked this 'confession under pressure'). This acquittal was granted despite confirmation from midwives of a sexual assault in which the victim had lost her virginity. In both these cases the sentence was based on arguments we should now consider weak – such as rumours, and confessions that may well have been fictitious. In those pre-DNA days, even the loss of virginity did not prove that the accused was indeed the perpetrator. In both cases the family, friends and protectors of the two accused men had been active in seeking to prevent the conviction. The lower middle-class family of de Pottere had no greater impact on the events than a short stay of execution.

In the case of Thuisy the rumours were countered by the influence of an efficient protective network, including the Archbishop of Rheims and influential lawyers from the *Parlement de Paris*. In the first case, a 'normal' decision had been taken based on 'facts', 'rumours' and 'witnesses', at least within the legal framework of the usual death penalty for rape. The second case did not follow these rules, because of more powerful interests.[22]

For centuries authorities had made great efforts to prevent and suppress violence toward women with moderate success. Criminal legislation regarding violence against women started in Flanders in 1191, when count Baldwin VIII prescribed the death penalty for abduction. In the following decades abduction remained one of the routes to an enforced marriage. In many cases abduction turned into seduction, as the girl gave her consent to her abductor/seducer, thus keeping most of her property – to the great displeasure of her family and the urban establishment. For this reason in 1297 a later count, Guy of Dampierre, proclaimed additional measures against both abduction and seduction. The abduction of women remained punishable by death or by exile for life. The punishment for seduction was a double one: banishment for three years, and the loss of the girl's inheritance should she have married her seducer. A philosophy of social stability and order was clearly a constant background to this civil legislation. Indeed, the decree allowed the partners to change their informal relationship (which could be defined as a form of clandestine marriage) into a traditional marriage by a friendly arrangement between the two families that restored the inheritance rights. In 1438, a year of famine and social disturbances, Philip the Good, duke of Burgundy and count of Flanders, sought to stop a new wave of forced marriages by rebellious children, as well as a new plague of abductions of marriageable girls from well-to-do families. This represented a clear hardening of former legislation. A woman who remained with her seducer of her free will, or who had married him clandestinely, or legally but without parental consent, lost all her property rights including her future inheritance – as if she were dead. The ordinance contained several incentives together with elements of financial and moral pressure to make the girl change her mind. If the girl left her seducer and was prepared to marry a candidate of her parents' choice she could recover part of her property and future inheritance. If the undesirable partner died, she was able to recover the whole of it. This search for a happy ending accords with the global elite view of marriage and the family.[23]

In sixteenth-century Flanders, rapists were seldom granted 'remission' (pardon). Pardons, however, were granted in a case of a collective rape in 1556, when five men were condemned together. Not only was the specific victim able to profit from an extra fine, destined to compensate for her suffering, but the five men had to pay the large sum of 1,000 karolusguilders to facilitate the marriage of other poor girls. In this instance, punishment effected the reconstruction of collective honour, and represented the view that society as a whole had the right to profit from the punishment of this crime. In many cases prince and towns worked in concert. In 1438 Philip the Good mentioned explicitly that he had published his decree at the request of the aldermen of Ghent, who represented the wealthy families of the city and its equally mighty guilds. The duke, who was then engaged in putting down a revolt in Bruges, clearly hoped to keep the political elite of Ghent on his side. The earlier legislation on violence against women must have been the result of similar alliances of counts and urban elites, though this alliance was not formally mentioned in the justification of these earlier decrees. Such decrees represented the union of the prince's agenda for social stability and social elites' concern to protect property. There were also informal ways of keeping social peace: the Metteneye, a wealthy merchant family in Bruges, put considerable pressure on the city aldermen to banish a young man who courted one of their daughters, 'pour faire mariage avec elle, sans le conseil du père et mère'.[24]

Gender-based discourse and practice: public morality and the preservation of ethical norms

The transgression of moral standards, considered as an offence to God and religion, was observed and suppressed by ecclesiastical authorities in Europe, from the local priests to the episcopal judges. Canon law formulated the standards and the sanctions. Some ethical issues, however, fell under the jurisdiction of civic authorities. This is true of immoral behaviour, including those involving violence, such as rape and abduction. There were also other forms of sexual activities that were considered as social disturbances and fell under civic jurisdiction.[25] Several legal regulations and decisions discriminated along gender lines. The universal phenomenon of prostitution, for instance, forced the cities of the Low Countries to take measures of control, restriction and gender discrimination, similar to those taken throughout Europe. Civic authorities sometimes restricted prostitution to a specific 'red-light' district, and obliged the women to wear specific clothes and signs of identification, and profited from the income of brothels and bathhouses. Conversely, there was also tolerance: in some instances prostitutes were regarded as a safety valve against sexual violence, and to provide a solution to the sexual energies of unmarried young men.

In contrast to southern cities, where the town established official municipal brothels, either directly run by the civic authorities or leased out, the cities of the Netherlands never witnessed the development of such a *prostibulum publicum*. Nor did the Low Countries adopt the model of the small-scale *Frauenhäuser*, known to exist between the fifteenth and sixteenth centuries in southern and central Germany which were often run on behalf of the urban community. In Bruges and Ghent the free market controlled this essential part of urban social life. If both church and lay authorities condemned prostitution as morally unacceptable, both also accepted the fact of its existence and tried to bring it under control. They made considerable efforts to bring repentant prostitutes into semi-religious communities to facilitate social reintegration. Real repression focused on those disruptions to public order and violence which were allied to prostitution. In a rich commercial city such as Bruges there was a vast network of prostitutes: they ranged from those women driven by economic necessity through to the cultivated courtesan, offering her clients a variety of sexual services, often in the luxury club-style surrounding of a bathhouse. Prostitution in Bruges closely reflected the laws of the market: when more and more foreign merchants left the city, the supply of love for sale collapsed. There were, however, peaks of activity. During the key epoch of Burgundian court life in Bruges in the 1430s, at least 30 brothels were in operation, as well as around 20 bathhouses (about 1 prostitute for every 312 inhabitants). Among the operators of the brothels roughly a quarter can be linked to administrators and successful local entrepreneurs: prostitution clearly was an investment opportunity such as any other – which explains the lack of any truly repressive approach toward it.[26]

Another area of interest to public authorities was sodomy, a term preferable to 'homosexuality' which has been borrowed from nineteenth-century medical discourse. Sodomy referred to any non-procreative sexual practice: homosexuality, bestiality and masturbation. Sodomy was considered an unacceptable and unforgivable form of sexuality and as such was persecuted mercilessly by canon law, as the 'enemy from within' to be defeated. Civil authorities also violently punished a behaviour that was seen as threatening as it militated against society's ability to reproduce itself. They even called it a form of *lèse-majesté*, an offence against earthly majesty, as well as one against divine majesty. From professional preachers, such as St Bernardino of Siena, to town and state officials, legislation and special courts instituted to deal with sodomy displayed a more than ordinary interest in what even the routine accounts of Flemish bailiffs labelled 'the terrible, evil and detestable crime and sin of sodomy'. In almost every town a number of capital executions (death by burning) can be found; extenuating circumstances, which could save the accused from the stake, had little effect. There were however exceptions granted on the basis of the youth of a participant; the claim that one of the partners was passive; or, in some cases, if the participants were female. There were an exceptional number of capital executions in Burgundian Bruges (1385–1515): 90, with a clear concentration of more than 30 per cent taking place in the last 45 years. This represents the period in which Bruges increasingly became the scene of the Burgundian theatre-state, while remaining one of the most competitive commercial centres of North-western Europe. Several examples indicate that the ultimate decision over the life or death of the accused lay with the duke himself, or his political right hand, the Chancellor of Burgundy. The numerous denunciations of sodomy are a strong indication of the extent to which this collective obsession influenced the behaviour of rank-and-file burghers. In the early fourteenth century charges of sodomy tended to be levelled primarily at prominent figures, such as kings, prelates and the order of Knights Templars. However, a century later it had become an issue involving individual burghers, and their behaviour and morals. As in the North and Central Italian cities, the Burgundian Netherlands proved a fertile breeding-ground for the development of this collective fear.[27]

Other non-normative sexual behaviours, such as adultery and concubinage, involved consenting partners and did not involve violence. The medieval church classified these behaviours as transgressing moral boundaries, and limited its sanctions to spiritual penalties, such as excommunication. However, from the fourteenth to the sixteenth centuries in the majority of cases, such penalties were commuted into fines, adjusted to the social status of the sinners. In the absence of violence, civil authorities did not consider these actions as crimes. Some cities in the Low Countries, however, viewed adultery as an aspect of social disorder. In 1491, the city of Ghent decreed that one act of adultery would be punished by two weeks' imprisonment on bread and water. In Ypres an urban ordinance of 1535 banished any man, who did not repudiate his adulterous wife.[28]

Not only was private morality at stake here, the issue was also one of collective honour. The collective identity of a city, the body politic to which the majority of the people referred when defining their position in society, was based substantially on its privileges, the so-called 'freedoms' enjoyed by all of its inhabitants. Collective responsibility implied a strong sense of rights and duties, and hence a strong drive to regulate the behaviour of city-dwellers, obliging them to reflect in their private life the honour of the collective. This was expressed through communal responsibilities such as payment taxes, service in the ranks of the city's militia and leading an honourable life. The last implied close control and intervention in even the most private matters of citizens. Although few judgments promulgated by the guild deans of Ghent survive, in those that do, honour was a crucial element when the behaviour of one of the guilds' members was to be judged. There were, of course, varieties of honour such as honour linked to professional pride; honour in the way the guild, its delegates, deans and sworn representatives were respected; and finally honour in the strictly personal field. Sexual behaviour could be closely scrutinized and in 1402 concubinage led to the exclusion of the offending merchants from trading in the marketplace. Throughout the period, the natural or legal birth of guild members' children was a matter of great concern; over and above the question of entry into the guild, it reflected again an obsession with the notion of honour central to urban society. The drive to control the behaviour of other people was therefore not only a matter of control imposed from above by ecclesiastical and lay authorities, but was also a by-product of the role played by institutions, coming from below, and expressing the free association of citizens.[29]

Gender was a crucial variable in determining the way in which sexual activities were viewed and how sexual 'transgressions' were punished. Discrimination was the rule in several Italian cities where men were not punished for adultery while women were. Selective punishment was less present in the Low Countries, which levied equal fines for both sexes. However, a municipal decree of Breda in 1454 exempted adulterous women aged less than ten and over sixty; but it also stipulated that a man could bring a criminal charge for 'loss of honour' against his adulterous wife, and also bring civil proceedings. Women in the same position only had recourse to civil charges as the first step towards a separation. Greater discrimination can be found in a town ordinance from Aardenburg (Flanders) of 1320–40 that stipulates 'that a husband may beat his wife, since the wife is part of his household effects'. A husband might discipline his wife, but not the other way round. The legal definition of a 'domestic quarrel' had its limits; however, these were never clear or explicit. Every year the accounts of the various bailiffs register fines relating to a husband who had 'misused his wife'. We may presume that there was considerable under-reporting of matrimonial disputes.[30]

Imagining gender: femininity and masculinity in visual arts and fiction

Gender specific images in late medieval painting and literature in the Burgundian Netherlands indicate a predilection for the tropes of female 'tricks' of seduction, betrayal and domination. Images and narratives of ways in which women deflected men from their masculine duties were also popular, as were those of female vanity. Erotic ironies were also popular. As, for instance, in the motif of a semi-naked man standing with a small key before a woman who hides her genitals behind a casket with a large keyhole.[31] Such moralizing images and warnings are symbolic representations of the power-relations between men and women, and indicated how men and women were to behave if the existing patriarchal society was to be perpetuated. These tropes functioned as role-confirming patterns for both sexes. The fear of the alleged powers of women to weaken the will of even the most venerable and learned men, engendered the *horribile visu* images of Aristotle as a quadruped mounted by his mistress.[32] This motif of a woman riding on the back of her lover symbolizes the power of love to make fools of men. In such images and narratives, we see the tricks women use to impose their will on powerful men, who despite warnings are constantly ensnared. The moral message is: men, if you don't want to resemble this fool, beware of falling into the same trap: women, if you want to preserve your honour, be honest, be chaste and be faithful. There were also traditional depictions of women using their wits to achieve rightful goals, and these functioned as didactic examples of good behaviour for a female public. Moralists presented the world turned upside-down to perpetuate the perennial gendered allocation of tasks and maintain the relative power of men and women.

In pictorial art, young beautiful women were often represented with mirrors, which has been interpreted as signifying female vanity. In fact, the mirror can also be seen as a warning against female pride. The mirror makes its user aware of her physical flaws and moral weaknesses and compels her to remain humble and modest.[33] Bad women were always portrayed as voluptuous and led by their senses and men are shown as also falling victim to passion. The power of love as a disease that can infect healthy young men was a permanent theme in drama and romance. In these narratives the dominant character is always female.[34] Erotic and sexual topics were also favourites in the art and literature of the Burgundian Netherlands. One of these erotic scenes, that of the woman with the casket and the man with the key described above, can perhaps be linked to the myth of the medieval 'chastity belt'. Mostly these erotic scenes have an ironic tone and use humour, even slapstick, to dispel the husband's anxieties about his ability to satisfy his wife; about being mocked as a cuckold, or over his ability to beget male heirs. Women were frequently depicted as insatiable, voluptuous creatures, always ready to betray their husbands, especially with priests and monks, who were reputed to be more suitable and subtle lovers than their lay brothers. These women are portrayed as sexually enterprising and who often sexually initiate inexperienced youths. In tales and plays, women challenge men in sexual matters and they have recourse to a full arsenal of artifices with which to achieve their goals.

These images of adulterous and sexually uninhibited women are in sharp contrast to the prevailing marital and familial norms and ethics of chastity, honour and dignity. They are also in contrast to the sexual and other violent attacks inflicted on unprotected women in real life. Once again we observe that fiction and art were outlets for male frustrations and anxieties. Fiction and art created a world apart from harsh reality, instantiating an area where men could forget their own obligations and pressures, failures and miseries, and instead reflect ironically on the topics which in real life frightened them.

Conclusions: early emancipation and discrimination in the Low Countries

Legal equality did not reflect social status and social behaviour. Women, for instance, were not really absent from economic life, especially not as widows, but they are very rarely found in political positions. In daily life and in recreation, there was more or less voluntary segregation. Men and women sat separately in church. Miniatures suggest that they enjoyed separate spaces for leisure time: drinking and playing cards in alehouses for men, chatting at the front door in the evening for women. In bourgeois houses there were separate parlours – along gender lines – for indoor pastimes.

In many ways married women and men in medieval Flanders enjoyed an equal legal position, more so than in Northern Italy, which was similarly urbanized and economically 'modern' though more deeply influenced by patriarchal Roman Law.[35] A key factor in Flemish 'modernity' was its progressive inheritance legislation. In this area daughters and sons were treated equally, except in the area of feudal inheritance rights.[36] Flemish girls could inherit from their parents, just as did boys, and they did not need a specific female dowry, as did girls in most of Europe. In other countries the dowry system made women totally dependant on the goodwill of their parents. This was not the case in Flanders, where inheritance was a right. However, this meant that daughters, as much as their brothers, became components in the family strategies for expanding the patrimony through connections with economically important families. Many daughters, as we saw earlier, were hindered in their free choice of partners should their choice not accord with such parental strategies. It should not be forgotten that the medieval concept of 'family patrimony' included not only property, but also social capital, prestige, culture and connections. Succession legislation was not the only definitely egalitarian aspect of law in medieval Flanders. The regulations regarding joint property within a marriage were also based on the equal rights of both partners. The two of them enjoyed a full or qualified community of property. The system explains why women and widows in the Low Countries had a stronger social position than in many other parts of Europe, where on a husband's death most of the inheritance went to his heirs.[37] In particular, small family businesses benefited from a system in which the principle of a community of goods dominated. The equal rights of daughters and sons did not, however, prevent divergent social and cultural behaviours. Girls usually married younger, boys rarely before they were 25. Late marriages for men created the problem of a gap between puberty and legitimate sexuality within marriage. Young men satisfied sexual desire through various ways: prostitution, trial courtships and petting marriageable girls. Pre-marital sex, however, caused many unwanted pregnancies and unmarried mothers.[38]

Paradoxically the overall equality of men and women in Flemish property and inheritance laws did not prevent married women from having fewer legal rights than they had as unmarried girls and could have as widows. Throughout the marriage a husband had the right to dispose independently of his own property as well as the right to the partial disposition of joint conjugal property and his wife's property. He needed, however, his wife's formal agreement to such dispositions. In contrast, a married woman needed her husband's permission for every legal action or transaction. She had, however, full authority to act without her husband's permission should he be mentally deficient; she could act as an authorized agent should he be abroad, or if she became an independent merchant.[39]

Orphans enjoyed a well-protected legal status in Flanders which provided full equality to girls and boys. Should both parents die, material care was organized by legal guardians; in general this was provided by close relatives. Should they not wish to take on these responsibilities, the municipal authorities could force them to do so.[40] The material interests of the orphans were secured by the parents' will, or in absence of such a document, by the rules of general succession. This sophisticated legislation required a detailed inventory of the parents' property, and a document that summarized available resources and the obligations of the guardians. The orphans were brought up by them on income derived from their inheritance. The responsible guardian was allowed to reimburse himself from this budget, and this explains the eagerness of extended families to take in rich orphans. Differences of gender played no role in the regulations on food, clothing and nursing, nor in education. Orphaned girls had equal opportunities in these respects, and certainly with regard to elementary schooling.[41]

Guardianship could come to an end in three ways: by the orphan marrying; by entering a convent, or by being 'breaded out' (i.e. formal emancipation).

The law made no discrimination between the sexes here. In practice, however, different routes were taken. The great majority of orphan girls in Flanders were released from guardianship by marriage; with a minority, some 20 per cent, being 'breaded out', at an average age of 24.7 years old. With regard to the males, 57 per cent left guardianship by 'breading out' at the average age of 24.4, and only a minority were released through marriage. Males married much later than females, because of their longer apprenticeships. The release from guardianship meant that the young people had acquired full disposition of their property. Guardians were therefore prone to postpone as long as possible the three forms of emancipation and the unconditional transfer of total property to the orphan.[42] The guardians were indeed the first heirs of the child if it should die during their guardianship. The wider family, especially the guardians, also monitored the choice of marriage partner particularly with regard to girls, as matrimonial alliances with other wealthy families also constituted an advantage for the extended family, over and above the orphan's marriage. Indeed, an orphan girl, when she married, took her whole inheritance with her. Even within marriage she kept her property rights, so that if she died her children inherited and, only in the absence of children, would the relatives of her original wider family inherit.[43]

Promotion by socially mixed marriage was one form of social mobility in the fifteenth and sixteenth centuries. A close statistical summary of the success of this option is not possible yet. However, it is possible to compare the Burgundian and Habsburg Netherlands with the equally urbanized Italy. Specifically in Florence in the fifteenth century no fewer than 37 per cent of partners appear to have married outside their own social class.[44] In the late medieval and early modern Low Countries, however, it would appear that the trend towards an 'open society' was in vigorous competition with a strong reactionary trend, whose aim was social immobility. The patrician elites in the cities, in alliance with the local counts, later with the dukes of Burgundy and the Habsburg emperors, opposed all attempts to cross social boundaries by the way of socially mixed marriages.[45]

The early appearance of new social trends in the Low Countries was due in part to the permanent influence of international trade networks, together with the cosmopolitan nature of the Burgundian and Habsburg dynasties. These rulers had an extremely strong impact, with the prince and his court functioning as a huge theatre-state, and thus providing a model for individual behaviour. The court may be seen, apart from its obvious political function, as a centre of decision-making, as a meeting-place and as a trend-setter for aspirant social groups. As the court was peripatetic, many cities in the Netherlands were the location for the princely display of taste and conspicuous consumption. The creation of the Burgundian state and the

GENDER AND EARLY EMANCIPATION IN THE LOW COUNTRIES

Habsburg empire allowed these dukes, princes and emperors to set rules of etiquette and ceremony for a large segment of continental Europe. Even in those parts of Europe in which they did not exert direct power, the Burgundian ideal of *vivre noblement* had cultural currency.[46] The courtly life-styles also exerted a strong appeal to urban populations. The courtly world was both enviable and yet unattainable for city elites. At the individual level, the opportunities available to citizens with regard to social mobility and the exercise of creative ambition, which is characteristic of an urban environment, collided with the closed world of the princely court. Indeed, recent research suggests a 'cultural transfer' from the Low Countries to other geo-political areas less constrained by the suffocating grip of centralized institutions and the powerful and draining model of the princely court.[47]

CHAPTER THREE

'So was thys castell layd wyde open': Battles for the phallus in early modern responses to Chaucer's Pardoner

ROBERT S. STURGES

My aim in this chapter is to bridge the historiographical gap between late medieval and early Tudor representations of the relationship between gender and power. I shall do so by extending a discussion, begun in my recent book *Chaucer's Pardoner and Gender Theory: Bodies of Discourse*, of the Pardoner's literary afterlife.[1] That book examines the Pardoner in the light of medieval and twentieth-century theories of the sexed body, gendered behaviour and erotic practice, and finds that the Pardoner occupies multiple positions in each of these categories: he cannot be reduced to a univocal definition or identity in any of them. In the conclusion, I argue that later writers responded to this figure's irreducible ambiguity by using him, and figures like him, to initiate – sometimes by their mere presence – an exploration of the rule of the phallus, whether to subvert or to reinscribe it, or indeed both. Whereas my earlier discussion is theoretical, drawing on feminist and Bakhtinian methods for its analysis of a historically wide-ranging set of texts, here I shall attempt a more historical reading, primarily of one of those texts, John Heywood's early Tudor interlude entitled *The Foure PP*.

However, a few remarks on an earlier text, the fifteenth-century Prologue to *The Tale of Beryn*, will be in order first, to provide a link between Chaucer and Heywood. These two texts are linked not only by the presence of a Chaucerian Pardoner, but also by imagery of battles, at once violent and funny, in which women appropriate the phallus. Both are thus marked also by the kind of gender disruption associated with the Pardoner. Furthermore, each text also situates its gender disruptions in a context of power relations appropriate to its own period.

This essay has benefited from the suggestions of my colleagues Catherine Loomis and Miriam Youngerman Miller, whom I take the opportunity to thank here.

In the past decade, various historians have explored the social consequences of the Black Plagues of the fourteenth and early fifteenth centuries,
concluding that peasants who survived the plague benefited from it socially.[2]
As the labour supply decreased, the peasants' standard of living increased;
anxious governmental measures such as the statutes of labourers and the
sumptuary laws suggest that the peasants were imitating the gentlefolk, and
that this imitation was also imagined as a source of unruliness and, indeed,
rebellion. It is a short step from counterfeiting class and upward social mobility
to overthrowing 'proper' class relations altogether.[3] Another long-term effect
of the Black Death and subsequent epidemics was an increase in the rate of
urbanization. These economic and demographic shifts affected young women
in particular. Historians have found that women were attracted to town life
in even greater numbers than men, and that they found there both economic
survival and a degree of independence unavailable to them in the countryside. P.J.P. Goldberg suggests that real economic recovery from the Black
Death did not occur until late in the fifteenth century, and that in the
meantime the labour shortage created new opportunities for women.[4]

In the fifteenth-century Prologue to the *Tale of Beryn*, a spurious addition
to *The Canterbury Tales* depicting the pilgrims' adventures after arriving in
Canterbury, especially the Pardoner's pursuit of a tapster named Kit, such
class anxieties are discernable in the Pardoner's and his fellow pilgrims'
behaviour throughout their stay in Canterbury. They may be 'counterfeiting
gentilmen' (l. 150),[5] but they pose no real threat: the text keeps these lower-
class pilgrims in their place by comically exposing their pretensions as mere
counterfeits. But Kit is a more threatening figure. She is precisely the sort of
woman Goldberg describes, unmarried and exercising the power of choice
– not only in marriage but, in Kit's case, in extramarital sexual relations –
over the men who are interested in her.

The Pardoner, though he engages in a false performance of class, also
performs his masculine gender in a way that would have seemed culturally
appropriate: he claims masculine phallic power over Kit. His belief in his
own phallic power is badly mistaken, however, for he has already symbolically
given up the phallus itself to Kit. Upon his arrival at the inn, the Pardoner
hands his pilgrim's staff – often, in medieval literature, 'suggestive of a
tumescent phallus', as in the well-known ending of the *Roman de la rose* –
over to her.[6] The Pardoner thus symbolically hands the phallus over to Kit
at the very outset of their relationship, and with it the masculine authority
and privilege that he continues trying to exert throughout the rest of the story.
A climax of sorts is reached when Kit commands her lover to beat the
Pardoner with his own staff, or, as she puts it, to 'dub hym knyght' (ll. 454–
8). The discourses of class and of female independence operate in tandem
here: the Pardoner is ironically made a knight through a 'dubbing' with his

41

own phallus, a conferral of phallic authority that will really be a drubbing, a demonstration of the Pardoner's lack both of status and of masculine potency.

Gender privilege and class power are linked here by the symbolic appropriation of the phallus, and they continue to be linked in the battle that ensues. Beaten with his own phallus, the Pardoner tries to fight back but succeeds only in parodying his own earlier attempts at counterfeiting gentle status, and thus unwittingly reinforces Kit's mockery of him: needing to arm himself, he can do so only with kitchen equipment (ll. 569–75).

Kit and her friends represent exactly the kind of social disruption being prosecuted in society at large, which in turn reflects the social disruptions of class and gender, and the cultural anxieties about them, discussed above. The new social arrangements coming into being after the Black Death posed, for late medieval and early modern culture the question of who possessed the phallus, and the frightening possibility that it might be passing from the upper to the lower classes, and from men to women, is addressed throughout this tale. The Pardoner, as a lower-class pilgrim, is reassuringly unable to wield the phallus, but whatever comfort the audience might gain from seeing him get his come-uppance is disturbed by the fact that it comes from an even lower-class, uncontrollable, disruptive young woman.

In the long run, it is the story's comic or carnivalesque tone that contains Kit and renders her harmless. But perhaps it is not the comic tone alone that does so. Also noteworthy is the fact that Kit wields the phallus only through men, specifically by passing it to her paramour and the hosteler, a fact about Kit's authority that perhaps brings the tale closer to the true nature of female power in the late Middle Ages and early Tudor period. At all social levels in this period, from urban trader to queen, women exercised power primarily through their husbands. Female traders most often worked in their husbands' trades and were usually allowed guild memberships only in their husbands' names,[7] while even queens in the later Middle Ages lost much of their direct political power and exercised influence primarily as intercessors with their royal husbands.[8] In any case, all such women, like Kit, exercised what power they possessed only through men, while women who might be imagined as independent of male control – like whores – usually remained at the lower ends of the economic spectrum.[9] Though women gained some economic power and independence in late medieval towns, and though these gains were a source of the cultural anxieties expressed in the Prologue to the *Tale of Beryn*, in reality they were comparatively minor and short-lived in comparison to male power and authority. The cultural imaginary that produced literary representations like Kit may have found in her a source of anxiety, but real-life Kits wielded little power against the forces of patriarchy.

Historians and critics have discerned both continuities and disruptions in women's roles and status between the fifteenth and sixteenth centuries. Most of the historians of medieval women cited above (Goldberg, Karras, Mate, Bennett) extend their analysis at least into the early decades of the sixteenth century, and their conclusions thus apply to the 1520s as well as to the 1420s. Indeed, the economic status and public authority of most ordinary women improved little, if at all, in the early Tudor period, and may well have gotten worse, as Renaissance historians have also noted; although greater opportunities for social mobility were open to men due to a 'vigorous land market, agricultural commercialization, and the expansion of education', the same was not true for most women because 'institutions and the law discriminated against them . . . common law regarded wives as *femmes couvertes*: their legal existence was vested in their husbands'. And 'single women were especially vulnerable, while literature stereotyped women as "scolds" or gossips'.[10] In fact, whatever material advances in economics, independence and the power to choose single urban women may have gained after the Black Death had, for most women, been lost again by the 1520s:

> In the later fifteenth century it seems these opened doors were being
> pushed back on women's faces. . . . So women's 'always precarious hold on
> the labour market', in Goldberg's phrase, was easily pushed aside and their
> economic potential marginalised. By the end of the period urban women
> were being faced with the stark alternatives of marriage or perpetual
> servanthood.[11]

If anything, then, ordinary women's material power had weakened by the early decades of the sixteenth century; probably they saw little positive change in their real-life status, and the description of medieval women's position offered above may be taken as representative, or even optimistic, for the early Tudor period as well.

The status of women as described in the context of certain intellectual debates, however, did undergo some improvement. Ian Maclean's work demonstrates the ways in which theories about women, as distinct from the realities of their lives, continued the primarily misogynous tradition of medieval scholastic thought, but also took it in new and more positive directions in the sixteenth century. If women remained subordinate to men in theological and medical thought,[12] and even if this subordination was theoretically justified by 'arguments from naturally preordained function' (i.e. marriage and motherhood), still this is also a period of what Maclean calls 'dislocations' in these theories, 'caused by changes in society such as the activities of queens, queen regents and court ladies, and the emergence of a class of women possessing the leisure and the aspiration to fill it profitably'.[13] Whereas in the Middle Ages exceptional women tended either to confirm misogynous stereotypes (the Virgin Mary, the repentant prostitute, saints) or to be perceived as a threat (Kit the tapster), in the sixteenth century some intellectual space was opening up for the praise of exceptional upper-class and wealthy women, a topic with particular resonance in the England of Henry VIII. Feminist historians following Maclean have tended to emphasize either one or the other of the intellectual positions he excavated: on the one hand, early modern women are described entirely in terms of their 'subjection';[14] on the other, challenges to the misogynous orthodoxy found in the formal controversies on the topic of women's worth mentioned above are taken to be of primary importance.[15] All these contrasting elements in the early modern (primarily male) perception of, and intellectual debates about, women are evident, conflictingly, in John Heywood's *Foure PP*.

The date of *The Foure PP* can only be approximated: it was first printed some time in the 1530s or 1540s, and composed, in the opinion of most scholars, in the 1520s or early 1530s; Heywood's most recent editors date it to 1531.[16] Heywood's interest in Chaucer, and the Pardoner in particular, is well known; he also composed a second play about a Chaucerian Pardoner, and a number of nineteenth- and twentieth-century critics have investigated the influence of Chaucer's Pardoner both on that character and on the one who appears in *The Foure PP*, primarily in terms of their shared association with false relics.[17] As in *The Canterbury Tales* and the Prologue to the *Tale of Beryn*, the Pardoner's presence here is used to investigate the rule of the phallus; like the latter, *The Foure PP* makes women, as much as or more than men, the focus of its conflicting responses, both positive and anxious, to perceived problems in gender and phallic power.

In the play's rudimentary plot, after the Pardoner and the second P, a 'Potycary' or apothecary, have both made obviously false boasts about their respective powers to cure souls and bodies, the third P, a 'Pedler', challenges them, along with the final P, a 'Palmer', to a lying contest, which is to be won by whomever tells the biggest lie, the tale 'most unlyke to be true' (l. 702).[18] At this point their lies, still about their own healing powers, turn specifically to the healing of women.

Heywood's Pardoner – the second to speak – tells a tale about one Margery Corson, who closely resembles Kit the tapster. She is subjected to the same discourses concerning working-class single women and unruliness as Kit, discourses that are relieved of their threat by the same carnivalesque humour. Given its context of a play written in the 1520s or 1530s, in fact, the Pardoner's speech is remarkably backward-looking, its continuities with the medieval concerns of the Prologue to the *Tale of Beryn* and, indeed, of Chaucer, emphasizing the continuities between the late medieval and the early modern periods far more than their differences (though signs of change are perhaps also visible).

In this case, however, the Pardoner depicts himself as cooperating with Margery, in fact as rescuing her. Even as he aligns himself with female transgression, he thus retains his own masculine authority, specifically that of the Church (rather than the exalted civil status claimed in the Prologue to the *Tale of Beryn*); indeed, this is his reason for telling the story, to demonstrate that he has 'done greater cures gostely/Than ever [the Potycary] dyd bodely' (ll. 773–4). Margery Corson may claim certain male prerogatives, but she appropriates the phallus only briefly and without posing any threat to the Pardoner. The Pardoner's authority as an ecclesiastical employee also links this play with the medieval Church; it contains the incipient Reformation just as it contains the threat of gender transgression.

The Pardoner's speech about Margery concerns his successful attempt to rescue from hell the soul of his friend, who died without absolution. The Pardoner retains his spiritual authority throughout: Lucifer himself accepts the Pardoner's boast that 'Thorough out the erth my power doth stande' (l. 919) – an obviously false claim if it is taken to include hell, as it apparently does here. Indeed, Lucifer urges the Pardoner to keep as many women as possible out of hell because they are too unruly even for devils to control:

> For all we devyls within thys den
> Have more to do with two women
> Then with all the charge we have besyde.
> Wherfore, yf thou our frende wyll be tryed,
> Aply thy pardons to women so
> That unto us there come no mo.

> (ll. 937–42)

Like Kit the tapster, Margery Corson and other women cause 'to-do' even in hell: the familiar medieval accusation of female unruliness is reinforced with little change.[19] Margery also resembles Kit in her standing as a working-class and apparently single woman involved in the victualling trades: although we learn little of her life on earth, her job after death is to roast meat in hell's kitchen. In reality, the roasting of meat, especially in an institutional setting, would have been men's work; the spit thus serves as a sexual double-entendre, according to the play's editors: 'Margery turns a spit but is not herself spitted. . . . A playful double-entendre links her punishment in hell with her sexual life on earth ["here" 955] and the burning diseases associated with it.'[20] Margery, like Kit, thus briefly appropriates the phallus, and in doing so makes things too hot even for the devils:

> For many a spyt here hath she turned,
> And many a good spyt hath she burned,

45

And many a spyt full hote hath tosted,
Before the meat could be halfe rosted.

(ll. 955–8)

Margery is too hot for hell to handle, and the devils rejoice when the Pardoner takes her away. The devils, in fact, as the victims of a working woman's sexual unruliness, play the same role that the Pardoner himself played in the Prologue to the *Tale of Beryn*, whereas the Pardoner is now not a victim but a rescuer, his authority to save souls from hell unquestioned despite his new alignment with the threat of female power. Margery herself is rather passive compared with Kit: her phallic spit does not become a masculine weapon as the Pardoner's staff does when it passes to the tapster. Instead, Margery simply waits to be delivered by an authoritative man. The earlier discourse of women as sexually disorderly remains intact but now is considerably less disturbing to masculine power, perhaps as a result of the diminution of genuine economic power and independence for real working-class women after the early decades of the fifteenth century.[21]

Margery does not remain entirely untroubling, however: at the end of the Pardoner's speech she becomes a 'common woman' or whore:

Wherfore, thys tale to conclude brevely,
Thys woman thanked me chyefly
That she was ryd of thys endles deth,
And so we departed on New Market heth.
And yf that any man do mynde her,
Who lyste to seke her, there shal he fynde her.

(ll. 971–6)

Margery remains humbly thankful toward the Pardoner, but he lets her loose to roam the heath ('a gathering place for witches and an entrance to hell'[22]), where she will be available to any man who seeks her. Margery is now 'common' to all and is therefore associated with whoredom and the social disorder it represents; she may not assert phallic power over the Pardoner, but she remains a potential source of trouble for others.

That potential is not, however, pursued in the play. The Pardoner's masculine authority remains in place, even though it is now paradoxically aligned with the threat of the female sexual unruliness that he releases. This alignment might in itself, of course, be a cause for concern: in both *The Canterbury Tales* and the Prologue to the *Tale of Beryn*, the Pardoner's own disorderliness – his unauthorized sexual behaviour and overall corruption – calls

46

for a severe punishment, which is meted out in the narratives. No such punishment occurs in *The Foure PP*: the genially comic tone is retained throughout. Heywood recognizes the Pardoner's corruption and his association with gender disruption, but punishing them seems less important to him, perhaps because of the shifting religious attitudes of the early sixteenth century. Whereas the recognition and reformation of corruption within the Church was of paramount importance in the fourteenth and fifteenth centuries (the period of Lollard critiques of the Church), in the 1520s and 1530s it may well have seemed, to a Catholic like Heywood, that the preservation of the Church was of greater importance than its reform. As a favourite royal entertainer, Heywood was surely aware of the potential for a break with Rome in the context of Henry VIII's desire for a divorce from Katherine of Aragon. As John Guy suggests, Henry's quarrel with the pope was inevitable 'from the moment he ventilated his doubts about his marriage in the spring of 1527'.[23] It must have seemed even more so after Cardinal Wolsey's fall in 1529 and the threat of interdict in the early 1530s – that is, at precisely the moment Heywood was composing *The Foure PP*. Heywood's Catholicism is well documented, and it may account for the indulgent tone taken toward the Pardoner's transgressions: in the atmosphere leading toward the break with Rome, it may have seemed expedient for a Catholic at court to present as harmless the corruption and gender transgression associated since Chaucer with the figure of the Pardoner. As a courtier, Heywood invites laughter at the Pardoner's foibles; as a Catholic, he suggests that they are contained by the Church's universal authority.[24] Despite its corruption, now indulgently rendered non-threatening, the Church, like the Pardoner himself, must, in Catholic eyes, retain its spiritual authority, as Heywood makes clear in the play's final pages: the Palmer assures the audience that

> *To passe the tyme in thys without offence*
> *Was the cause why the maker dyd make it.*
> *And so we humble beseche you take it,*
> *Besechynge our lorde to prosper you all*
> *In the fayth of hys churche universall.*

Gender transgression poses no real threat – is, indeed, harmlessly entertaining – as long as figures like the Pardoner remain subject to the universal Church. The possibility of transgression is raised only so it can be contained by the Church – as well as by humour. We are also reminded in this passage that the Pardoner's entire story is presented as a self-conscious lie: in the context of the play, the threat of gender transgression is, after all, to be taken only as a joke. Unlike the lies of Chaucer's Pardoner and of the Pardoner who appears in the Prologue to the *Tale of Beryn*, this Pardoner's lies are not intended to fool anyone, and the play's audience, interpret as Catholic, shares in the joke.

It is no accident that the Pardoner tells not the first, but the second lie about women. His assertion of authority paves the way for this final insistence on the Church's universal power, and thus moves the play away from the Potycary's preceding, and potentially more troubling, lie. It is the Potycary rather than the Pardoner who, in the first lie, tells a tale of a more dangerous female appropriation of the phallus, and who posits this transgression as a threat – though not only as a threat – in terms of politics and religion as well as gender, a threat that will be contained or defused by the Pardoner's lie.

The woman whom the Potycary claims to have cured is strangely anonymous: not only does she remain nameless, she is also classless, lacking the markers of social status that located Kit so precisely in the social hierarchy (and that will do the same for Margery Corson). The Potycary's patient is little more than a female body, though she is morally a 'wanton' and physically afflicted with epilepsy inherited from her mother (ll. 714–15), 'the fallen syknes' (l. 713) for which she is seeking a cure, a sickness that, given the following reference to 'short heels', appears to be a double-entendre on female sexuality:

> How ofte she fell were muche to reporte.
> But her hed so gydy and her helys so shorte,
> That with the twynglynge of an eye
> Downe wolde she falle evyn by and by.

> (ll. 720–3)

The female body that insists on 'falling', that indeed cannot remain upright, suggests the Aristotelian and medieval belief – one that continued into the sixteenth century – that 'the uterus makes women eager to procreate, and desire the male', and that this desire causes women to be 'more prone to illness', as Maclean punningly notes.[25]

The Potycary's description of the treatment for this ailment (the insertion of a 'glyster' [l. 731]) is filled with further double-entendres relating to sexual intercourse, conception and childbirth – and to gunpowder artillery – as well as, appropriately, to medicine, since, as Axton and Happé point out, '[i]t was thought that in the case of women sexual intercourse was beneficial' as a treatment for epilepsy.[26]

> I thrust a thampyon in her tewell
> And bad her kepe it for a jewell

But I knewe it so hevy to cary
That I was sure it wolde nat tary,
For where gonpouder is ones fyerd
The tampyon wyll no lenger be hyerd.
Whiche was well sene in tyme of thys chaunce:
For when I had charged this ordynaunce,
Sodeynly, as it had thonderd,
Even at a clap losed her bumberd.

(ll. 732–41)

The woman's body is metaphorically transformed into a cannon, the language of 'tampions', gunpowder, ordnance and bombards specifically denoting heavy artillery ('tampion' refers to the wadding used in firing muzzle-loading guns). At the same time, such terms additionally refer to the female anatomy, 'tampion' also suggesting a pessary (or suppository inserted into bodily orifices, especially the vagina, for medical reasons), and 'bumberd' including, in addition to its primary meaning, 'the traditional play on bum-beard'.[27] These sexual references are confirmed by their result: this woman having expelled the 'tampion' is 'delyvered, with suche violens/ Of all her inconveniens' (ll. 765–6). This is the language of parturition for the early modern period, in which childbirth is typically imagined primarily in terms of the mother's delivery: 'The primary work of childbearing . . . was not the production of a child but the deliverance of a woman. Attention focused on the female body and its punishing trials and tribulations.'[28] The metaphorical sexual intercourse suggested by the Potycary inserting his 'tampion' into the woman's body, which in turn is the cause of a burden 'hevy to cary', thus issues in a metaphorical childbirth, as is also confirmed by the Potycary's exclamation, 'But in a good houre maye these wordes be spoken!' (l. 762), appropriate, as Axton and Happé point out, 'to heralding delivery of an infant'.[29] The 'tewel', or anus, is also metaphorically a birth canal.

If the discourse of childbirth is present in this description, however, it is a peculiarly destructive parturition; paradoxically, the 'tewel' is also a phallic cannon. Following the 'clap' of line 741, the Potycary continues:

Now marke, for here begynneth the revell:
The tampion flew ten longe myle levell
To a fayre castell of lyme and stone –
For strength I knowe nat suche a one –
Whiche stode upon an hyll full hye,
At fote wherof a ryver ranne bye
So depe, tyll chaunce had it forbyden,

Well myght the Regent there have ryden.
But when this tampyon on thys castell lyght,
It put the castels so farre to flyght
That down they cam eche upon other,
No stone left standynge, by Goddes mother . . .

(ll. 742–53)

This explosive metaphorical birth, described as a carnivalesque 'revell', has the power, like all carnivals (and bombardments), to bring down at least the signs of aristocratic and phallic power, in this case a distant castle that literally loses its 'stones'. This birth has the power to turn the world upside down: not only is the high castle levelled, its stones fill the river and turn it into land, so 'That who lyste nowe to walke therto,/May wade it over and wet no shoo' (ll. 758–9).

Gunpowder weapons were, by the late fifteenth and early sixteenth centuries, well established as the phallic symbols they still are today.[30] The Potycary's speech, then, is, like the Prologue to the *Tale of Beryn*, about the violent appropriation of phallic power by a woman. As we might expect, this appropriation is a threat to the symbols of patriarchal authority, a threat contained, like those posed by Kit the tapster and Margery Corson, by carnivalesque humour: the female body itself becomes a phallus, and that which this phallicized female body produces not only brings down the castle of patriarchy, but makes it accessible to all who desire entry, 'who lyste'. As the Potycary says, 'So was thys castell layd wyde open': the image of impenetrable masculine authority itself is penetrated and opened up, feminized, by the disturbing power of the phallic female body. (Female unruliness was, in fact, traditionally associated with the gathering of women in the birthroom.[31])

Also as in the Prologue to *The Tale of Beryn*, this phallic power is exercised by the female body in conjunction with men: the Potycary's patient requires the insertion of his 'tampion' in order to achieve her full destructive potential. (Conception as well as childbirth – at which only women would normally be present – is thus emphasized at this point.[32]) In this case, however, the circumstances are somewhat different: the Potycary, unlike the Pardoner in the fifteenth-century tale, cooperates fully in handing over phallic power to this woman, and finds the results pleasurable, a revel. And this woman needs no assistance such as Kit's paramour in wielding the phallus once it is in her possession: she looses her own 'bumberd'. In addition, the language of the speech links this power to the uniquely female realm of childbirth as well as to masculine warfare; the woman does not give up her female identity in taking on masculine power. The play, unexpectedly, both recognizes the potential destructiveness of female power and also refuses to limit it or even to condemn it, radical though its results may be. As in the case of the Pardoner's speech, it is important to recall that this one is self-consciously presented as a lie. Here, too, female phallic power is primarily a joke. On the other hand, we might also inquire why Heywood chooses this specific lie or joke for the Potycary to tell.

The Potycary's speech is both remarkably similar to the Prologue to *The Tale of Beryn* (a man hands over the phallus to a woman, who then wields it as a military weapon) and very different in its effect. Given both the similarities and the differences between them, we might ask what exactly has changed? What anxieties in the 1520s and 1530s about childbirth and the future of the patriarchy, as represented by the castle, might contribute to this image of the childbearing woman as destructive of masculine authority, yet also as not to be condemned?

If we pose the question in this way, it may be possible to see that this speech participates in the discourse of royal (and national) anxiety over the question of succession during Henry VIII's marriage to Katherine of Aragon, just as the Pardoner's speech suggests anxiety about the future of the Church in the same period. Katherine of Aragon never produced a living male heir who might succeed Henry on the throne; her pregnancies resulted in miscarriages, stillbirths and children who died in infancy, as well as a living daughter, Mary, in 1516. By 1525–26, according to J.J. Scarisbrick, Henry was seriously involved with Anne Boleyn;[33] and by 1527 he was expressing his intention to divorce Katherine. In 1533 the divorce was granted, Anne Boleyn became pregnant and Henry married her. As in the case of the incipient break with the Roman Church, Heywood's composition of *The Foure PP* coincides exactly with this period of upheaval and national anxiety over the issues of childbirth and succession. Axton and Happé have suggested that the reference to the devils' troubles with the 'two women' mentioned in the Pardoner's speech 'may cloak a jibe . . . about the great trouble in the realm caused by Anne Boleyn and Katherine of Aragon',[34] and I would argue that the Potycary's speech does the same.

Specifically, the image of a woman who takes on masculine authority and phallic power by the paradoxical means of her own female anatomy and traditional role as mother, and who thereby brings down, opens up and feminizes the symbol of royal patriarchy, participates in the same controversy over female rulership as the texts discussed by Maclean; so might the anticipated real-life succession of Princess Mary to the throne (hence, perhaps, the reference to 'Goddes mother' Mary at the end of the passage quoted above). Maclean reviews the arguments both favouring and opposing women's ability to rule directly; both positions were argued throughout the sixteenth century and, while those opposing it were perhaps regarded as more convincing, the possibility of female rule was undoubtedly also acknowledged, and is the best example of the theoretical improvement in women's status in this period mentioned above.[35] Certainly Henry VIII desired a male successor yet, at the time of Heywood's composition of *The Foure PP*, Princess Mary was his only living heir.

While I do not necessarily wish to claim that Heywood intended the Potycary's speech as an allegory of this historical situation, the image of the phallic woman presented therein resonates powerfully with it. The description of the castle, for example, irresistibly suggests Windsor Castle, the main royal residence outside London, and one that Henry VIII had restored as part of his project of castle building;[36] Henry's extravagant life at Windsor in the 1520s has been documented by Christopher Hibbert.[37] Of all the castles associated with Henry VIII, only Windsor matches the castle described by the Potycary:

> . . . *a fayre castell of lyme and stone –*
> *For strength I knowe nat suche a one –*
> *Whiche stode upon an hyll full hye,*
> *At fote wherof a ryver ranne bye*
> *So depe, tyll chaunce had it forbyden,*
> *Well myght the Regent there have ryden.*

(ll. 744–9)

The mention of *Regent*, one of the king's warships, associates this description with Henry VIII.[38] Furthermore, the description of a stone castle perched on a high hill with a navigable river running at its foot corresponds closely to the topographical situation of Windsor Castle, 'a steep chalk cliff rising abruptly to a height of 100 feet above the bank of the Thames, which flows under its northern front'.[39] The reference is even more piquant if, as Bolwell suggests, *The Foure PP* were performed at a court dinner – perhaps at Windsor itself.

As the main royal residence, and an edifice first built by William the Conqueror and occupied by every English monarch since, Windsor serves as a peculiarly apt symbol of patrilineal royal power. And it is this same royal patrilineage that Katherine of Aragon – or, more precisely, the products of Katherine's womb – threatened with destruction and, indeed, with feminization, in the person of Princess Mary and the prospect of her succession. For Heywood, once again his double position as courtier and as Catholic seems to have posed the same sort of problem expressed in the Pardoner's speech: he recognizes here the threat to Henry VIII's patrilineal line posed by Katherine and Mary, and yet the prospect of a Catholic queen may have seemed less problematic to him than to the king, especially if the re-establishment of the male line required, as it clearly did in the late 1520s and early 1530s, a divorce from Katherine and marriage to the more reform-minded Anne Boleyn. (Heywood was, in fact, on friendly terms with Mary throughout her life.[40]) For this brief moment in Henry VIII's reign, women may have seemed to possess, at least in potential, the formerly masculine power of rule theorized in the intellectual debates of the period, that is, to have appropriated the phallus precisely through their female bodies. From this perspective, the Potycary's speech may anticipate the image of the 'Queen's Two Bodies', female in her private life but male in her public functions, later to be developed with regard to Queen Elizabeth I.[41]

It is all the more important, then, for Heywood to conclude his play on a less ambivalent, more clearly pro-Catholic note, and his return to the Pardoner allows him to do so, as we have seen. The very fact that the Pardoner's speech looks backward to medieval discourses on gender, and indeed specifically to Chaucer, suggests such a return to traditional authority. Heywood's appeal to the specific authority of the universal Church places gender transgression, like all transgression, in its place as no more than a joke or foible to be contained within the Church's ultimately patriarchal power. Thus the Palmer finally wins the contest by having his positive valu-ation of women ('I never sawe nor knewe, to my consyens,/Any one woman out of paciens' [ll. 1002–3]) declared the greatest lie of all, a reassertion of misogyny followed in short order with the assertion that all judgements must follow those of the Church: 'But as the churche doth judge or take them,/So do ye receyve or forsake them' (ll. 1213–14). Both judgements, antifeminist and pro-Church are, significantly, delivered by the same voice, the Pedler's; the Church and patriarchy are thus re-established as one and the same. Whereas the Pardoner represents the anxieties surrounding gender transgression for both Chaucer and the author of the Prologue to the *Tale of Beryn*, for Heywood he becomes the means of subsuming those transgressions within the greater patriarchal power of the universal Church.

The specific historical situations that I am positing as the underlying problems being addressed in Heywood's interlude are not the only discourses present in it. As I suggested earlier, the Potycary's speech is not to be taken as an allegory, but as a multivalent discursive site, one element of which is the national debate over female succession, focusing on Princess Mary. As a literary rather than a political or religious text, however, this speech also draws on a number of other discourses for its comic effect. For example, it may also anticipate the discourses of monstrous birth that, according to David Cressy's recent study, would shortly appear as warnings of God's displeasure in the context of the religious controversies fostered by the Reformation.[12] The Potycary's speech additionally reflects the discourse of the female body out of control, and thus in violation of early modern strictures on bodily integrity, that has been explored by Gail Kern Paster. It may also be conditioned in part by early modern discourses on the 'fundament', meaning both 'rectum' and 'foundation'; from that perspective, the image of the fart that in destroying a castle also lays a new foundation provides evidence for Jeffrey Masten's contention that the Renaissance rectum signifies not abjection, but an originary groundwork. The image of a body of water giving its easy access to an English castle might additionally reflect fears of a French invasion. The Pardoner's speech, too, draws together various late medieval discourses about women, male authority, whoredom, etc., in addition to the religious discourse I emphasized above. Literary texts are, in part, the sites where numerous such discourses intersect, with or without the author's conscious intentions; the discourse of gender and power is only one of them. But where those specific discourses are concerned, Chaucer's Pardoner provides a literary model that seems to have been particularly appealing in this transitional period between late medieval and early Tudor literature.

The importance of a name: Gender, power and the strategy of naming a child in a noble Italian family: The Martinengo of Brescia

MARCELLO ZANE

Introduction

The study of first and family names (onomastics) reveals a great deal about a family's connections to a particular locality.[1] Names carry symbolic values which give prominence to complex plots that interweave lives, mentalities and the fortunes of important families of the Italian nobility. Names show alternations in the fortunes of a family: they disappear or reappear repeatedly across the generations, with the addition of numerals, diminutives, and plurals which tend to distinguish and rescue the individual from oblivion and homonym.[2] In the following pages I shall try to explain the system of imposing and transmitting names in relation to one of the most important families in the history of Brescia, the Martinengo.

This was a noble family, which exerted a primary role both in the public life of the town and in Venetian territory during almost four centuries of domination by the Most Serene Venetian Republic between 1427 and 1797. The wealthy Martinengo were frequently public officials, notaries, leaders, high-ranking prelates and condottiere in other Venetian cities. The family was interrelated with the powerful Doges of Venice and had dominions in some areas of the province, with *merum et mixtum imperium*, that is to say supreme penal and civil jurisdiction.[3] They are considered the most powerful Brescian family of this period.

The genealogical materials in the historical documents used[4] have been formalized through the help of a structured and informative database, which allows the study of the demographical, onomastic behaviour, as well as the gender relationships in this important family. This database also makes it possible to study a significant split in Italian patrician society of this period and specific family behaviour patterns. Names are never chosen at random.[5] Issues such as religious beliefs and political strategy are important elements in the motivation and dynamics of name selection. Interpersonal relationships play their part in name choice and, very importantly, the relationships between men and women of the family. Moreover financial and patrimonial issues, always important to families, play a predominant role in naming.

Names for a surname

The Martinengo name and its variants emerge around the tenth and eleventh centuries when the disappearance of the powerful dominions system permitted the formation of family groups.[6] These settlements were based on territories. The castle and the land functioned as the concrete symbol of family origin and provided a common and distinctive nomenclature among families with the same surname. In addition, the Martinengo used names of places and palaces, for example, from Padernello to Villagana, from Cadivilla to Villachiara, from Mottella to Barco and others (Novarino, Pallata, of the Palle), names connected to precise geographical places in the Brescian surrounding countryside or to well-known urban symbols.[7] A surname extends and is recast as time goes by and becomes the identification mark between families, and an indicator of original wealth. Thus names define the position of individuals and family groups in the ideal referential space of the town nobility.[8] The characteristics of the Martinengo name signal individuality and establish identity, through a variety of denominations. Throughout his life, every Martinengo had a precise onomastic placing. This person is not simply called Martinengo, but this name also indicates the family branch to which he belongs, with geographical specifications of the castle and the locality assigned to the founder. It also includes a Christian name, often followed by his father's Christian name and sometimes even by a nickname. A truly univocal research into surnames, names and nicknames is at variance, as we will see, in the mass of the very frequent homonyms and at times with the fluctuations of an individual's name. This research depends on the historical sources used, such as religious, testamentary and military materials, or on the historical period or on the variability of the social condition. Name choice, over which the women of the family had no power of say or decision, nevertheless, quite often held surprises in the subtle interplay between the different families both of the mother and father of the newborn.

Genealogical charts

The number of names used by the Martinengo between the fourteenth century and the beginning of the eighteenth century, is made up of 188 source names, which took on feminine inflections, diminutives or pet names. These could also be combined in compound form as a second or third name. These names mostly cover the 996 Martinengo who are studied in the course of this research. This set is much higher than the number utilized in different studies. In studies of Florence in the fourteenth century and Puglia in the sixteenth and seventeenth centuries 195 different names were used for more than 4,000 individuals. In the France of the seventeenth century, for example, in the area of Limousin about 120 names were used in this study and about 50 in the case of Marseilles.[9] In this case I refer to thousands of christened individuals of different social extraction.

Table 4.1 shows an ideal classification of the most commonly used names, and also the percentage of Martinengo who, during the course of the centuries, are thus named:

Table 4.1 Names used with major frequency

Name	Individuals	%
Francesco/a	67	6.73
Giovanni/a	45	4.52
Camillo/a	40	4.02
Mario/a	38	3.82
Paolo/a	37	3.71
Giulio/a	31	3.11
Marco	30	3.01
Carlo/a	26	2.61
Marcantonio	25	2.51
Eleonora	25	2.51
Luigi/a	22	2.21
Pietro	20	2.01
Lelio/a	19	1.91
Emilio/a	17	1.71
Bartolomeo/a	17	1.71

Naturally this table must take into account the inevitable gaps in the available documentary sources and there must be some reservation with regard to the exact formation and composition of the Martinengos' genealogical charts. It is in the criteria adopted in the drafting of the genealogical charts, in their omissions and in the precise dispositions of the same, that the role played (or not played) by the female becomes evident. Because of their negligible responsibility in the symbolic evolution of the family, the Martinengo women adopted a subtle strategy in order to withstand the masculine role and hence to construct their own spaces.[10] The patrilineal succession system, that is the relationships organized around the male line that had been adopted by Italian nobles, automatically discriminated against females who were seen merely as intermediary links between the lineages of different families.

The degree of permanence of the family is well indicated and made evident by appearance over time in the genealogical charts. The female side appears for a limited period of time: from the time of birth up to the time of marriage, which is followed by their leaving the family nucleus, or from the date of marriage to death (or widowhood), for women who enter a new family. The anchorage to genealogies is precise and male and, cleansed of the female presence by marriage or death, codifies with precision the domination of the Martinengo blood relationship over those acquired by marriage.[11] For this reason the birth of a daughter is not always registered in the deeds or put into the genealogical charts, especially if she died at a very tender age. More often, there is a simple registration of the birth with an indication of the sex of the child, but with no indication of date or name; this means that the heraldic sources are full of gaps and incomplete. However, they also provide evidence of the important difference of gender.

An analysis of the naming system of the new-born members of the Martinengo families allows us to perceive the rule of onomastic transmissions and its links to accepted customs. These were so deeply rooted as to make even the choice of a name for children a strongly formalized matter. In particular, let us try to understand when and why a new-born child is made the namesake of a relation (on the male or female line). What are the different channels of transmission for a name, and what is the role played by the Martinengo women? This female role was often seen as a real and probable danger for the acknowledgement and safeguarding of the family patrimony.[12] The choice of the name indicates the separation between the males and females of the family.

Saints and godfathers, the deceased

The religious factor in the choice of names, which derives from images of saints or symbols of the Catholic Church, does not seem to have mattered greatly to the Martinengo. In fact, there are very few examples that we can trace back to this practice. There are, also, very few instances in the family where individuals are named after patron saints of a territory belonging to the Martinengo or after the patron saint of the parish of residence. This very scant affection for saints and Catholic precepts is confirmed, for example, by the family register of the noble Silla di Cesare Martinengo Cesaresco, who married Domicilla Gambara with whom he had no less than fifteen children. The document has entries for the date of each child's birth (with the name of the saint of the day), the names of the godfathers and godmothers, and additionally details of the registrations of births in the family of their son Giorgio and subsequently their grandson, Silla.[13] Of the twenty-nine births registered from 1666 to 1763, not a single new-born child bears the name of the saint of the day or the name of a godfather, the preferred names being those of parents taken from the family onomastic stock.[14] This naming practice is carried out even though the Catholic Church, especially after the Counter-Reformation, encouraged the custom of naming children after saints and patrons, of taking these as models to be imitated during the life of the new-born child and, furthermore, forbidding the feminizing of the names of the Apostles and major saints.[15] The attempt to use the act of naming as a means of education, seeking to put the latest new-born child under the protection of a particular saint, was a purpose carefully avoided by the Martinengo. They acknowledged saints' names only partially, through the use of multiple names in an attempt to reconcile the family's requirements with the indispensable patronage of the church.[16] Of course, there are Martinengo names such as Francesco, Giovanni, Paolo, Marco and others which clearly derive from Christian martyrology, but their lasting use was dictated more by family reasons than by religious practice.

The use of names deriving from the Christian calendar is almost unknown in this family; had it been employed, it would reveal a particular devotion of the Martinengo parents to an individual figure, a devotion which could be reaffirmed in the name chosen at baptism. It is true that there are three Martinengo men bearing the name of Angelo. No one is called Rocco to plead for protection against pestilence, and no one is called Domenico to celebrate a birth or christening on a feast day.

In the other areas dealt with in analogous research, the name Maria accounts for up to 50–60 per cent of the female names. Among the Martinengo this name is chosen at baptism in only about 10 per cent of cases. However deeply symbolic the name Maria may be, it is clearly evident that the method of selecting names adopted by the Martinengo is even more deeply concerned with honouring the memory of a deceased member of the family. In these cases the religious aspects, the pain of personal loss, the exorcizing of death and the world of the dead, form the essential motivations for decisions connected to patrimonial succession.

This is typical in the case of a child born posthumously, a not uncommon event in a family of military leaders and condottiere, destined to lead an adventurous and dangerous life. These were sons who, conceived during rare intervals at home, never saw their fathers, and their mothers (on their behalf) followed the family tradition and named the child after the deceased father. For males born posthumously to the Martinengo family the index of homonyms is 100 per cent of the known cases. There are no genealogical charts in which posthumously born daughters appear: the obvious sign of a difference of gender and importance in the management of heredity networks. This is a standard that endured from generation to generation through the centuries and the many branches of the family as in the unfortunate case of the Cadivilla Martinengo. In this case, Ettore I of Giacomo had a sixth son, the posthumous Ettore II, whose wife, in due time, bore a posthumously born son, naturally called Ettore III. In none of these cases do the Martinengo women have the power to decide: the rule is applied strictly and without exception by the males of the Martinengo family.

The homonym between father and posthumous son is clearly not the only case in which the child is given the name of a deceased relative. Often the family named the most recent new-born child in memory of family members who had died at a very young age and around the same time as this new birth. This naming practice is common in families that suffered a high percentage of stillbirths. This naturally led to the repetition of the same name at every birth that follows that of the new-born.[17] A custom emerged, underlining the constant attempt to achieve the rebirth of the deceased child, that amounts to a sort of reincarnation of the child and its name.[18] Another common usage was the adoption of names belonging to brothers or sisters who had died either unexpectedly or violently shortly before the birth of the son. This was one of the rare occasions when consent was given to the introduction of a name from the distaff side, even if it was not in keeping with the general rules in force. This name was often one that was foreign to the traditional Martinengo onomastic (since it was inherited from in-laws) and its intrusion was justified only to the extent that it was taken from a recently deceased close relative of the wife, preferably, of course, if he or she belonged to a prestigious or important family. Sentimental reasons were stronger than economic ones. However, we must remember that the choice of a name could play a new role in more complex strategies involving the process of public mourning and become a sign of homage on the part of the Martinengo male toward the powerful family of his wife.

As already mentioned, it is a different matter when death comes through other agents. Someone dying from plague or smallpox will hardly ever be honoured by having a descendant named after him. However, precise distinctions can be made in cases of homicides and duels, or the execution of those sentenced to death. No member of the Martinengo family, for example, ever bore the names of the brothers Troiano or Ulisse, the first having been assassinated by a third brother, and the second having been poisoned by relatives in a tragic family feud. However, Marcantonio Martinengo Barco, who was killed in a duel in 1750, had at least two nephews who bore his name, the sons of his brothers Silvio and Massimiliano. Subtle strategies and fine distinctions come into play, therefore, in cases of violent death. These strategies can be clearly seen in the case of the descendants of Giovanmaria Martinengo Motella, husband of Taddea Martinengo Padernello, both members of the same family. Three of their sons were assassinated between the years 1527 and 1533: Luigi was killed in 1527 by mercenaries of the powerful Nassino family, and Scipione in 1533 by Girolamo Martinengo Padernello, a relative on his mother's side, during bitter family feuds over patrimonial inheritances. In the midst of this, we note the death of the other brother Giulio, which occurred in 1531 at the hand of Carlo Averoldi. The names of Luigi and Scipione, killed for internal Martinengo causes, are quickly forgotten, because they have upset the patrimonial order of the family. They had no homonymous descendants in either of the two family branches involved. Conversely, Giulio, killed by an external hand, was able, in memory of his sacrifice, to unite the family and shortly after his death his name was given to a nephew, the son of Camillo, the fourth brother who survived. Therefore, there are three elements that seem to play a major part in the decision to name a son after a deceased member of the immediate family circle. First of all, there is the freedom to take action regarding inheritance and patrimonial obligations; secondly, there is the need for commemoration within the family as a reaffirmation of power that is clearly visible both inside and outside the family; lastly, the length of time separating the date of birth from the death of the relative who is to be remembered.

The lapse of time between a death and the naming of an infant in memory of the deceased is almost always proportional to the grade of relationship and the age of the deceased. The Martinengo, judging by the available data, gave a deceased grandfather's homonym to a new-born grandson within an average time span between the death and the birth of about 8–15 years. The interval for giving a deceased uncle's homonym to a new-born nephew was shorter, on average 1–5 years, and for other relatives and a new-born child less than 3 years. After a period of two years, every name that could bear reference to the memory of a maternal ancestor is lost. For the same reason the death of a first wife was rarely commemorated in the names given by a father to children born in marriages that follow. He applied the rules, however, by giving the name of his deceased mother to a daughter. It is clear, above all, that matrimonial union has a strategic and patrimonial function, rather than being the crowning moment of an affair of the heart. A wife's family line concerns the Martinengo circle only for the length of time that the two families are united: on the death of the wife it is consigned to oblivion.[19]

Prestige and heritage: Choices which count

The circumstance that is of great significance in the naming of new-born babies is the link to the patrimonial legacy. In this case the names cease to be a simple system of identification bound to family traditions, but become an element of the hereditary system of the Deed of Trust where, often inevitably, names are inherited, as are palaces and family riches.[20] As an institution, the Deed of Trust satisfies the need to conserve family power, retaining the integrity and stability of the patrimony and defending it against the division and the claims of the female branches of the family.[21] On the other hand, the Brescian statutes establish that in cases where fathers die intestate, the inheritance passes to the male line: to sons and, in their absence, to brothers and nephews. Only in cases where there are no male heirs can the inheritance pass to women. This is only a remote possibility, but for the Martinengo, it is one to be avoided at all costs. A consequence of such an inheritance would be the loss of all power to the advantage of the family of their female in-laws.

For the Martinengo the struggle to retain the inheritance always had powerful consequences for the structure of the family, imposing continuity and conferring on family groups a cohesion and behaviour privileging a masculine orientation. However, in the Martinengo family the practice of the Deed of Trust was applied even more rigidly in the form of the law of primogeniture. In their case the inheritance passed to descendants through the first-born, exclusively through the male line. Quite often the Martinengo apply the bond of the Deed of Trust to primogeniture, in order that the inheritance can pass intact from first-born to first-born without dissipation. These Martinengo children are thus invested with their hereditary rights even before they are born. Each appropriate heir claims the inheritance in its entirety exactly as the first testator did leading, as can be imagined, to numerous quarrels, but also to various new onomastic traditions. The visible possessions of the family: palaces, thousands of hectares of land, farmsteads, mills and money, passed from one to another without being consumed along the way.[22]

It is useful to illustrate some of the Deeds of Trust established in various Martinengo epochs, in order to show how the selection of names was influenced, noting that the female branches of the family were excluded from the selection process. However, they were frequently involved against their will in name changes. Bartolomeo I Martinengo Villachiara established a Deed of Trust on 24 October 1425 for the descendants of his three sons – Taddeo, Carlo and Prevosto. Carlo and Prevosto died very young, and the relatives had a precise onomastic strategy for dealing with the inheritance.[23] Then Taddeo also died young, while the father, Bartolomeo, was still alive, leaving his nephew Francesco, who was in bad health. This created concern, because the will stipulated that should the three sons predecease the father, the nephew Francesco di Taddeo, would become the first possible heir of the Deed of Trust. Coming to the aid of the family in the event of the nephew also dying (with the consequent dispersal of the inheritance) there is a further safeguard for this particular family group. The posthumously born son of the original testator Bartolomeo, inevitably given the name of Bartolomeo, later had a natural child, Vittore, who was promptly acknowledged as legitimate, thus becoming the sole upholder of this branch of the family and heir of the original Deed of Trust. Thus the loss and dispersion of the property was avoided. The uncles and cousins having died childless, Vittore's son was naturally named Bartolomeo, as the new heir to the Deed of Trust instituted more than a century earlier by his homonymous great-grandfather.

In 1634 Francesco Martinengo da Barco, a bachelor, and son of Carlo (Bartolomeo I's second son) created a Deed of Trust in favour of his nephews, his brothers' sons and, but only in the event of his descendants dying out, in favour of his maternal uncles Paolo and Battista Martinengo (Carlo had married Isabella di Frederico Martinengo Palle).[24] Even though his father and mother belonged to the same family, the difference of gender became a discriminating factor. The name of the testator Francesco Martinengo da Barco was extensively used: each of his brothers promptly called one of their sons Francesco. However, the maternal branch adopted its own strategy: Battista Martinengo Palle, having given his sons the names of their paternal ancestors, called his last born daughter Isabella. His last child, born in 1645, was a son, and he called this potential heir by the name of the Martinengo Barco testator Francesco, thus introducing a new onomastic tradition to his family. This name had been entirely absent in the preceding two hundred years amongst the 46 Martinengo Palle males born up to that point. It seems that Battista was declaring his family ready, in case of need, to inherit what had been instituted by his testator relative.

The importance of the name is also indicated by the will of Camillo Martinengo Cesaresco, born in 1612 to Antonio and Claudia Caprioli who, on 5 November 1690, founded a particular Deed of Trust with the object-ive not only of maintaining property but also the perpetuation of the name Camillo. This name was given to his father in memory of his paternal grandfather (Camillo di Giovanni Antonio Martinengo Cesaresco, born in 1557, and also of his mother Claudia's grandfather, the powerful Count Camillo Caprioli). The following passage is a part of this document that forbids any degree of derogation on penalty of forfeiting the very substantial patrimony. Having listed the details of his possessions, Count Camillo records having:

> resolved that on these should be founded a specific Deed of Trust confined to a perpetual line of first-born males with the obligation on all beneficiary first-born males to bear or to assume the name Camillo in order that the total property remains intact in perpetuity . . . the beneficiaries and . . . the Ill. Sig. Count Antonio my nephew has the obligation to name himself Antonio Camillo, this failing to be [the property] shall immediately pass on to 3rd Count Camillo my great-grandson, first-born son of the 3rd Count Lodovico, brother of the above mentioned Sig. Count Antonio, and continuing thus from first-born to first-born, in perpetuity, to the last male descendant, always with the obligation that all first-born are to be named at baptism or to assume the name Camillo; if there be anyone not so named or who does not desire to be so named, he shall immediately be deprived of the aforesaid benefits.[25]

Over the years, however, things did not go as the testator Camillo hoped they would because, though his first-born nephew, Antonio, did change his name to Camillo, he did not have any descendants. Lodovico, the second-born, added the name Camillo as required and took his place with his descendants, inheriting his rich uncle's estates. After the will was drawn up, the frequency with which the name Camillo was used naturally increased enormously. Before the year 1690 – the date of the will – the name Camillo had been used by only six individuals, 9 per cent of the Martinengo Cesaresco; however, now the name Camillo became an essential require-ment for those wishing to aspire to the inheritance. The name was adopted 11 times, i.e. almost 21 per cent of the individuals subsequently born into the heritable branch of the family, and the family will be known by the nickname of 'Martinengo Camilli'. Notably, even if not themselves directly able to inherit, the female members of the family were also constrained to use that name.

The right name for the right heir

The reasons for the use of a particular name are various. In fact, in practice, the Martinengo patrimony of 188 names was subject to restricted use in the family. Of this stock, 69 names appear only once in the numerous family histories and then usually during the fifteenth century. Twenty names are sufficient to christen more than 50 per cent of the Martinengo. Canon law concerning the transmission of names to descendants is understood by medieval and early modern historians as a system in which the eldest son is named for his paternal grandfather, the second for his maternal grandfather, with subsequent sons taking the names of paternal and maternal uncles in alternation.[26] This alternation sought to honour the line of male descendants.

With regard to the sole paternal Martinengo branch, the application of this rule in a non-restrictive sense demonstrates the frequency of use as shown in Table 4.2. Here, the data (reconstructed from computerized

Table 4.2 Homonymy between paternal grandfather and nephew

Family	Grandfather-nephew	%
Barco	20	50.0
Cadvilla	9	50.0
Cesaresco I	7	100.0
Cesaresco II	4	23.5
Cesaresco III	5	62.5
Cesaresco IV V	6	60.0
Colleoni	9	50.0
Delle Palle	13	72.2
Motella	7	35.0
Paternello	5	45.5
Palatini	6	33.3
Pallata	6	42.9
Villachiara	6	40.0
Villagana	10	52.6
Total	113	48.5

(The percentage is calculated on nuclear families with at least one male child)

analyses) are presented subdivided into single family branches, using as comparison the 262 Martinengo families with progeny.

This is a rule that is followed only partially. If we examine the analysis carefully and narrow our field of comparison we will find that, among the Martinengo, 39 per cent of paternal uncle and nephew cases involve the transmission of the paternal uncle's name to the nephew, whereas 28 per cent of the paternal aunt and niece relationships involve homonymous transmissions (percentages calculated on families with more than one son).[27] This is sufficiently interesting to make us examine the case of homonymy between a niece and a paternal grandmother (who is not originally a Martinengo, but has for a long time been a member of the family). Unfortunately, the incompleteness of the data compromises this research, but 30 per cent of the families with daughters (excluding marriages between consanguineous Martinengo) show a homonymous relationship.

Everything was done to give the first daughter a name that will be 'useful'. The new Martinengo baby girl was given a name with clear endogenous origins. This pays homage to the maternal family and unites the two families with symbolic name bonds. Above all, the name given to a female child had significance in the field of matrimonial dowries, which were regulated by numerous conditions. Among the nobility, in an even more complex structure of economic relationship, the name represents an important formal signal. According to the city statutes, a dowry does not become the exclusive property of the husband's family, but belongs to all the children, male and female, born into the marriage. Furthermore, women were not obliged to leave their property to their sons. Thus, dowries have a precise economic influence, which affects the descendants of both genders, and even bypasses strict regulations, to the extent that part of these riches went to the daughters, who then left them to their daughters.

In many cases, the taking of a name originating from the mother's side, allows these female practices to be maintained, as a clear symbol both linking affection and the transfer of wealth both inside and outside the Martinengo family. There appear to be fewer cases that show father and son homonymy. As far as the Martinengo are concerned, this occurs in only 21 cases. Therefore, in approximately 8 per cent of Martinengo families with children there exists homonymy capable of generating confusion. However, this is a percentage which coincides with the average level of cases studied in Italy and Europe.[28] The almost complete absence of mother/daughter homonymy is in line with the patriarchal Martinengo tradition, which categorically excluded direct female homonymy.

The defence of the rule

This rigid line of descent through the father, which is revealed by the choice of names, remains significant in marriages between Martinengo men and women from other branches of the same family. Only three sons (equal to 7 per cent of the known cases), bore the name of their maternal, non-Martinengo grandfather in contrast to the degree of paternal grandfather/nephew homonymy which comes to 48.5 per cent. It seems clear that only rare departures from the rule of naming children after the male line were acceptable – even when the name to be inherited from the maternal grandfather was part of the Martinengo family stock of names. This behaviour satisfies the non-heritable nature of the patrimony possessed by the female branch: the wives entered into the new branch with merely a large but unchangeable dowry. Subtle strategies were also employed, which tend to reorganize the in-law relationships through other channels and with modest homonymy concessions. Such concessions were only allowed to the most important families of Brescian patricians, and were determined by reasons of power or discrimination.

For example, Francesco Martinengo Villagana married Taddea Caprioli in 1624. She was the daughter of a rich and powerful city family, and her husband named his two children Bartolomeo (born in 1628) and Medea (born in 1633). These names were taken from those of his Caprioli in-laws. For those times, this practice would have been a sign of weakness and an indication of a lack of authority on the part of Francesco Martinengo Villagana, both inside the family and with regard to the patrician power struggles, which were dominated at the time by the Caprioli family. Above all, this is a clear signal of the economic marginalization of the Francesco Martinengo Villagana family. Francesco, who was widowed in 1653, almost immediately entered the priesthood, dying in 1675.[29]

In this outline, the variations of family and male strategies appear to follow mandatory routes. Silla Martinengo Cesaresco and his wife Domicilla Gambara had 17 sons. The succession of their names confirms, to some extent, the patterns outlined: they show a stronger inclination toward the conservation of homonyms from the paternal line while preserving a certain degree of symmetrical alternation in the choice of names between paternal and maternal homonyms. The succession of these children follows below. In brackets I give the degree of homonymy that is most likely chosen, understanding *paternal* to mean the Martinengo branch and *maternal* to mean Gambara (another very rich and noble Brescian family) and the in-laws thus acquired:

1666 Lelio	(paternal grandfather and/or abbot brother)
1667 Fulvia	(paternal grandmother)
1668 Margherita Teresa	(paternal grandmother and/or paternal aunt)
1669 Fortunato	(paternal great-grandfather)
Orsolina	(?)
1670 Ottaviano	(?)
1671 Chiara	(?)
1674 Cesare	(father)
1675 Giorgio	(maternal uncle)*
1676 Chiara Teresa	(predeceased daughter)
1677 Eleonora	(paternal great-grandmother)
1678 Ippolita	(maternal aunt)
1680 Francesco Sarra	(maternal grandfather)
1682 Giulia	(paternal aunt)
1687 Geronimo	(?)

If we are dealing with a tradition, then the best thing to do is to verify the method of adopting names in the generations immediately following those that have already been studied, namely that for the sons of Giorgio (marked*). His first wife was Giulia Chizzola – who gave him an only child, a daughter called Domicilla – and who married for the second time Paola Fenaroli Calini:

1712 Domicilla	(mother)
1720 Chiara	(sister who died in infancy)
1721 Silla	(father)*
1722 Giulia	(deceased first wife and/or sister)
1723 Giovanni Francesco	(brother Francesco)
1724 Eleanor Margarita	(two sisters who became nuns)
1725 Laura Teresa	(sisters and/or in-laws)
1727 Cecilia Francesca	(paternal grandmother Cecilia, or son Francesco who died in infancy)
1728 Maria Rosa Polissena	(paternal grandmother, Polissena)

(The relationship referred to the parent: the paternal line is Martinengo and the maternal lines are first Chizzola and subsequently Fenaroli Calini.)

Finally, I shall now compare the choices of the third generation, that of Silla (marked*) born in 1721, who married Maria Soardi:

1751 Paola	(mother)
1752 Giacomo	(maternal grandfather and/or in-law)
1755 Luigi Fortunato	(paternal great-uncle)
1763 Paola Maria	(predeceased daughter Paola)

(The relationship refers to the parent Silla. The paternal line is Martinengo and the maternal line is Soardi.)

As is evident, the theoretical rule undergoes notable exceptions, as time goes by. Above all, the death of a relative appears to determine the name chosen for sons other than the first-born. Commemorating a deceased relative, either from the Martinengo line or the in-laws, seems to be an accepted reason, though there are some distinct exceptions. This is a tendency that seems to become general in cases where the family of the wife acquired by marriage is rich and rooted in the history and public life of the city. For the Gambara, as we have seen, the homonymistic influence is quite evident, as also, for example in the case of the marriage of Cesare Martinengo Cesaresco and Ippolita Gambara in 1495. Six of their twenty children bore a name of distinct Gambara origin and, for nine other births, a name of definite Martinengo derivation. Conversely where the prestige of the wife's family is insignificant, the presence of non-Martinengo names will be limited or non-existent. Therefore, for Martinengo fathers there is a determination first of all to select the name of first-born sons, giving them the name of their own father or grandfather (almost as if to satisfy as early as possible the onomastic demands of the close family). This is followed by the names of the family's illustrious dead, and then namesakes alternating between the relatives of the two families were selected.

Conclusion

Giving the eldest son the same name as that of his father's father was meant, therefore, to designate him explicitly as the legitimate heir, while names supplied by other branches of relatives were reserved for younger children. Guarding against the dispersal of the patrimony was always a priority and planning by descendants was meticulous. Women 'outsiders' to the Martinengo family entered it before the age of twenty. They bore children at regular intervals with not less than two years between one birth and another, and the use of the same name assured the imperative for a male heir to whom the family fortune is assigned. Those born into the Martinengo family followed precise paths through life: the first-born was the keeper of the family heritage and had to marry a woman chosen by his father and father-in-law in a precise framework of matrimonial alliance.[30] For the other sons the options were a life of celibacy, priesthood or a military career and, for the women, either marriage predetermined by the father or the cloister.[31]

A name is a search for identity, able to create confusion as well as distinction. It can specify family order precisely or express the limits of freedom, but it is also an historical source capable of revealing some of the elements that enable us to understand differences between family structures and, more generally, to reconstruct the mentality and sensibility of an aristocratic society in the early modern period.

CHAPTER FIVE

'Our Trinity!': Francis I, Louise of Savoy and Marguerite d'Angoulême

ROBERT KNECHT

Each year, as thousands of tourists visit the châteaux of the Loire valley in France, they are made aware of King Francis I, who built or refurbished many of them and whose emblem, the salamander, adorns so many gateways, chimney-pieces and dormer windows. In his own day Francis was commonly described as 'great', but over time his reputation has slumped. It began to suffer in the seventeenth century when a new royal dynasty – the Bourbons – came to rule France and sought to enhance its own achievement by depreciating that of its predecessor – the Valois. However, it was in the nineteenth century that Francis I came to be seen by historians as little more than a playboy. None was as influential as Jules Michelet. While admiring the period, which he himself first christened as 'the Renaissance', he came to despise Francis, who had contributed so much to its manifestation in France. The reason stemmed essentially from Michelet's hostility toward the Catholic church. In his view, Francis had missed a great opportunity offered to him by the Protestant Reformation. Instead of emancipating France and her people from the trammels of papal Rome by joining forces with Luther, Calvin and the other reformers, he had capitulated to Rome and tried to suppress religious dissidents. This for Michelet was an unforgivable error that eclipsed any credit the king may have earned by his patronage of the arts and of learning.[1] But Michelet had too low an opinion of Francis even to hold him entirely responsible for perpetrating that error. In his estimation the king had compounded his error by allowing himself to be manipulated by his mother.

For all his physical endowments and his prowess as a soldier and sportsman, Francis was, according to Michelet, a weak character, incapable of standing up to the women in his entourage. 'Women and war', he writes, 'war to please women'. He was completely under their spell. Women made him all that he was, they were also his undoing.'[2] Among the women who allegedly 'made' the king, two were outstanding: his mother, Louise of Savoy, and his sister, Marguerite d'Angoulême. 'This dangerous object who was to deceive everyone', writes Michelet, 'was born one might say between two prostrate women, his mother and sister, and thus they remained in this ecstasy of worship and devotion.'[3] Elsewhere Michelet writes of Francis: 'he was framed and beatified by his family. One saw him wear the halo that is shared by all who are loved, a noble vision between two women and two loves, his mother, passionate and still handsome, and his sensitive and charming sister, the Marguerite of Marguerites, who used to speak of "Our Trinity!" . . .'[4]

Every historian is to some extent conditioned by his or her upbringing. Michelet worshipped his mother and came to attach an enormous import-ance to maternal influence generally. 'All superior men', he wrote, 'are the sons of their mother; they reproduce her moral imprint as well as her traits.'[5] Thus, if Francis I acted as he did, the responsibility could be ascribed, so Michelet thought, to his mother, Louise of Savoy. She was, in his judge-ment, the king's 'evil genius'. 'This royal figure', he writes, 'who seemed to understand everything and spoke wonderfully, was in reality a splendid automaton in the hands of his mother, the crafty, violent and wily Savoyarde, and of Duprat, a businessman, shrewd, lowborn and base, whom she chose as chancellor.'[6] Louise loved her son passionately, Michelet continues, yet she was prepared to act behind his back. Thus, she boldly declared to a papal legate: 'Speak to me and we shall go our own way. If the king grumbles, so be it.'[7] Michelet's snobbish xenophobia also persuaded him to blame Louise for the matrimonial ties established between the royal house of France and the upstart Italian family of Medici, or, as he put it, between the lilies of France and the pills of the Medici. Having married off one of her sisters to Giuliano de' Medici, the pope's brother, she persuaded her son to give a princess of the French blood royal (Madeleine de la Tour d'Auvergne) to Lorenzo, the pope's nephew. The latter died soon afterwards of syphilis, as did his wife. They left a child, Catherine de' Medici, whom Michelet describes as 'a fatal gift'. In short, at his mother's instance, Francis played into the hands of the papacy: instead of becoming Italy's protector and of encouraging the German reformation, he 'let everything go by default, and like a new Esau, sold everything for a mess of potage'.[8]

If Louise of Savoy was the personification of evil to Michelet, her daughter, Marguerite of Angoulême, was, by contrast, all sweetness and light. Although only two years older than her brother, Francis, the age gap between them was, according to Michelet, widened by the all-consuming love which she bore him. She was, he writes, 'the mother, the mistress, the little wife'. Her love, Michelet writes, was the 'decisive, capital event in Francis's life: he owed her the charm by which he has seduced posterity'. Legend has it that Marguerite was the result of a pearl which her mother had swallowed. Still according to Michelet, Marguerite owed her upbringing to Madame de Châtillon, an accomplished lady who had secretly married cardinal Jean du Bellay. Thanks to her influence, Marguerite had been trained for the role of protector of all free spirits, a role which she fulfilled to the best of her ability despite the harsh treatment which she received from her brother. Michelet expresses his admiration of Marguerite in a fervent prayer: 'Our eternal gratitude will be yours, sweet mother of the Renaissance, whose hearth was that of our saints and whose charming bosom was the nest of Liberty.'[9] Michelet blames Francis I and ultimately Louise for such unhappiness as Marguerite had to endure. The all-consuming love which she felt for her brother, he argues, was to prove her misfortune, for he lacked her breeding and spirituality. 'Cradled by the intoxicating vines of the Charente . . . and poorly educated by women of Poitou . . . he was born with a material soul. Beneath the man and even the child, lay the faun and the satyr.'[10] In other words, the Trinity was cankered.

In addition to being a historian, Michelet was also a kind of poet who gave free rein to his imagination and deeply felt prejudices. Logic never was his strongest suit and he was prepared to manipulate history as ruthlessly as, in his judgement, Louise of Savoy manipulated her son.[11] Much of what he writes about the Trinity is too patently absurd to deserve close scrutiny, yet there is some semblance of truth in his account. Although never a queen, Louise did share actively in her son's government of France in spite of the Salic law which debarred women from the throne and the widespread belief that they were intellectually unfit to rule.[12] She was also reckoned by contemporaries to be excessively ambitious and avaricious. As for Marguerite, she did demonstrate a deeply felt spirituality which earned her the praise of evangelical and Protestant reformers. So we need to ponder the exact nature of the Trinity. Was it more than the bond which normally exists between a mother and her offspring? Was it as cankered as Michelet supposed? Was Louise evil and Marguerite saintly? How far were they responsible for Francis I's policies? These questions deserve an answer.

Louise of Savoy was the daughter of Philip, count of Bresse, who became duke of Savoy in 1496, and of Marguerite de Bourbon. Following her mother's death in 1483, she was brought up by Anne de Beaujeu, the daughter of King Louis XI, who ruled France with her husband, Pierre, during the minority of King Charles VIII. Anne married off Louise in 1487 to Charles, count of Angoulême, the impoverished first cousin of Louis, duke of Orléans. Charles died in 1495, leaving his nineteen-year-old widow to bring up their two children, Marguerite (born in 1492) and Francis (born in 1494). When Louis of Orléans succeeded to the throne as King Louis XII,

Francis became his heir presumptive. In 1499 Louis confirmed Louise's guardianship of her children and invited her to his court at Chinon. Soon afterwards, however, he entrusted them to the care of Pierre de Rohan, seigneur de Gié and a marshal of France. An ambitious and powerful man, Gié angered Louise by trying to control her household too closely. She slept in the same room as her children and protested vehemently when her privacy was broken by one of Gié's more zealous underlings.[13] It seems, however, that she was allowed a free hand in educating her children. Michelet unfairly accuses her of allowing them to grow up in a small, easy-going, and morally rather lax court. 'Tender and with few scruples', he writes, 'she shut her eyes.' But all the evidence contradicts this. Within her entourage, Louise was frequently identified with Prudence. Symphorien Champier called her 'another Pallas and very wise Minerva'. In 1530 she was praised by Jehan de Bourdigné as 'the Pallas of Savoy'. Louise's contribution to her son's education was given symbolic recognition in several books which were dedicated to her. One contains an illumination depicting a tall woman dressed entirely in black, holding a small boy in one hand and a huge compass in the other. The boy is easily identified as the Dauphin Francis since he is flanked by a dolphin. It follows that the tall woman is Louise. As for the compass, it is meant to conjure up the idea of the circle as the perfect form given by God to the whole of creation. Its task is to indicate the 'points' or moral principles to which the prince must adhere strictly. Even allowing for flattery, Louise is known to have commissioned serious books for her children and employed François Demoulins as her son's tutor.[14] He was a distinguished churchman who became Grand Almoner of France and also a bishop. A keen Erasmian, he counted Lefèvre d'Étaples and Budé among his friends. Among several manuscripts due to his pen is one that seeks to promote a grand style of French oratory and another that seeks to deter his pupil from indulging in games of chance. In a work on the four cardinal virtues dedicated to Louise, Demoulins deals harshly with bad priests and deceitful theologians. Yet, humanism seems to have had no place in Francis's education: he grew up, like Shakespeare, knowing 'small Latin and less Greek'; but he did learn Italian, presumably from his mother. Contemporaries thought him unusually well educated for a nobleman. His childhood companion, Florange, believed that no prince had been better taught, and Castiglione paid tribute to his love of learning in his *Book of the Courtier*.[15]

Until recently nothing was known of Francis I's artistic education. But a letter has recently come to light which suggests that he was quite precocious in this respect. On 12 June 1504, when Francis was barely ten years old, the Florentine Nicolò Alamanni wrote to the marquis of Mantua asking him to send some Italian paintings. 'My very illustrious Lord', he wrote, 'as I am the servant and familiar of our little prince of Angoulême, he has told me that he would like me to obtain for him some pictures of those excellent Italian masters, because they give him much pleasure.' Alamanni suggests that Andrea Mantegna might be persuaded to oblige and tells us also that he has ordered pictures from Florence and elsewhere. But to whom did the young prince owe this taste? Almost certainly to his mother, for another letter, this time dating to 1516, indicates that she too was fond of Italian art. On 23 May 1516 Gian Stefano Ronzone wrote from the French court to Isabella d'Este as follows: 'I will tell you of an idea of mine: it would not be a bad thing, in fact a good one, for Your Lordship [Seigneurie] to offer her [Louise] some perfect painting of a male or female saint, for she takes much pleasure in this and is also knowledgeable.' 'It is therefore very likely', writes Marc Hamilton Smith: 'that the mother of Francis of Angoulême, played a decisive role in his artistic education.'[16]

It is often said that Louise extended the same education to both her children, but this is by no means certain. In the fifteenth century a literary education was generally regarded as a male preserve; girls were prepared for marriage, child-bearing and running a home. Princesses, however, were sometimes taught letters. This may have been true of Marguerite, though much that has been written on the subject is speculative, resting on assumptions drawn from her subsequent literary career. Marguerite rates only two mentions in the *Journal* of Louise of Savoy. This underlines the all-devouring love which she felt for her son. However, Marguerite was undoubtedly brought up in a bookish environment and became in time one of the most well-read women of her time.[17] Her grandfather, Jean d'Angoulême, had built up an excellent library which his son enlarged and, when Louise and her children went to court, they may have gained access to the royal library at Blois. According to Brantôme, Marguerite 'was much addicted to letters in her early years', a statement echoed in the eulogy given by Scévole de Saint-Marthe at her funeral.[18] He stressed the moral and philosophical education which she had received as a child. By 'philosophical', he meant not merely the writings of Plato and others but also 'evangelical philosophy which is the Word of God'. Otherwise, one might ask, would Marguerite have assimilated so readily the arcane spiritual teaching of Bishop Briçonnet in 1521? In the words of Pierre Jourda: 'she could not at the dawn of the sixteenth century and within the limited means then available receive an appropriate education. But for the time that education was exceptional'.[19]

Louise was the archetypal possessive mother. She placed all her hopes in the advancement to the throne which the holy man, Francis of Paola, had predicted for her son even before his birth. Her *Journal* enables us to follow all her mood swings as various incidents threatened to frustrate that advancement. Every pregnancy of Anne of Brittany, whom Louis XII married in 1499, was a cause of alarm in case it produced a son, who would displace

Francis in the order of succession to the throne. When such a son was born in 1512 only to die immediately, Louise could not contain her joy. 'Anne, queen of France,' she wrote, 'gave birth to a son on 21 January, the feast of St Agnes; but he was unable to prevent the exaltation of my Caesar, for he was still-born.'[20]

When Francis did eventually reach the throne in January 1515, Louise immediately assumed a prominent role at court. She was also rewarded by her son for all her support. He gave her the proceeds from the confirmation of office-holders; raised her county of Angoulême to the status of a duchy and, in addition, gave her the duchy of Anjou, the counties of Maine and Beaufort-en-Vallée and the barony of Amboise.[21] Her half-brother, René, was appointed *Grand sénéchal* and governor of Normandy. Equally significant were the promotions of men who had served Louise before the king's accession. Foremost among them was Antoine Duprat, who, as Chancellor of France, became, in effect, Francis I's chief minister.[22] An Auvergnat by birth, he was both shrewd and hard-working, but also ruthless and grasping. He became universally unpopular but could always count on Louise's support. Francis reciprocated his mother's love and devotion. He wrote to her whenever he was separated from her, keeping her informed of his activities. Some of these letters have achieved immortal renown, notably that which he wrote after his defeat at Pavia, reporting 'all is lost save honour and my life'.[23] Louise was also given pride of place at court. At Fontainebleau, she occupied a suite of rooms so desirable that the king adopted them as his own after her death in 1531.[24]

Louise was by all accounts an impressive woman. Antonio de Beatis describes her in 1517 as 'an unusually tall woman, still finely complexioned, very rubicund and lively and seems to me to be about forty years old but more than good, one could say, for at least another ten. She always accompanies her son and the Queen and plays the governess without restraint.'[25] This description can hardly be faulted. Throughout her life Louise played such a key role in public life that she is often and quite wrongly referred to as 'queen mother'. She never was a queen, only a regent on two occasions. The first time was in 1515 when Francis I set off on his first invasion of Italy. But the powers given to her on that occasion were limited by the fact that the king took with him the Great Seal, used to authenticate the most important state documents.[26] The second regency was prompted by another royal campaign in Italy, but this time it lasted far longer and assumed a quite different character as a consequence of the king's defeat and capture at Pavia in February 1525. His captivity, which lasted nearly two years, left Louise to govern the kingdom with the assistance of a council headed by Duprat. The crisis was huge: France was still at war and threatened by foreign invasion. Her army had been largely wiped out at Pavia, and such survivors as remained were trickling back across the Alps bedraggled and unpaid. Louise set up her government at Saint-Just, an abbey near Lyon, leaving the defence of northern France largely in the hands of the Parlement of Paris, the highest court of law under the king. But her right to deputize for her son in this way caused serious misgivings in certain quarters. Under the Salic law, women were debarred from the throne, and many people believed that they were unfit to rule. Although there was no hard and fast rule governing a regency, it was generally accepted that this should be entrusted to the king's nearest male kinsman. Charles de Bourbon-Vendôme, the governor of Picardy, qualified for this role, and it seems that an attempt was made to unseat Louise in his favour, but he refused to cause a division in the kingdom at a time of national crisis.[27] So Louise was allowed to rule and did so with considerable success. Not only did she ward off the threat of foreign invasion, she also succeeded in splitting the Anglo-Imperial alliance against France by negotiating the Treaty of the More with England. This marked the first step in the building up of an international coalition designed to put pressure on Charles V to release Francis I from prison on reasonable terms. Louise also sought the aid of the Ottoman sultan, Suleiman the Magnificent, a move which bore fruit later in the form of military coopera-tion against the Emperor in the Mediterranean.[28] Her task was not made easier by the readiness with which the Parlement of Paris seized the oppor-tunity of the king's absence to try to reverse some policies that he had followed since his accession. It wanted to rescind the Concordat of Bologna of 1516 which Francis I had signed with Pope Leo X. This had seriously curtailed the privileges of the French or Gallican church, notably the right of cathedral chapters and religious houses to elect their own superiors. Acting in defiance of the Parlement, Louise appointed Duprat, her own chancellor, as archbishop of Sens and as abbot of Saint-Benoît-sur-Loire against the wishes of their respective chapters. The move prompted a violent confrontation between the regent and the Parlement, which even tried to call the chancellor to account. But Louise stood firm and, when Francis eventually returned home, he confirmed all that his mother had done in his absence.[29]

Even when Louise was not regent, she exerted a strong political influ-ence, especially in foreign affairs, so much so that Cardinal Wolsey, Henry VIII's chief minister, called her 'the mother and nourisher of peace'.[30] In 1519 she worked hard to bring about a meeting between Henry VIII and Francis I. Henry had taken an oath not to shave his beard until he had met Francis. When soon afterwards he was seen clean-shaven, French observers grew worried, but Louise pointed out that 'the kings' love lay not in their beards but in their hearts'.[31] The summit did in fact take place near Calais (the Field of the Cloth of Gold). Afterwards Louise announced that the two kings had decided to meet each year and to build a chapel dedicated to 'Our Lady of Friendship'. Letters written to Wolsey by various English ambassadors at the French court in the 1520s amply testify to the importance of Louise's political role. She was a leading member of the king's council, often acting as its mouthpiece. She would ask ambassadors probing questions aimed at discovering the true intentions of their government or would deny a report which might damage her son's interests. Thus on 23 April 1521 she asked Sir William Fitzwilliam for his opinion on the breakdown of Franco-Imperial relations. 'Think ye not verily', she asked, 'the breach of this amity cometh of the King Catholic?' The ambassador replied that he had only heard one side of the dispute, but believed Francis to be a prince of his word. Whereupon Louise assured him that her son spoke only the truth. On 15 September she denied a report that Francis was sending the duke of Albany to Scotland with the aim of causing trouble for Henry VIII. Albany, she said, was in Paris, but she added that Francis could not stop him going to Scotland if he so wished.

Francis had the reputation of being ruled by his mother. In July the pope was reported as saying that the king's word could not be trusted as long as he was ruled by his mother and Admiral Bonnivet. Louise was accused of receiving foreign bribes, notably a coffer of gold worth 5,000 ducats from the duke of Ferrara.[32] Thus in July 1521 Fitzwilliam asked Admiral Bonnivet, who was leaving for Guyenne, whom he should approach to know Francis I's pleasure. The admiral advised him 'to resort to my Lady as formerly, and after to Robertet'.[33] On 2 August, as the war between Francis and Charles V gathered momentum, Louise seemed to Fitzwilliam 'somewhat accrased'. Before the month was out, she said, the strength of France would become clear to all. Fitzwilliam was saddened to hear her speak 'so like a man of war'. She was evidently sabre-rattling with a view to deterring Henry VIII from joining the Emperor's side in the war. But, in August 1521, as the tide of conflict turned against France, Fitzwilliam noted a change of mood at the French court. 'And though the French king and his mother bear a good face', he wrote, 'yet I hear divers gentlemen and many right substantial, that some curse Robert de La Marche for beginning [the war], and some curse my Lady the King's mother, and say it was never well in France when ladies governed.'[34] In October the ambassador advised Wolsey to write to Louise in support of a truce: 'I have seen in divers things since I came hither', he wrote, 'that when the French king would stick at some points, and speak very great words, yet my Lady would qualify the matter; and sometimes when the king is not contented he will say nay, and then my Lady must require him, and at her request he will be contented; for he is so obeissant to her that he will refuse nothing that she requireth him to do, and if it had not been for her he would have done wonders.'[35] On 18 January 1522

Fitzwilliam reported that Francis had gone to Le Havre. Chancellor Duprat, Florimond Robertet and all the council had remained at Saint-Germain with Louise.[36] On 15 February she thanked Wolsey for trying to keep the peace between her son and Charles V. She said that 'rather than this good amity should break, she had liever never to see the king her son whiles she liveth; which word she spoke with a sorrowful countenance, for I ensure your grace that the waters stood in her eyes'.[37] Louise's role in the government is made clear in many diplomatic dispatches. On 8 September the Emperor reported that Francis was spending all his time hunting with the cardinal of Lorraine and that he left all public business to his mother, the Admiral and the Chancellor.[38] By the autumn of 1524, Louise was most anxious to end the war. The Imperial army had invaded Provence only to be thrown out and Francis was about to cross the Alps in pursuit. Louise hastened south in a bid to stop him, but he gave her the slip. Had her mission succeeded, he would have been spared the greatest humiliation of his life on the battle-field of Pavia. Following his defeat and capture, Charles V gave instructions to his captains in Italy to keep Louise fully informed of her son's health. When Francis received the Emperor's terms for his release, he only gave a provisional response, leaving the final decision to his mother. She turned them down flatly, yet eventually it was at her insistence that he agreed to give away the duchy of Burgundy in the Treaty of Madrid. She said that it was not worth losing a kingdom for a duchy. Louise was more often than not a peace broker. In 1529 she played a leading role in negotiating with Margaret of Austria, the regent of the Netherlands, the treaty of Cambrai, otherwise known as 'the Peace of the Ladies'. By using his mother in this way, Francis was better able to ditch his allies while freeing himself from the obligation of accepting any settlement that did not suit him. Women were often used as diplomatic pawns, not merely in the obvious sense of being matrimonial baits, but also for the expression of views which might seem impolitic in the mouths of the king or his ministers.

But if Louise made a positive contribution to the government of France, can she be entirely cleared of the charges levelled at her by Michelet? Was she her son's evil genius? In two respects, her record does seem blemished: the treason of the Constable of Bourbon and the prosecution of the finance minister, Semblançay. In both cases Louise appears as rapacious and vindictive. Charles III, duke of Bourbon, is generally regarded as the last of the great feudal lords in France. He owned a huge territory in central France and, as Constable, commanded the royal army. In 1523 in the thick of a war between Francis I and Charles V, Bourbon turned traitor. The event which prompted this dramatic move was the death of Bourbon's wife, Suzanne, in 1521. As an important landowner in her own right, she had made a will leaving all her property to her husband, but this was challenged by Louise, who, as Suzanne's first cousin, claimed to be her nearest blood relative. The will was also contested by Francis, who argued that Suzanne's property had escheated to the crown. The dual challenge was submitted to the judgment of the Parlement of Paris, but even before its verdict was given, Francis gave part of Bourbon's inheritance to his mother. Eventually, the Parlement ordered the confiscation of the Constable's entire inheritance.[39]

Suzanne's death also raised the thorny issue of Bourbon's re-marriage. As she had died childless, he needed to remarry if he wished to perpetuate his family line. It has been suggested that Louise, who was still only forty years old, offered him her hand and that he rejected it, causing her to hate him bitterly, but the evidence for this story is slender and serious historians have generally dismissed it.[40] What is indisputable, however, is that Bourbon was put under intolerable pressure to marry a princess of royal blood, if not Louise, then perhaps Queen Claude's sister, Renée. This would have avoided the danger of Bourbon marrying abroad and of his lands eventually passing into the hands of a foreign power, possibly even of an enemy of France. This threat in fact materialized when Bourbon accepted an offer from the Emperor Charles V to marry one of his sisters. How far Louise was responsible for the Constable's treason is hard to establish, but it seems that she and her son put such pressure on him that he was forced to choose between surrender and treason. The end result of the affair was, of course, satisfactory to the crown as Bourbon was forced into exile, leaving his lands to be annexed to the French royal domain and thereby strengthening the territorial unity of the kingdom.

Louise's role in the Semblançay affair is controversial. Jacques de Beaune, baron of Semblançay, became Francis I's chief finance minister after serving as bursar in Louise's household. Indeed, he continued to serve as her treasurer while overseeing the king's finances. He was also a merchant-banker in his own right. This conjunction of roles offered the temptation of borrowing from one purse in order to replenish another. In 1521 Francis became involved in a protracted war with Charles V which he could ill afford. Louise implored Semblançay to do all in his power to assist her son out of his predicament. He assumed that she intended him to use her savings as well as his own. Even so, he was unable to satisfy the king, who had to resort to all kinds of expedients. Eventually, the temptation to accuse the king's financiers of corruption proved irresistible, and steps were taken to prosecute them and confiscate their assets. Louise wrote in her *Journal*: 'In 1515, 1516, 1517, 1518, 1519, 1520, 1521, 1522, my son and I were continually robbed by the *gens de finances* without being able to do anything about it.'[41] According to the memoirs of du Bellay, after the French army had been defeated at La Bicocca in 1522, the commander Marshal Lautrec blamed Semblançay for the disaster on the ground that money intended for his troops had never reached him. Semblançay allegedly explained that, just as the money was about to be sent, Louise seized it, saying that it belonged to her. Francis is said to have accused his mother of losing him Milan.[42] However, the story, seized upon with relish by Michelet as evidence of Louise's avarice and of a jealous plot on her part to unseat her son's mistress Françoise de Châteaubriant by bringing shame on her brother Lautrec, is not supported by archival evidence.[43] The army's pay had, it seems, been sent to Italy but had been held up in the Alps.[44] What really happened is less damaging to Louise. Semblançay was accused of corruption and his accounts were duly investigated, only to reveal that he had been insufficiently careful in distinguishing between the king's purse and that of his mother. The investigation also demonstrated that Semblançay, far from being in debt to the king, was actually owed money by the king. This may have sealed his fate. In 1527, following Francis's return from captivity, Semblançay was put on trial on a criminal charge. Many of his judges were his personal enemies. Nothing, not even his age (he was about eighty years old) could save him from the gallows. Semblançay was found guilty and publicly hanged.[45] Brantôme saw his death as the only serious blot on Francis I's escutcheon. Louise should perhaps bear some of the blame for that tragic event, but Philippe Hamon, the latest scholar to examine the 'Semblançay mystery' in depth, thinks it may have been quite simply a forceful assertion of royal authority. Though Louise was a party to the prosecution, Hamon does not hold her responsible for its tragic outcome.[46]

Louise of Savoy died at the age of 54 at Grès-en-Gatinais on 22 September 1531.[47] Marguerite was with her, but Francis apparently was not. He made up for his absence by giving her a magnificent funeral. On 28 September he wrote to the Bureau de la Ville de Paris ordering for her a funeral on the same model exactly as had been given to his first wife, Queen Claude.[48] The significance of this command has, to my knowledge, been overlooked by historians. Francis was, in effect, giving his mother posthumously the status of queen to which she had never been entitled in her lifetime.[49] After her body had been taken to Saint-Maur-les-Fossés and embalmed, it was carried to the monastery church of Saint-Martin-des-Champs just outside Paris where it lay in state until 17 October. On that day a huge procession of dignitaries from all walks of life accompanied Louise's body and effigy from Saint-Martin-des-Champs to the cathedral of Notre-Dame for the funeral service. The effigy was, it seems, crowned and held a sceptre – the symbol of justice – in one hand. It was borne on a litter under a canopy, and the corners of the gold cloth on which it rested were each held by one of the four presidents of the Parlement wearing their scarlet gowns. Everyone else was in deep mourning, and the houses overlooking the cortège were draped in black. As was customary on such occasions, the king was not among the mourners.[50] His presence would have detracted from the life-sustaining illusion created by the effigy. The next morning the funeral cortège made its way to the abbey of Saint-Denis where the body of Louise was buried in the crypt alongside the remains of France's past kings and queens. Her death, of course, elicited eulogies in plenty from court poets, including Clément Marot, and also condolences from European princes.[51] Writing from Abbeville on 28 December, the Venetian ambassador, Giovanni-Antonio Venier, described Marguerite's reception of the Republic's message of sympathy. 'Ambassador', she said, 'the Signory has in truth incurred a great loss, for Madame greatly loved and honoured the Republic, and to the last desired its welfare and peace.' Venier replied that the Doge thanked God that Madame had left her own image in her daughter both in respect of virtue, wisdom and integrity, but also by reason of Marguerite's love of the Republic. He felt that the compliment was appropriate given the high repute which the queen of Navarre enjoyed at the French court. 'They apparently communicate everything to her, as they did to her mother', Venier wrote, 'after whose death, when she purposed retiring with her consort to Navarre, Francis insisted on her remaining and following the court.'[52]

Close as were the relations between Marguerite and her brother, they were not as close as Michelet has suggested.[53] The notion that their love was incestuous is a nonsense based on the misreading of one of Marguerite's letters. However, that is not to suggest that their love was not deep. Marguerite's copious correspondence endlessly idolizes her brother, calling him 'her second Christ, her father, her brother and her husband'. After his death, she told her nephew that she and Francis had been 'one body, one heart, one will, one desire'. As she lay dying, she said that a letter from him would revive her and she kept as a 'relic' his last letter to her.[54] Throughout her life she devoted herself body and soul to Francis, who did not always treat her with as much concern. Only a few examples can be given here. Following Francis's defeat and capture at Pavia in February 1525, Marguerite wrote, urging him to stop fasting and sent him the Epistles of St Paul to read. But her sisterly devotion was best demonstrated when she undertook the hazardous journey to Spain later that year in the hope of securing his freedom. She arrived in Madrid only to find Francis dangerously ill. However, he suddenly recovered as he was taking communion. Witnesses spoke of a miracle, but one may assume that Marguerite's timely arrival at Francis's bedside had contributed to his recovery. Thereafter, she worked hard to secure a favourable settlement with Charles V, but returned home empty-handed. Francis was only able to secure his freedom after his mother had persuaded him to give up the duchy of Burgundy in the Peace of Madrid, a promise which in the event he failed to honour.[55]

Marguerite is best remembered for her writings. In addition to the *Heptaméron*, a series of stories modelled on Boccacio's *Decameron*, she also wrote many religious poems which are important for the light they throw on her faith. This has always puzzled historians, who have posed the question: was she a Protestant? The answer seems reasonably clear: though deeply devout and fervently committed to an evangelical faith, Marguerite never managed to solve in her own mind the crucial problem of justification. She was drawn to Luther's idea of justification by faith alone, yet retained a belief in the efficacy for salvation of good works, and contributed much herself to charitable bodies. She never severed relations with the Roman Catholic church and seems to have cherished the hope that it would reform itself in accordance with her beliefs.

Marguerite married Charles duc d'Alençon in 1509, yet she continued to spend much of her time at the French court and to act as a mouthpiece for her brother's government in audiences with foreign ambassadors. Her words, however, should always be taken for what they were: diplomatic ploys. Thus in 1521, as Henry VIII seemed inclined to ally with Charles V against Francis, Marguerite chided Fitzwilliam, the English ambassador. She expressed surprise that foreign princes rejoiced over the misfortunes of the French king who had always treated them honestly. Fitzwilliam denied that Henry VIII was one of them, whereupon Marguerite laughed, saying that if that were so, he must be the only one. In September she raised doubts about Cardinal Wolsey's peace-making efforts. 'See ye not', she asked, 'how the Cardinal is ever treating of peace almost to the day of battle?'[56]

However, we cannot assume that Francis and his sister, fond as they were of each other, necessarily always saw eye to eye or that other members of the royal entourage were not as influential or even more so in certain contexts. In an age of personal monarchy, the responsibility for the conduct of foreign policy lay with the king alone, but, if he had any sense, he would consult members of his council. In the absence of council minutes for the reign of Francis, the historian has to rely on evidence largely culled from the dispatches of foreign ambassadors to find out whose voices were loudest in the king's council. Following the death of Louise of Savoy, the most influential councillor was certainly the Grand Master, Anne de Montmorency, who in 1538 became Constable of France.[57] Marguerite's attitude toward him was strangely variable. Originally she was on excellent terms with him.[58] However, in 1535 she persuaded Francis to banish from court Madame de Châtillon, Montmorency's sister. The bishop of Faenza interpreted her action as evidence of her hatred of the Grand Master. Yet, a year later, as hostilities between Francis I and Charles V were resumed, Marguerite looked to Montmorency as the only man capable of providing the necessary military leadership. She wrote to him, assuring him of her affection and, after visiting his camp outside Avignon, praised him to the skies in letters to her brother.[59] By early 1540, however, Marguerite was again hostile to Montmorency, presumably because he was trying to reconcile Francis with Charles V. The duke of Norfolk described her in February as 'the most frank and wise woman he ever spoke with'. She spoke of her enmity for the Constable. 'What doth he mean?' she asked, 'Will he have no equal? Will he be God?' Yet she advised the duke to 'make a great trust' of the Constable, for it would be premature to attack him. She also urged Norfolk to 'speak fair' with Chancellor Poyet who enjoyed great credit with the king and also the duchesse d'Étampes.[60] This was Anne de Pisseleu, the king's second official mistress. She had been one of Louise's ladies and the king had fallen for her in 1526 when she was only eighteen. Combining intelligence with beauty, she was also ambitious and grasping.[61] About 1534 Francis married her off to Jean de Brosse, seigneur de Penthièvre, and in June he gave them the county of Etampes, raising it later to ducal status. Thus did Anne become the duchesse d'Étampes, the title by which she is best remembered. Her influence on the king seems to have been very strong. Politically, she became the focus of a war party at court in the late 1530s in opposition to Montmorency, who arranged for Charles to travel across France on his way to the Netherlands during the winter of 1539–40. The Constable hoped that the Emperor in return for the lavish hospitality which he received would cede the duchy of Milan to Henri, the king's younger son. England was extremely concerned at the rapprochement between Francis and the Emperor which threatened to leave Henry VIII out in the cold. The duke of Norfolk tried to find out what was going on, and Marguerite was only too happy to oblige. In addition to advising him as to whom he should seek to win over at the French court, she poured scorn on her brother's marriage with Charles V's sister, Eleonor. No man could be less satisfied with his wife than her brother. For the past seven years 'he neither lay with her, nor yet meddled with her'. When the duke asked Marguerite to explain, she replied: '*Purce quil ne le trouve plesaunt a son apetyde* [Because he does not find her to his taste] . . . when he doth lie with her, he cannot sleep; and when he lieth from her, no man sleepeth better.' As Norfolk pressed Marguerite further, she said: 'she is very hot in bed and desireth to be too much embraced'. Then laughing loudly, she added: 'I would not for all the good in Paris that the king of Navarre were no better pleased to be in my bed than my brother is to be in hers.'[62]

Montmorency's policy ended in failure. Charles V, following his visit to France, gave the duchy of Milan to his son, Philip. Madame d'Étampes blamed the Constable for what had happened. 'He is a great scoundrel', she exclaimed, 'for he has deceived the king by saying that the Emperor would give him Milan at once when he knew that the opposite was true.'[63]

Francis did not dismiss Montmorency immediately, but from April 1540 onward the Constable ceased to influence royal policy. Anne d'Étampes was described by the imperial ambassador as 'the president of the king's most private and intimate council'. 'I hear from a good quarter', he wrote to Charles V, 'that the reason for her angry feelings is that when Your Majesty passed through the kingdom you did not make so much of her as she expected which has hardened her heart in such a way that it will be very difficult, nay, almost impossible to appease her.'[64] In April 1541 Mary of Hungary received the following report from France: 'As for the government of the court, Madame d'Étampes has more credit than ever. The constable . . . is paying court to her; his credit is diminishing each day.'[65] In May 1543 the papal nuncio, Dandino, wrote: 'The king is more than ever addicted to his lascivious pleasures, being totally in the power of Madame d'Étampes, who, in order to appear wise always contradicts others and lets the king believe that he is God on earth, that no one can harm him and that those who deny this are moved by selfish interest.'[66]

Two major factors affected Marguerite's relations with her brother after 1527: the first was her second marriage to Henri d'Albret, king of Navarre, in that year, and the second was the growth of religious dissent in France. Navarre was a small kingdom lying astride the Pyrenees. In 1513 its southern half had been annexed by the Spanish king, Ferdinand of Aragon, and ever since the ruler of the northern part had looked to the king of France for help in regaining his lost patrimony. However, Francis I was more interested in recovering the duchy of Milan for himself than in regaining Spanish Navarre for his brother-in-law. This became manifest in the talks with the Emperor Charles V which led to the Peace of Cambrai in 1529. Disappointed by Francis's failure to champion his cause, Henri d'Albret entered into secret negotiations with the Emperor with a view to getting what he wanted. Marguerite thus found her loyalties divided between her husband and her brother.[67] Her own lifestyle was not significantly altered by her marriage. Now and again she accompanied Henri to their estates in the south, but most of the time she remained at Francis's court. She looked after his children and continued to take a keen interest in public affairs. Foreign ambassadors continued to call on her to pay their respects, to find out what Francis I and his ministers were up to, and to ask her for some favour. But Marguerite's relationship with her brother was further complicated by the birth of her daughter, Jeanne d'Albret, in November 1528.[68] Like all high-born princesses at the time, Jeanne soon became another pawn on the chessboard of European matrimonial diplomacy. Marguerite, perhaps mindful of her husband's principal concern, hoped that Jeanne might be married off to Charles V's son, Philip; but Francis I had other ideas. In 1540, after falling out with the Emperor, he sought to revive his alliance with the German

Protestant princes and offered the hand of Jeanne to William, duke of Cleves. Marguerite opposed the match, but in the end had to give way to her brother, as she always did. The little girl was forcibly carried to the altar.[69]

Religion became a major problem for the French monarchy in the reign of Francis I as early manifestations of Protestant dissent began to challenge the monopoly of doctrinal teaching enjoyed by the Catholic church. Francis himself was no theologian, but he was obliged to take up a position in respect of this crisis. Was he to persecute heretics, as the Parlement of Paris and the Faculty of Theology of the University of Paris pressed him to do or tolerate them? For a long time Francis hesitated. He protected certain evangelical writers and preachers in response to the wishes of his sister Marguerite. In 1521 she began to correspond with Guillaume Briçonnet, bishop of Meaux, and through his teaching imbibed the teaching of Jacques Lefèvre d'Étaples, a leading humanist whose ideas on justification were close to Luther's.[70] Marguerite was not a Lutheran. Her personal faith, as Lucien Febvre has argued, was essentially idiosyncratic, but she certainly shared Luther's interest in the writings of St Paul and sympathized with the views of members of the Cercle de Meaux, a group of evangelical writers and preachers, who helped Briçonnet reform his diocese.[71] As the king's sister and a duchess, later a queen, in her own right, Marguerite was well placed to protect members of the Cercle and other evangelicals from persecution. Thus it was at her instance that Francis ordered the release from prison of Louis de Berquin, a young aristocratic scholar, whom the Parlement had imprisoned for heresy. It was Marguerite, too, who doubtless informed Francis during his Spanish captivity of the Parlement's harrassment of the Cercle de Meaux, thereby prompting him to order the Parlement to suspend its proceedings against Lefèvre and two other members of the Cercle.[72] Marguerite was regarded by Parisian Catholics as a fellow traveller. During the king's captivity, a masquerade was held in the cloister of Notre Dame. It included a woman on horseback (almost certainly a portrayal of Marguerite) being pulled by devils wearing placards inscribed with Luther's name.[73] Following the king's release from captivity in 1526, members of the Cercle de Meaux, who had been driven into foreign exile, returned to France and took up positions at court. In Lent 1531 Gérard Roussel, who had become Marguerite's almoner, was accused of preaching heresy in her presence at the Louvre. Francis pacified Roussel's critics by ordering him to give advance notice of what he intended to say in future sermons. Even so, there was more trouble in 1533 when Roussel's enemies accused Marguerite's husband of heresy. Francis rounded on them, prompting one to say that their only hope was for Marguerite, who was pregnant at the time, to die soon.[74] Much of the university's resentment was directed toward her. In October 1533 students at the Collège de Navarre put on a play in which she was shown preaching heresy at the instigation of a fury called Mégère (a pun on Roussel's name) and bludgeoning anyone who would not listen. The college was raided by the police but the culprits seem to have escaped punishment. Later that month, Marguerite's poem, *Le miroir de l'âme pécheresse*, which had been published anonymously, was banned by the university. A huge rumpus ensued as the king launched an enquiry. Those responsible for the ban denied that they had intended to offend Marguerite.[75]

In October 1534 the religious situation took a decisive new turn when some placards or printed broadsheets attacking the Catholic mass in the most vitriolic terms were put up one night by persons unknown in the streets of Paris, triggering a wave of public hysteria. A savage campaign of persecution ensued. Francis had no time for any religious demonstration which threatened public order. A royal edict was issued banning all printing until further notice, and on 21 January 1535 the king took part in a gigantic expiatory procession through Paris. Soon afterwards he made a speech urging his subjects to denounce heretics, even relatives or friends. A number of executions followed.[76] Even Marguerite may have been shocked by the extremism displayed in the so-called 'Affair of the Placards', for she kept a low profile at the time. She withdrew from the court and accompanied her husband to their kingdom in the south, where she offered protection to religious escapees from the persecution in Paris, including Roussel, who became bishop of Oloron, the poet Clément Marot and John Calvin. Yet Marguerite's love for her brother remained undimmed. Before long the religious situation became less fraught as Francis tried to undo the damage which the persecution had inflicted on his relations with the German Protestant princes. In June 1535 he invited Philip Melanchthon, Luther's lieutenant, to France for discussions with Catholic theologians. It has been suggested that Marguerite was behind this move, but there is no documentary evidence for this. The initiative in any case came to nothing. Marguerite's religious stance is mystifying. Théodore de Bèze, Calvin's lieutenant, concluded after reading her poem the *Miroir de l'âme pécheresse* (Mirror of a sinful soul) that around 1536 she 'began to behave in a quite different way, plunging into idolatries like the rest' without realizing their significance. Yet Florimond de Rémond stressed her ties to the Reformation. She worked on her brother, he claimed, and 'in small doses tried to instil into his soul some pity for the Lutherans while calling to her assistance the duchesse d'Étampes'.[77] Yet at the same time she remained on good terms with the papacy. While Pope Paul III recommended his nuncio to her and lavished praise on her, saying that she was the person in whom he placed his highest hopes, Protestant towns in Switzerland thanked her for helping reformers in France. This dualism persisted for the rest of her life. In the summer of 1538 she had several meetings with Pope Paul III. On one occasion he listened to her discussing scripture with cardinals Contarini and Sadoleto. Yet in February 1542 Marguerite was quite venomous about the pope. Talking to Sir William Paget, the English ambassador, she said that Henry VIII and she were 'both of one opinion in religion, for neither of us loveth the Pope; and I think he would be glad to see both our destructions, for the which purpose he practiseth with th'Emperor, that is to say, with hypocrisy; for the Emperor is hypocrisy and the Pope the Devil'. When the ambassador remarked that he saw no greater Popery anywhere than in France where ten or twelve people had just been imprisoned for saying that the pope deceived the world, Marguerite blamed the 'maskers in red caps' (i.e. the cardinals) who were of the king's council for this state of affairs. She reckoned that other royal councillors, notably Admiral Chabot, cardinals du Bellay and Tournon, and the seigneur de Langey were good Christians as was the duc d'Orléans.[78] Was Marguerite a hypocrite? Not so, writes Jourda; 'religious hypocrisy [*tartufferie*] was never part of Marguerite's character'.[79] She combined her own brand of Catholicism with ultimate subservience to whatever religious policy her brother wished to enforce.

As Francis grew older and his health declined, factions developed around his two sons, Henri and Charles. Whereas Henri remained loyal to Montmorency after his fall from power, Charles became the darling of Madame d'Étampes. When war broke out in 1542, the rivalry between the brothers was embittered by their military performance. Whereas Charles conquered Luxemburg, Henri had to retreat from Perpignan. At the heart of much of the strife at court was Anne d'Étampes. At the same time she used her influence to advance members of her family. She was very effective in finding ecclesiastical benefices for relatives in holy orders. Two of her brothers became bishops, while her uncle, Antoine Sanguin, rose to become archbishop of Toulouse and Grand Almoner of France.[80] Culturally, Anne is best remembered for her patronage of the artist, Francesco Primaticcio and her relentless hostility to his rival, Benvenuto Cellini. Her efforts to wreck Cellini's presentation to the king of his statue of Jupiter are among the most entertaining stories of his Autobiography. Meanwhile, Marguerite, who was always on good terms with Anne, withdrew to her kingdom of Navarre, where she was able to devote more time to her literary pursuits, while her husband served Francis as governor of Guyenne and other provinces in the Midi. She and her brother kept up a lively correspondence and exchanged poems. At times Marguerite assisted her husband by assuming various administrative and military responsibilities.[81]

Where does all this leave Michelet and his view of the royal Trinity? He was clearly correct in believing that an unusually close bond existed between Francis I and his mother and sister, but his interpretation of their respective characters and roles does not stand up to scrutiny. To cast Louise of Savoy as her son's evil genius is to ignore all that she did that was positive for his education, for the defence of his kingdom during his captivity and for peace. Not without reason did the Parisian authorities describe her in 1531 as 'the conservator of the kingdom and the restorer of peace'.[82] As for Marguerite, she was certainly an exceptionally well-read and devout woman, who did what she could to protect like-minded men from persecution. She also took a lively interest in politics and played an active role in diplomacy, but in adoring her brother she tended to overlook his faults, and her influence upon him, while real enough, was not always sustained or effective. Thus she failed to check the religious persecution that followed the Affair of the Placards in October 1534. This may have been partly a result of the confusion in her own religious ideas: thus, while sympathizing with Luther, she remained within the Roman church; while fraternizing with the pope, she denounced him as a devil. Such inconsistencies must have interfered with effective action. Far from being subservient to his mother and sister, as Michelet suggested, Francis was his own man. He believed himself to be God's anointed and always behaved autocratically. He undoubtedly loved his mother and sister and listened to them. In the case of Louise, he even relied on her to run the government when he felt that he had better things to do, but he also consulted others such as Chancellor Duprat, Admiral Bonnivet, Anne de Montmorency, Admiral Chabot and Madame d'Étampes, to mention but a few. Ultimately, however, he did what he wanted to do. Thus Louise tried in 1524 to stop him from going to Italy, but he went there just the same, to his cost and shame. But if Michelet can be criticized on several counts, he deserves credit at least for indicating the important role played by women in the public life of Renaissance France.

> The participation of women in politics [Eliane Viennot has written] is an established fact of the sixteenth century. The chronicles of the time, whether they describe wars and battles or concentrate on royal or princely courts, are full of details concerning their political role, both direct and indirect. Queens, of course, played a pre-eminent role, but women of the high nobility . . . were also in front of the stage. . . . Despite the existence of the Salic law which formally denied them access to the supreme power, despite their total exclusion from the central government and parlements, despite an ideology which refused to acknowledge their authority however high, they intervened at all levels of public life to a degree hitherto unseen in western Europe and which declined steadily after the Fronde.[83]

The popular notion that high-born ladies in Renaissance France spent all their time weaving tapestries or listening to madrigals needs to be firmly set at rest.

CHAPTER SIX

Elizabeth I as Deborah: Biblical typology, prophecy and political power

ANNE MCLAREN

On 14 January 1559, the day before her coronation, the City of London presented a pageant series to honour Elizabeth Tudor. On this occasion London became a vast stage, focus of attention for other parts of England and abroad. The pageant series displayed, in superficial harmony, the political views and values of a significant swath of the political nation, for the court, the queen and the city had all collaborated in the production. These were more widely disseminated through the publication immediately afterwards of a pamphlet entitled *The Quenes Maiesties Passage through the City of London to Westminster the day before her Coronacion*. Written by the schoolmaster and author Richard Mulcaster, the pamphlet was popular enough to run to two editions in 1559 and to warrant republication, in the context of another monarchical accession, in 1604.[1]

Two of the devices presented along the route that Mulcaster describes are particularly noteworthy for the instruction they offered this female ruler. At the lower end of Cornhill Elizabeth encountered 'the seat of worthy governance', a royal seat covered with the cloth of state, occupied by a child representing the queen. The throne appeared to be detached from the arch below, supported only by four virtues – Pure Religion, Love of Subjects, Wisdom and Justice – each of which, while supporting the 'queen's' seat, trampled underfoot antithetical vices. When Elizabeth approached the scene another child interpreted the device in verse. He reminded her, in Mulcaster's words, that 'like as by vertues . . . the Queens Majesty was established in the seat of government: so she should sit fast in the same so long as she embraced virtue and held vice under foot'. The Venetian ambassador translated the device to mean 'that hitherto religion had been misunderstood and misdirected, and that now it will proceed on a better footing'[2] The last, climactic, device suggested how it would be that a female ruler would effect this outcome, so fervently desired by the articulate and committed Protestants among Elizabeth's subjects: the 'Protestant ascendancy'.[3] Elizabeth arrived at Fleet Street where she encountered another 'seat royal', this time backed by a palm tree to indicate a change of scene from sixteenth-century London to ancient Israel. The figure seated in the chair, representing simultaneously Deborah and Elizabeth, was 'apparelled in parliament robes, with a sceptre in her hand'.[4] Flanking her were representatives of the three estates – two nobles, two clergymen, two commoners. This device adjured Elizabeth to follow the example of Deborah the prophetess, 'restorer of Israel', whom God had appointed 'for the judge of his elect'.[5] Mulcaster's account glosses 'judgeship' – a key attribute of monarchical authority in the context of providential rule – as the queen's receptivity to good counsel. The device reveals, he writes, 'that it behooveth both men and women so ruling [that is, by God's immediate volition] to use advise of good counsel'.[6]

We can see what such receptivity entailed by looking at an analogous production, this one from ten years later in the reign, the 1569 *Bishops' Bible*. Both Elizabeth's chief minister, William Cecil, and her Archbishop of Canterbury, Matthew Parker, played leading roles in producing this official version of God's Word. Its title page featured Elizabeth enthroned and surrounded by four virtues, in a pose similar to that assumed by her representative in the device enacted at Cornhill in the 1559 pageant series. In this image her 'seat' is effectively supported by the underlying cartouche containing the title *The holi bible*. Added support is provided by 'Fortitude' and 'Prudence', while above 'Justice' and 'Mercy' are poised to place a closed, imperial crown on the queen's head – how characteristic of Elizabeth's reign that attitude of anticipation becomes! (See Figure 1) Beneath the cartouche the engraver has included a border scene which indicates how it is that, under Elizabeth, 'religion will proceed on a better footing'. It features a minister in his pulpit preaching to a large congregation. At his side is a 'grave senator', William Cecil.[7] The immediate focus of his attention is a woman – Elizabeth. She ignores the opened Bible on her lap to listen instead with rapt attention to the preacher. The message is clear. England's queen, although scripturally literate – indeed, like Deborah a prophetess – will, in common with her subjects, understand God's will through the exposition of godly men. For in the sixteenth century the word 'prophet' contained an ambiguity that became central to the politics of Elizabeth's reign. It referred not only to those who spoke immediately on God's behalf through divine inspiration but also, even primarily, to men who interpreted or expounded the Scriptures.[8]

This conception of the queen's role is – at first glance perhaps surprisingly – entirely consonant with John Knox's highly qualified acceptance of female rule, written, like the London pageant series, at Elizabeth's accession

Figure 6.1   *The holi bible* (1569), Shelfmark G.12188 T.P.
By permission of the British Library.

in 1559. For Knox, who played a much more central role in English politics in Elizabeth's reign than historians have acknowledged, too drew on the identification of Israel's Deborah with England's Elizabeth. He did so to justify what he believed would be, without God's immediate intervention, utterly contrary to His revealed will: female rule. As a man who regarded his plain speaking as evidence of his godliness, Knox did not mince words in conveying his message about its ungodly status. But the difference in tone between these productions and Knox's should not hide from us their common ground. They shared, and responded to, the conviction that female rule was 'prodigious' and hence inherently incompatible with good, and godly, order. After her accession, Knox wrote Elizabeth a letter denying any need to apologize for his book *The First Blast of the Trumpet against the monstrous regiment of women*, written during her sister's lifetime to demonstrate these self-evident propositions. Interestingly, he did not argue that his timing was off – that he would not have made this case (or at least expressed himself so forcefully) had he known that Catholic Mary was soon to die, leaving the throne to Protestant Elizabeth, although that is what modern historians customarily assume.[9] Instead, he asserted, not that his critique was wrong, but that Elizabeth might prove to be a partial exception to its strictures – if she proved herself to be a true Deborah. The *Blast* could only be 'prejudicial' to her regiment, he told her, if she proved to be 'ungrateful' to God, by transferring 'the glory of that honour in which ye now stand, to any other thing, than to the dispensation of his mercy'.[10] For Knox this meant specific-ally and continuously acknowledging God's immediate overlordship rather than claiming to rule autonomously, as 'king' rather than as godly vessel. Knox reasons that this 'humiliation before God' will, paradoxically, secure her continuance in authority, for two reasons. If she understands, and acts in accordance with, her position in Reformation history, God will continue to bestow His favour on the nation. But also, and importantly, this self-abnegating stance will persuade godly men that obedience to the queen constitutes, in an immediate sense, obedience to God Himself. (This is also one way of interpreting the message of the *Holi bible* marginal border discussed above.)

What, then, did the identification of the queen with Deborah mean during Elizabeth's reign? As J.N. King has shown, the figure of Deborah became a powerful one at her accession, as Englishmen once again encoun-tered the political problem of legitimating a queen regnant. On one level recourse to this biblical typology obviously enhanced Elizabeth's monarch-ical authority. It fused the mediatory symbolism of medieval queens, presented as figures capable of interceding on behalf of mercy between just kings and their subjects, with the claim traditionally made by kings to rule as divine agents or little 'gods'.[11] But this period of reformation history made available alternative meanings, meanings that challenged Elizabeth's monarchical autonomy as they problematized relations with her counsellors.[12] The meaning that achieved political salience in Elizabeth's reign read the identification as positioning the queen, not as interpreter or arbiter of God's word and will – a role now devolved to men of God – but as the medium of His grace. Through their labours, and her obeisance to God's will, England will become a truly reformed commonwealth.[13] In this context, then, the figure of Deborah proposed a female ruler whose claims to regal power were to be validated by her spiritual status. And to conceive of queenship in this way allowed for the conceptualization of the relationship between the queen and her godly (male) subjects as a new kind of partnership, one that included, even, a species of parity. Her 'just and lawful authority' depends, finally, on their reckoning of her virtue.[14] Ambiguous as an emblem of regality, the typology thus speaks to the major issues of Elizabeth's reign. These issues were to reverberate through the reigns of her successor kings, James VI and I and Charles I. The identification of Elizabeth with Deborah provided a powerful source of legitimation, in a culture profoundly hostile to female rule. But it did so in ways that simultaneously constituted the 'country': a body of spiritually elect men self-righteous enough to envisage, in the last resort, a mode of political existence independent of kings whom they deemed to be ungodly. In this chapter I want to explore one dimension of this political configuration, the identification of godly counsellors. For reading Elizabeth as Deborah, her governance as providential, left open the issue of who would be interpreters of God's will in the body politic, and what their relationship would be to the queen.

First, though, we need to consider contemporary presuppositions concerning female rule. Why the intensely felt need to bridle a female ruler who, by position if not necessarily by personal inclination, ascended to the throne as a Protestant princess? To answer this question we need to look not only at sixteenth-century views on women's rule but also at post-Reformation English history. Merry Weisner-Hanks describes early modern Europe as 'a time when the public realm – politics in the broadest sense – was becoming increasingly male again, in theory and practice'. Other historians relate this development to the growth and consolidation of centralizing monarchies.[15] At this time too both humanism and religious Reformation powerfully fused ideas about women from classical and Biblical sources, and infused them with a new immediacy and specificity. Women were seen as lacking the capacity for judgement and prudence (hence political 'virtue') present in a developed form in adult males, as potential in young boys. This view found expression in the rank-ordering of preferred successors to kings in early modern dynasties, which gave young males second place over adult females when no suitable adult male candidate could be found. In many ways representing a triumph of hope over experience – and privileging gender status over blood claims – this hierarchy underwrote, for example, the invention of the French Salic Law as an immutable identifier of the French state that specifically excluded women from inheriting the crown.[16] Invented it may have been, but Englishmen looked longingly at that guarantor of a virtuous male state at intervals from Edward VI's reign onward, when demographic calamity invested the strongest blood claims to the English imperial crown in women: Mary and Elizabeth Tudor, and their cousin Mary Stuart of Scotland.[17]

Moreover, Reformation ideology problematized a key element in monarchical authority, the ruler's will. Reformation theologians argued that after the Fall woman became subordinate to man not because she recognized him as her superior (a feat of which she was only capable in her unfallen state), but as punishment for her seduction by Satan. The bondage was secured, her humiliation announced, by the terms of their union. After the fall, God ordained that woman would lust after man with the full force of her newly dominant bodily desires.[18] The fall into lust thus posited reinforced the prevailing Aristotelian model of gender relations. This model positioned women as more consumed by desire for men than men were for women because, like other imperfect things, women strove after perfection. The conflation of the two ideologies helps to explain the view of women as having a stronger sexual drive that was commonly held, despite the gradual supersession of Galenic scientific theories, until the late eighteenth century.[19] It also informs the distrust of women rulers, single or married. That distrust accompanied and was exacerbated by the accession to political power of an unprecedented number in sixteenth-century Europe.[20] If a woman, ruled in her own person by her physical body, acquired self-control only through her subordination to her husband, whom God had decreed should be her head, what then of a woman not so constrained? And what of a woman whose acquisition of supreme political power nullified conventional constraints? Could any man, in the role of husband and king consort, subordinate a woman prince, his superior in rank and power? What woman, in the role of king, would possess sufficient virtue to voluntarily accede to such, or any, due subordination? Sixteenth-century logic dictated that a woman elevated to a crown in her own person would exercise her newly authoritative will according to the vagaries of her instinctual desires. Tyranny or conquest of her unfortunate realm would be the result, effected either through her own unbridled exertions or through the machination of men to whom she ceded power in order to satisfy her desires. From this point of view the unmarried queen (like Elizabeth) represented only a variation on a theme – although one that left open the door for a persistent fantasy that anticipated her marriage to a godly king who would be her superior.[21]

Finally, because it was centred on a true reading of Scripture, Reformation ideology in Europe collapsed the traditional division between temporal and spiritual authorities, symbolized before the Reformation by the relationship between pope and monarch, in ways that starkly problematized female rule. The problem was particularly acute in England, where the Henrician Reformation invested 'absolute' spiritual and temporal dominion (in relation to external powers) in a monarch newly denominated both an emperor and 'Supreme Head of the Church of England'. This new conception of imperial kingship raised a whole host of issues that reverberated through English political discourse from the time of Henry VIII's break with Rome through to the English Civil Wars. In a Bible-centred theocracy, whose role would it be to interpret Scripture? Was the task of establishing authoritative interpretation a matter for the king or some other form of spiritual authority? What should be the relationship between the two? If the king, as temporal authority, took it upon himself to fulfil this role, did this make him a priest? A bishop? A pope? What constraints, if any, might apply to this new creation, the imperial king? The legal writer Christopher St German (who feared that Henry's failings as a person included caesaropapal proclivities) tried to establish limits for the imperial king. He did so by figuring supreme headship as a collaborative endeavour enacted by king-in-parliament: 'Why should not the parliament then which representeth the whole catholic church of England expound scripture?'[22] This proved to be an influential model of the English imperial crown. In Elizabeth's reign, it privileged male political capacity, enacted pre-eminently in Parliament, the 'body of all England'. The role of authoritative scriptural exegete (or prophet) might, then, be available to a king, especially one joined in consultation with the 'whole catholic church of England'. It *might* extend to a minor king, imagined as a new Josiah attending to the wisdom of his godly councillors; hence the image of Edward VI as governed by godly preachers propagated in Elizabeth's reign.[23] (See Figure 6.2) It would not be available under any circumstances to a queen whose gender disqualified her from exercising authority in spiritual or even what John Guy calls 'semi-spiritual' matters.[24]

How then could a woman – any woman – exercise godly rule as incumbent of the English imperial crown? This central problem was camouflaged during Mary I's reign. Because she repudiated the Protestant definition of England's imperial status, she rejected the title of Supreme Head of the Church of England. She also acknowledged two species of overlordship, consonant with her 'two bodies': the Pope's spiritual supremacy and the headship of her husband, the Spanish king Phillip II.[25] The problem recurred in force, however, with Elizabeth's accession, as the debate over the 1559 religious settlement attests. In that debate a consensus emerged, across confessional lines, that Elizabeth would be Supreme *Governor* (not Head) of

Figure 6.2 'A description of Maister Latimer, preaching before Kyng Edward the syxt, in the preachyng place at Westminster' from John Foxe, *Acts and monuments of these latter and perillous days* . . . (1563). Shelfmark C.37.h.2 p.1353

By permission of the British Library.

the Church of England.[26] Nor was this compromise between ideological conviction and political necessity a stable one, as the politicization over Elizabeth's reign of religious controversy and conceptions of monarchical authority reveals.

In important ways this background complicates the model of Catholic versus Protestant allegiances that Tudor historians customarily adopt when explaining Elizabeth's untroubled accession to the throne and her success at maintaining her rule for forty years. According to this model, the English nation gradually became Protestant in the years following Henry VIII's break with Rome, and joy at the accession of a Protestant monarch largely kept at bay whatever hostility toward female rule simmered in the breasts of elite males. (Or at least displaced it – and much perceptive recent work has been done on the remarkable range of such displacement activities.[27]) But the model needs to be reworked to take account of this ideological context if we want to understand the dynamics of Elizabeth's reign. What are we to make, for example, of David Loades's finding that discontent with Mary I's reign was mollified by news of her (false) pregnancy? The child – assumed to be a boy – would be three-quarters Spanish, Catholic and (assuming that he survived to adulthood and reproduced) guarantor of an Anglo-Spanish Catholic dynasty. 'The evidence suggests the English people were prepared to welcome such a child', he concludes, and describes how disappointment when the pregnancy proved to be false was much exacerbated by rumours which had spread all over London that Mary had been safely delivered of a son.[28] And the enormous pressure on Elizabeth to marry and establish the succession throughout her reign gives further evidence of how deeply entrenched was the commitment to rule by men, and if not by men directly, then by men controlling the queen.[29] This commitment was shared by men across the confessional spectrum, but it achieved a politically significant centrality in the thought of conviction Protestants, including stalwarts of her Privy Council – the Earls of Bedford and Leicester, Sir Francis Knollys, Sir Francis Walsingham and of course William Cecil himself. For such men control of the queen would be necessary to legitimate what was otherwise directly contrary to God's law and hence to allow for the establishment of a godly realm.

Elizabeth's unexpected accession at Mary I's death thus proved deeply unsettling to her militant Protestant constituency. On one level it must be acclaimed as God's peculiar providence, He having seen fit to replace Catholic Mary with a Tudor Protestant heir by natural means. But . . . a female. Faced with this conundrum, John Knox approached Heinrich Bullinger, the doyen of reformed theologians in Europe, for advice on what to do. Bullinger's answer is instructive. Rule by a woman was, he said, self-evidently contrary to God's law. Godly men could tolerate such rule as the price of securing political order – if, he stressed, such a woman was suitably constrained: 'married to a husband, or in the meantime hold[ing] the reins of government by her councillors'.[30]

These ideological convictions gave rise to tensions concerning counsel discernible during the period – which proved to be the whole of Elizabeth's reign – when she, unmarried, '[held] the reins of government by her councillors'. Would she accept, and be seen to accept, godly counsel? Which members of the body politic would serve as interpreters of God's will to secure the godly commonwealth, to bridle the always potentially ungodly and tyrannical queen? In addition a species of public accountability came into play over the question of who would judge whether the queen's councillors themselves retained their rectitude in circumstances where their proximity to the queen was deemed to render the portents ambiguous. These issues lie at the heart of Elizabethan political culture. They appear as subtexts in political engagements of the queen with her councillors, with her parliaments – with the political nation more broadly defined, as well as in the actions and reactions of members of those corporations. I now want to examine some of the permutations that arose as different elements of the political nation, including the queen, jostled for the imprimatur of godly magistrate: interpreter of God's will in the Elizabethan body politic.

First, Elizabeth herself argued that she was the final arbiter of God's will in so far as it manifested itself with regard to her realm, or 'estate'. She did so through recourse to providential rhetoric, most strikingly when she faced pressure from the political nation, mobilized in parliament and without, which threatened to override her monarchical authority. One example dates from 1586, when she faced enormous pressure from all sides to execute her cousin, Mary Queen of Scots, in the wake of the Babington Plot. The pressure culminated in a petition – in effect a demand – for Mary's execution, presented to the queen by representatives from both houses. They also represented, on this occasion as on many others, the collective will of her Privy Councillors.[31] Elizabeth adopted a characteristic strategy to defuse this thinly veiled attack on her political authority. It centred on proposing that her status as medium or instrument of God's will in the body politic made her, and not them, uniquely qualified to judge the occasion. First, she suggested that her propensity for delay denoted her capacity for judgement. She implied that men of judgement (this status confirmed by their long past experience of her reign and knowledge of her character) will give her credit for possessing this key monarchical attribute: 'she thought they did not look for a present resolution; the rather, for that it was not her manner, in matters of far less moment, to give speedy answer without due consideration'. She then signalled the immediate connection between her capacity for judgement, as monarch, and her godliness, in terms that intimated that she alone could experience illumination on this matter: 'So in this [matter], of such importance, she thought it very requisite, with earnest prayer to beseech his divine Majesty so to illuminate her understanding, and inspire her with his grace.' She next hedged her bets, lest she had adopted too commanding a position to suit the political moment – one when she could really only safely seek to delay the enactment of their political will, not thwart it. She did so by describing herself as an instrument – of God's will and of *theirs*, those movers of the petition who might be deemed (by her charitable attribution) judicious members of the political nation. She besought God's illumination, she informed them, so that 'she might do and determine that which should serve to the establishment of his church, the preservation of their estates, and properties of the commonwealth under her charge'.[32] In this way she assimilated their agenda (notice the flattering reference to 'their' estates) in terms that proposed, but did not insist upon, her unique, even commanding, role in the commonwealth.

This kind of speech act, so very common throughout the reign, might lead us to conclude that, in David Starkey's words, 'government *by* the monarch was developing into government *under* the monarch by the Council' during Elizabeth's reign. Nor would this be wrong. But we will need to factor gender into our analysis if we are to avoid the two leading explanations for this political development, both equally anachronistic. The older Whig view, associated especially with J.E. Neale and Wallace Notestein, saw a House of Commons attaining to political self-consciousness and 'winning the initiative' that would enable England to become first past the post in achieving a modern parliamentary democracy.[33] The revisionist pragmatic, voiced by Starkey himself on this occasion, denies that this renegotiation of roles was a political development at all, seeing it only as a 'matter of style' that would change as soon as a different monarch came to the throne.[34] Factoring in gender reveals that this is a case where style and substance were inseparable. The acrobatics performed by the queen and the political nation to accommodate and maintain a female incumbent of the imperial crown changed the 'rules of the game' in ways that were to have a direct bearing on England's later career as a 'limited' (or 'constitutional') monarchy.[35]

Alternatively the queen's councillors, and especially her Privy Councillors, might claim to mediate between God and the commonwealth. Humanist reformers at the court of Henry VIII, and especially Sir Thomas Elyot, began to identify the king's councillors – his *synarchoi* – as the conduits for infusing virtue, both spiritual and political, into the corporate identity of 'king-in-council'. In a reformed commonweal, Elyot decreed, men would attain the status of councillors as a consequence of their virtue rather than simply by right of birth or kingly favour. These 'new men' would thus be in a position to rectify the deficiencies of the monarch's will through their intimate relationship with his person – in the Aristotelian model, the imperfect following the more perfect – and hence allow for an empire infused with grace.[36] Elyot's popularity continued unabated over the sixteenth century. Indeed, his ideas concerning godly counsel took on new currency, in different ways, with the accessions of Edward VI and Mary I. One reign featured a minor king whose godly councillors ruled in his stead, the other a queen regnant whose councillors should have compensated for her deficiencies of reason and judgement but (according to the view of Mary's reign that became dominant in Elizabeth's) did not. At Elizabeth's accession, the providential reading of English history that figured the new queen as Deborah suggested that her councillors would be (had better be, if this female ruler were to be bridled and the commonwealth sanctified) both grave senators and 'prophets'. John Aylmer voiced this primacy of godly counsel in his defence of Elizabeth's accession, *An Harborowe for faithful and trewe subjects*.

In his peroration he attempted to legitimate the new regime specifically by asserting that Elizabeth's councillors are, and will be – again that telling emphasis on the conditional future – godly men. 'She picketh out . . . such councillors to serve her (and I trust will do more) as . . . for their gifts and graces which they have received at God's hand, be men meet to be called to such rooms', the 'calling' ambiguously that of God and the queen.[37]

These councillors were perceived as being always in danger of declension because of their proximity to the person of the ruler. In Elizabeth's reign we can see how a time-honoured trope concerning relations between the king and his councillors changed form when the 'king' was a queen, the councillors functioning less to rectify than to constrain her potentially overmastering will. The danger was that they might bow to or be seduced by this force of nature, becoming 'flatterers' and 'caterpillars' in the commonwealth, as had happened in Mary I's reign (and, famously, according to Shakespeare, in Richard II's).[38] Again, as with the public reading of Elizabeth's fulfilment of the role of Deborah, we see the emergence of a species of parity, this time between councillors and other members of the political nation, specifically other men who might plausibly claim to know God's will. For in the last resort councillors' rectitude could only be affirmed by men who were not exposed to this temptation – or who were immune to it because the strength of their calling enabled them to put their duty to God above service to queen and realm conventionally defined. Hence the very common appearance in Elizabethan literature of exhortations to privy councillors to do their duty to God by moulding, if need be withstanding, the queen's will, and the equally common tone of expostulation when they appeared to have ignored that duty. In 1579 a Parson Prowde of Burton upon Dunmore wrote to William Cecil, now Lord Burghley, the Privy Councillor closest to the queen, to remonstrate with him over the slow progress of reformation in the body politic. His letter gives very rich evidence of this dynamic. He begins by announcing that he is merely relating what 'some say', in Burton upon Dunmore about Burghley 'and others now in great authority'. In Mary's reign they had bowed their knee to idolatry to preserve their positions: 'and so, by your dead doings therein, consented to all the blood of the prophets and martyrs that was shed unrighteously in Manasse's [e.g. Mary Tudor's] days.' The True Church thrives now, in these later days, but its survival, and England's status as potentially redeemed nation, owe nothing to such as Burghley, and everything to the godly (Marian exiles) who fought for the faith:

> ye came not to God's persecuted church, that he builded, maintained and
> defended . . . which was not corrupted, nor polluted with idolatry; wherein
> was the word of God purely preached, and sacraments godly ministered,

and discipline without partiality executed: and hearty prayer to God was made for God's afflicted church. By the which I persuade my self, and for the suffering of the just of that church, that both ye, and others now in great authority, and the whole land beside, fared the better. Ye came not I say, I say thither (viz to Frankfort, Strasburgh, Zurich, etc.) as others did, that were in your faith.

Moreover the word in Burton upon Dunmore is that, 'rid out of idolatrous bondage' (through none of their own doing), the queen's councillors, and specifically Burghley, are being lost to another species of idolatrous bondage: fear of the consequences of proffering godly counsel to an obdurate monarch. '[I]t is said, that you from time to time, fearing to exasperate the prince . . . have not dealt with her so plainly . . . as your knowledge hath required, both touching God's church, her own preservation, and the safety and profit of the commonwealth.' He closes by exhorting Burghley to remember that his duty to God, queen and country require him to 'be bold and courageous'. He must 'deal plainly' with Elizabeth, 'stirring and inciting' her to enact her role as Deborah, 'although it should cost you your life'.[39]

Prophets exercising this counselling function could be godly ministers of whatever degree, from Parson Prowde up to the primate of the Anglican Church, the Archbishop of Canterbury. Their power derived in large measure from their perceived probity and from their direct and indirect links with Privy Councillors. And the links could be both very immediate and surprisingly democratic – as with Prowde's approach to Burghley. Much evidence exists for the informal ties, based on shared ideological conviction, between Privy Councillors and godly ministers – men like John Knox, Christopher Goodman, Thomas Cartwright, and John Field.[40] Their counsel must inform and reform Elizabeth's realm if she is to be accepted as Deborah. In a 1572 parliamentary debate over the proposed execution of the Duke of Norfolk, Thomas Digges came close to characterizing the queen as reprobate because she implicitly disavowed this relationship. Her refusal to allow their reading of God's will to direct her own forces one of two conclusions. Either the true religion is false – or Elizabeth is not Deborah:

> The preachers have plentifully poured out vehement reasons, urgent examples and horrible menaces out of the sacred scriptures concerning the execution of justice [on the Duke]. . . . The contemning of these [the preachers] yieldeth unto God's adversaries great cause of triumph in advaunting our religion to be wicked and our preachers false prophets. For I suppose there is no enemy so malicious as will affirm her Majesty . . . so hardened in heart that such vehement exhortation of true prophets alleging the scripture of God should not move [her] to give ear to the lamentable cry of her whole realm pronounced by the mouth of the Parliament.[41]

Elizabeth could and did attempt to control the counsel that she received from this direction, most famously in the case of Edmund Grindal. Grindal was suspended from the archbishopric of Canterbury in 1577 because of his refusal to suppress prophesyings, those exercises designed to inculcate the habit of godly scriptural interpretation among men committed to the establishment of the True Church, in England and abroad.[42] In the age of print she could not, however, silence him or others of his ilk. Grindal went public with his claim to conscience, explaining, in terms at least humiliating to Elizabeth, if not damning of her queenship, why he must ignore her 'pleasure' in order to remain true to God's will:

> I am forced, with all humility, and yet plainly, to profess that I cannot . . . without the offence of the majesty of God, give my assent to the suppressing of the said exercises. . . . If it be your Majesty's pleasure, for this or any other cause, to remove me out of this place, I will with all humility yield thereunto. . . . Bear with me, I beseech you Madam, if I choose rather to offend against your earthly Majesty than to offend the heavenly majesty of God.[43]

In the context of Elizabeth's reign the queen's disapproval could actually signify the rectitude of the person under attack, to a significantly widened body of 'public opinion'.[44]

Other men too could claim the right to proffer advice to the queen on the basis of their zeal and ideological commitment. They could expect these claims to be respected and their advice to be heeded – at least by Privy Councillors, if not by the queen. Men like Thomas Norton, John Stubbs and Sir Philip Sidney spoke as prophets in their printed works to interpret God's will to a Protestant nation under female rule, and addressed a public audience in doing so. Like godly ministers, these men had links with the queen's 'innermost councillors', who often shared their convictions but who parted company with them, for various reasons, on the subject of their full and frank expression. Nowhere are these convictions – by the 1580s tinged with apocalyptic urgency – more tellingly displayed than in a letter written by Sidney to his father-in-law, Sir Francis Walsingham, during the Netherlands campaign. Elizabeth is God's instrument but simultaneously a weak reed, and God of His goodness will repair the damage to the True Church should she default from her role as His handmaid in these climactic times: 'If her Majesty were the fountain I would fear . . . that we should wax dry, but she is but a means whom God useth and . . . I am faithfully persuaded that if she should withdraw her self other springs would rise to help this action. For methinks I see the great work indeed in hand.'[45] John Stubbs lost his right hand in 1581 for insisting too explicitly in *The Discovery of a*

Gaping Gulf that Elizabeth would definitively lose her legitimacy as Deborah, and hence the allegiance of her godly subjects, if she were to persist in her plans to marry the French Catholic duc d'Anjou – a point Sidney had also made in his contemporaneous *Letter to the Queen's Majesty*. Stubbs's mutilation made a profound impact on contemporaries. Later historians have been more impressed by his ejaculation at the time: he is reported to have shouted out 'God save the queen' after his hand was chopped off. Yet from this vantage point the act reads ambiguously. Was it a patriotic declaration of unconditional loyalty to the Virgin Queen? Or was it a prophetic warning, delivered by a man (with close ties to both William Cecil, Lord Burghley, and Thomas Cartwright) conscious of that elect, and public, identity?

Finally – another development from later in the reign – godly councillors could be more radically defined as godly men whose spiritual and political rectitude was confirmed by their primary allegiance to the 'country', not the corrupt corporations of an unredeemed nation symbolized by the 'court'. This stance assumed political significance especially after 1587, once the execution of Mary Queen of Scots removed a powerful force urging loyalty to Elizabeth upon subjects increasingly dubious about her status as Deborah. Such men were likely to see themselves as affiliated through birth and breeding to centralized structures of authority – the court, the Privy Council, Parliament. But they resonated to a spiritualized identity as 'true Englishmen': an identity available to godly men throughout the country who shared an absolute commitment to God's truth. Job Throckmorton – and he was not alone – adopted this stance in a well-known speech made after the execution. In it he complained that MPs were granted only a show of freedom in their debates. What is truly radical about this speech is his privileging of the 'simple', the 'inferior sort', the 'country' over the court, 'private men' over councillors – and 'young men' over 'wise men'. For this truly was radical, in a culture that had hitherto, in its most spiritually charged moments, attributed political virtue to 'elders': men of worth and weight (it went without saying), whose godly lives entitled them to leading roles in spiritual and political matters:

> Ye shall speak in the Parliament House freely, provided always that ye
> meddle neither with the reformation of religion nor the establishment of
> succession. . . . In these causes . . . that reach so high and pierce so near the
> marrow and bones of Church and Commonwealth, if any of the inferior
> sort here amongst us do happen in some zeal to overstrain himself, surely
> you that are honourable . . . ought in equity to bear with them, because the
> fault is in yourselves. . . . When grey hairs grow silent, then young heads
> grow virtuous . . . it doth amaze us in the country that wise men of the
> Court should be so backward. . . . Is it a fault in a private man to be
> too busy, and can it be excused in a councillor to be too sleepy?[46]

What did the identification of Elizabeth with Deborah mean? In this paper I have argued that it was profoundly significant. First, it signalled a recourse to providentialism as the most effective means of legitimating a female monarch by anyone wanting to maintain the 'estate' of the last Tudor heir – including the queen. This connection inevitably fuelled the view of England as an elect nation, described by William Haller more than thirty years ago.[47] According to this interpretation of the recent past, Elizabeth was called to the English crown by God and on behalf of His people – a calling that revealed more about Englishmen's relations with the Almighty than it did about Elizabeth's monarchical capacity. By means of this extraordinary dispensation He gave the English nation a second chance to effect a spiritual reformation after the declension into idolatry that had accompanied Mary's reign. The taint of that declension touched the queen and many of her most powerful councillors through their collusion in Mary's regime. It proved to have a long-term half-life through Elizabeth's reign and into the reigns of her Stuart successors. In particular, polemicists conflated and demonized the figures of Mary I and Mary Queen of Scots – representing the Catholic past and the potential Catholic future – in order to shore up the Protestant settlement and Elizabeth's status as an exceptional queen.[48] Their very success accustomed men to fear subversion of the realm and taught them to believe that it might be effected through, if not at the behest of, the person of the ruler – especially if that ruler were female or (as was to be the case with Elizabeth's first two Stuart successors) deemed to be effeminate.[49]

In the circumstances of Elizabeth's accession, identifying Elizabeth as Deborah proposed a partnership between the queen and her godly male subjects for the exercise of English imperial kingship. It brought into polit-ical existence the concept of a fellowship of men who were potentially equal as men in their commitment to the enactment of God's will, as it were on behalf of the crown – or as citizens of the reform(ing) commonwealth: the 'country'. For, as the Marian exile Richard Bertie argued in his (qualified) defence of female rule – written, like John Knox's apology, at the outset of Elizabeth's reign – the members of a body politic will naturally compensate for the dangers and deficiencies of that condition. Indeed, they must do so '[f]or no man wholly committeth the conduct of his body to a head without eyes, neither cutteth off or refuseth the head because it is eyeless, and cannot direct him, but feeleth for the way with his feet, gropeth it out with his hands, and so supplieth the lack in the imperfect head. So must man do in the greater common weal.'[50] This imperative unleashed a contest over the provision of counsel, and monarchical identity, during Elizabeth's reign that retained its salience in the reigns of her Stuart successors. It surfaced when-ever men concluded that God had given them an idol in place of a king.

Figure 6.3 Frontispiece to John Dee, *General and Rare Memorials pertayning to the Perfect Art of Navigation* (1577). Shelfmark C.21.e.12

By permission of the British Library.

During Elizabeth's reign this political configuration came to be understood, following John Aylmer, as the 'mixed monarchy' or, following Sir
Thomas Smith, as the 'monarchical republic', with slightly different shades
of political meaning. Common to both official versions of the Elizabethan
polity was the conviction that Elizabeth must govern, and be seen to govern, in immediate conjunction with her godly councillors as a pre-condition
of political stability and the establishment of a godly realm. This prerequis-
ite was widely promoted in the iconography of the reign, where images of
the queen in proximity to 'three wise men', variously identified, abound.
On one level these figures serve as secularized versions of the magi, who
(aptly) symbolize godliness through their ability to recognize God's will
made manifest in the person of a weak and lowly child. On another level they
represent the 'commonwealth' element of the Elizabethan polity, whether
they are (as various historians and literary critics have posited) Elizabeth's
zealous unofficial counsellors, Thomas Norton, John Foxe and John Day,
or her chief ministers of state, William Cecil, Lord Burghley, the Earl of
Leicester and the Archbishop of Canterbury.

One example occurs in the frontispiece to John Dee's 1577 work, *General
and Rare Memorials pertayning to the Perfect Arte of Navigation*. (See Figure 6.3)
This woodcut features a ship, representing 'this imperial monarchy: or,
rather, the *imperial ship*, of the most part of Christendom: if so, it be her
Grace's pleasure'; that is, should Elizabeth agree to act as Deborah and
fulfil Protestant imperial destiny. At the helm sits Elizabeth, sanctified by
the beams of the tetragrammaton positioned in the top right-hand corner.
Below her in the ship stand three men who represent either her councillors
or (according to Frances Yates) the three estates.[51] On the shore kneels
Respublica Britannica, engaged, like these counsellors, in pleading with
Elizabeth to recognize and enact God's will. For under a female ruler the
respublica – the male domain of the political nation, significantly here imaged
as female – could be and was conceived of as separable from the person of
the ruler, with their linkage effected by the queen's male subjects. Elizabeth
as Deborah, I would argue, puts gender and power at the heart of the
'monarchical republic' of Queen Elizabeth I.[52]

CHAPTER SEVEN

Queen Anna bites back: Protest, effeminacy and manliness at the Jacobean court

MICHAEL B. YOUNG

Marriage

This is the story of a marriage. The husband was King James VI and I (so called because he was the sixth king of Scotland but the first king of England named James). The wife was Princess Anna of Denmark. Their marriage defies easy generalizations and forces us to reconsider some of today's commonly held assumptions about gender and power in early modern Britain.

James and Anna did not meet, fall in love and marry in the way that modern western couples are supposed to. Rather, they were both members of a small and privileged sector of society, the royalty of northern Europe, and they both needed spouses from that very select group in the year 1589. James was twenty-three years old. Originally placed on the throne of Scotland as a baby when the nobility drove his mother, Mary Queen of Scots, out of the country, he had just reached the point in life where he was genuinely beginning to take charge of his country. He was under increasing pressure to marry and start producing heirs, all the more so because he had shown no previous interest in women. Thomas Fowler, an English informant, reported that James 'never regardes the company of any woman, not so muche as in any dalliance'.[1] In fact, the one major love affair in his life up to this point involved his male cousin, the Duke of Lennox and that affair ended disastrously when the nobility drove Lennox out of the country and temporarily held James captive. It was a pattern that would repeat itself throughout James's life. Although he became an adept ruler in many respects, time and again he undermined his authority by becoming involved with these male 'favourites'.[2] As a French observer expressed it, 'he loves indiscreetly and obstinately despite the disapprobation of his subjects'.[3]

Figure 7.1   *Anna of Denmark*, oil on panel, attributed to Marcus Gheeraerts the Younger *c.* 1612
By courtesy of the National Portrait Gallery, London.

By 1589 James was secure on the throne but still precariously alone in the world.[4] In the absence of any immediate family, he had been raised by guardians.[5] He had no brothers or sisters. His father had been murdered. His mother had remained both geographically and emotionally remote during her exile in England and was executed in 1587. If James should suddenly die, there were no heirs waiting in the wings to take over the reins of government and prevent Scotland from slipping into chaos. James himself wrote a fascinating, open letter to his subjects explaining his predicament. He acknowledged that 'I was generally found fault with by all men for the delaying so long of my marriage'. The 'want of hope of succession bred disdain'. More than that, 'my long delay bred in the breasts of many a great jealousy [suspicion] of my inability, as if I were a barren stock'. This and other considerations drove James into marriage for the good of the state, 'for, as to my own nature, God is my witness I could have abstained longer'.[6]

These admissions from James remind us that he was not an entirely free agent. Had it not been imperative for him to produce heirs, he might never have married. Powerful as he was, James had to accede to the demands of his position and even, to some extent, to the wishes of his subjects. He was not entirely free in the choice of his wife. Factions formed around James, one advocating marriage to Princess Anna of Denmark, and another promoting marriage to a French princess. It was the Danish faction that ultimately prevailed, partly because the merchants of Edinburgh expected it would give them commercial advantages. In fact, the town leaders made threatening moves and showed a willingness to employ violence 'if the marriage with Denmark went not forward'.[7] Perhaps equally important to James was the fact that the French princess was eight years his senior while Anna was more than eight years his junior.

Anna's circumstances were quite different.[8] She was surrounded by a large and loving family. She had three sisters and three brothers. She was raised initially by her grandparents, and later by her strong, caring and intelligent mother, Sophia. In the spring of 1588, while the marriage negotiations between Scotland and Denmark were underway, Anna's family was struck by tragedy: her father, King Frederick II, died. However, Anna's younger brother smoothly succeeded to the Danish throne as Christian IV, and Queen Sophia continued during his minority to look out for the interests of the family, which included good marriages for her daughters.[9]

Thus Anna's marriage was arranged for her by people far more powerful than she, but it would be anachronistic to think of her as a mere pawn. Arranged marriages were the norm at this time, especially among the propertied classes. By facilitating the marriage with James, Anna's mother was doing what was best for her daughter. Although marriage did not mean freedom for Anna, it was infinitely preferable to remaining a single woman growing old in someone else's household. Marriage offered Anna status – indeed, considerable status since she was marrying a king.[10] Besides, the fact that a marriage is arranged does not necessarily mean it must be devoid of love. All the contemporary accounts show Anna eager to marry James. She was described as being so in love with James that 'it were death to her' to have the marriage negotiations broken off.[11]

James's emotional commitment to marriage was harder to discern. At first he was described as 'a cold wooer' who was 'not hasty of marriage' and unlikely to requite Anna's love.[12] These impressions could have been created intentionally by James, however, to extract better terms from the Danes. In any event, his affection soon grew to the point where he was writing love poetry to Anna, and he abandoned his demand for a huge dowry because, he said, he did not want to bargain like a merchant for his wife.

Any lingering doubts about James's feelings were erased by the heroic adventure he undertook to join his bride. Anna was technically married to James by proxy in a civil ceremony which took place in Denmark on 20 August 1589. In September she set sail for Scotland to join her husband, but ferocious storms forced her little fleet to take refuge in Norway. When James learned that his bride was stranded, he made the daring decision to embark on a rescue mission. He sailed to Norway and travelled overland to Oslo where Anna was waiting. A minor Scottish official recorded a story about their first meeting. James supposedly rushed 'boots and all' to see Anna. He had in mind 'to give the Queen a kiss after the Scottish fashion at meeting, which she refused as not being the form of her country'. Nevertheless, 'after a few words privily spoken betwixt his Majesty and her, there passed familiarities and kisses'.[13] The details of this story may be apocryphal, but it captures the public perception of events and the romance of the occasion.

Now joined in person, Anna and James were married a second time in a religious ceremony at Oslo on 23 November. Instead of trying again to reach Scotland by crossing the treacherous winter seas, the newlyweds spent the winter celebrating and travelling back to Denmark, where Anna had the pleasure of being temporarily reunited with her family. Finally, in the spring of 1590 they arrived in Scotland, where Anna's coronation occurred on 17 May. After six months of dizzying events, the honeymoon was over, and the new royal couple now had to tackle the difficult job of learning how to live together.

Living with James was not easy for Anna. To begin with, there was the great disproportion in power between them. On the surface at least, there was little Anna could do to counterbalance James's authority. She could use the arts of persuasion. She could play on his emotions. And she could scheme with allies at court who might have more influence than she did. But ultimately, it was James who had the final say, and often Anna had no choice but to submit to his authority, no matter how arbitrary and unfair it might be.

James's temperament did not help. He was not only a king, but a political theorist who subscribed to royal absolutism, which he elaborated in his books entitled *The Trew Law of Free Monarchies* and *Basilikon Doron*.[14] James did not believe his authority should be challenged by anyone, let alone his wife. Patriarchy was part and parcel of James's mental makeup. That was especially evident in his advice about how a husband should behave toward a wife:

> Treat her as your own flesh, command her as her Lord, cherish her as your helper, rule her as your pupill, and please her in all things reasonable; but teach her not to be curious in things that belong her not. Ye are the head, shee is your body; It is your office to command, and hers to obey.[15]

James's views on women were so misogynistic that the French ambassador once reported, he 'piques himself on great contempt for women . . . he exhorts them openly to virtue, and scoffs with great levity at all men who pay them honour'.[16]

James was also an intellectual with an inflated opinion of his own intelligence. He has justly been described as 'one of the most learned and intellectually curious men ever to sit on any throne'.[17] The other side of this learning, however, was a tendency for James to assume he knew best. Moreover, in a tradition that went all the way back to Plato, James believed that women were intellectually inferior to men.

Until recently, historians tended to see Anna through James's misogynistic eyes. In contrast to James, who was a deep thinker engaged with profound issues, Anna was assumed to be a shallow and foolish woman. David Harris Willson described Anna as 'incurably frivolous and empty-headed', 'childish', 'shallow and vacuous'. He sympathized with James because he 'had married a stupid wife'.[18] A.L. Rowse called her 'featherheaded'.[19] Maurice Lee Jr called her 'young, silly, and meddlesome'.[20] Maurice Ashley even called her a 'dumb blonde'.[21]

This caricature of Anna as the mirror opposite of James is a convenient literary device, but it is bad history. More recent studies have been more sympathetic and positive.[22] The shift in usage away from the Anglicized name 'Anne', back to 'Anna', the original name she herself preferred, is only a small token of this new respect for the authentic woman. In reality, as we shall see, Anna was an intelligent woman who displayed great determination and resourcefulness during twenty-nine years of marriage.

Scotland

Before examining how Anna fared in Scotland, it is worth remembering how young she was when she arrived there: she was only fourteen years old when she married James and fifteen at her coronation. She has been quite appropriately described as a 'child bride'.[23] On the other hand, this was no ordinary child. She had exceptional abilities. She communicated with James, for example, in the French language and quickly learned Scots. Equally important, she had an unusually high opinion of her own worth. Descended from royalty and married to royalty, she expected to be treated accordingly. Like her mother Sophia, whose example was apparently a lifelong influence, Anna had no intention of receding meekly into the background.[24]

It is true that Anna lived in an abominably patriarchal world, but she occupied a very privileged position in that world. It is a plain fact that she enjoyed far more wealth, power and influence than any ordinary man of her day could dream of possessing. Still, Anna's greatest asset derived from her proximity to one particular man, King James. In an age when courtiers competed feverishly to get 'the king's ear' and mere access to the king's presence was an inestimable political prize, Anna was in an enviable position. The first signs we have of Anna's involvement in politics are instances when she interceded with James on behalf of other parties. Roughly a year after her arrival in Scotland, court observers began taking note of Anna's efforts to influence the king.[25] It was no ordinary woman who could decisively affect another person's fortunes simply by putting in a good word with her husband.

Anna's political activities quickly extended beyond simple influence-peddling. The Scottish nobility were badly factionalized; and it was not long before Anna was taking sides in these mighty contests that affected politics at the highest levels. Indeed, Anna threw in her lot against one of the most powerful men in all of Scotland, the chancellor, Sir John Maitland. There were several reasons for Anna's dislike of Maitland. He had not favoured her marriage to James in the first place, preferring instead the French match. More importantly, he claimed ownership over land that Anna believed rightfully belonged to her as part of the traditional gift James had bestowed on her the morning after their wedding. Furthermore, upon her arrival in Scotland, Anna had befriended many of Maitland's enemies. This made her predisposed to take offence at any insult, real or imagined, attributed to the chancellor.

In 1592 Maitland was temporarily forced to withdraw from the court. The historian Maureen M. Meikle describes this exile of Maitland as Anna's 'triumph'. Another historian emphasizes that Anna held the key to the chancellor's return because it did not occur until he reached a reconciliation with the queen, in particular by giving up all claim to the land in dispute between them.[26] The reports of one contemporary observer support this view. He wrote that Maitland was 'hoping to be restored to the Queen's favour', that he had 'kissed the Queen's hand' and that he was tailoring his actions 'to please the Queen'.[27] Of course it is impossible to determine precisely how much Anna used Maitland's enemies to achieve her own ends in these matters, and how much they used her. But it strains credulity to believe that she was a mere pawn of other people. She clearly was a woman with a mind and a will of her own (though still only nineteen years old at the time of Maitland's restoration to favour).

Anna's arrival in Scotland had upset the status quo. She was a new factor in the bitterly divisive atmosphere of Scottish politics, and competing courtiers quickly learned it was advantageous to befriend her. There was nothing inevitable about this process, however. Anna could have been a docile wife who strictly confined her activities to the domestic sphere. Certainly that is what James wanted. In one of his formal writings, he declared that a ruler should keep his wife out of politics: 'suffer her never to meddle with the Politicke government of the Comonweale'.[28] Yet Anna brooked no interference from her husband and actively injected herself into politics, thereby challenging the boundaries between the private sphere and the public sphere. That Anna was able to do this suggests that James was not very good at practising what he preached. He allowed his wife more latitude and gave her opinions more weight than he needed to, if not because he respected her, at least because he cared for her (or feared her). Of course Anna could not have entered into this realm with any credibility if she had not also possessed solid abilities. This included the ability to make herself welcome and popular among strangers in an alien land. A less adroit woman could easily have been disdained and marginalized, but Anna was 'an instant success in Scotland'.[29]

In 1597 it was said that Anna routinely dealt in 'matters of importance to the greatest causes', and in 1598 that 'the Queen knows all'.[30] Nevertheless, it has to be added that historians who want to make Anna seem like 'a major player' or 'a queen to be reckoned with' instead of the frivolous lightweight of tradition are inclined to overlook certain other aspects of her behaviour.[31] Anna was not just 'one of the boys' at court. She was a woman in a man's world, and sometimes she resorted to using the only stratagems that were available to most women in her day, attempting to manipulate James through emotion. Sometimes Anna tried to cajole James with affection; sometimes she burst into tears, although this may have resulted more from frustration than calculation. As far above other women as Anna was in many other respects, she was quickly reduced to their level in this respect when James insisted, against all reason, on being obeyed. Indeed, Anna found herself in an even more exasperating predicament than ordinary women did when her husband gave her orders. If she defied her husband, she was not only challenging patriarchy but disobeying the command of a king.

For example, there was one occasion in 1592 when James flatly forbad Anna to visit certain friends. Anna was distraught. An observer reported that 'manye tymes she fallethe into teares'. Interestingly, though, she also expressed a desire to be back with her mother in Denmark, or to be able to speak with Queen Elizabeth of England.[32] This was not the only time Anna threatened to return to Denmark.[33] The threat to appeal to Queen Elizabeth would have seemed more ominous to James because he desperately needed to remain on the best of terms with the powerful woman he hoped to succeed on the English throne.

Anna's emotions were especially evident in 1600 in the aftermath of the Gowrie Conspiracy. For reasons that still remain a mystery, James had gone alone to an upstairs room with the Earl of Gowrie's younger brother. A struggle ensued in which James had to fight for his life and the Gowrie brothers were both killed. Anna, whom one would expect to be solicitous for the welfare of her husband in these circumstances, was furious instead. Anna may have suspected that James had allowed himself to be drawn into a sexual liaison that somehow went wrong, but historians have tended to find other explanations for Anna's strangely unsympathetic behaviour. They speculate that she was hoping to cultivate the Gowrie family as useful allies at court; and she certainly was angry that James removed the earl's two sisters from her court, where they were among her closest friends.

Whatever her reasons were, Anna responded by staging a strike of sorts that lasted at least two days. She refused to leave her bed or get dressed. There were rumours that Anna was threatening to go into seclusion or, alternatively, that James intended to keep her under house arrest. One report out of Scotland said the 'King and Queen are in very evil menage'. In public Anna warned James that she could not be treated like the Earl of Gowrie, and James exclaimed that his wife must be insane.[34] Two years later an observer reported that Anna was still 'that violent woman' who would not relent on this issue but, significantly, James was too far in love with her to heed warnings about her.[35] Later Anna met in secret with one of the banished sisters, a daringly defiant act that did alarm James.[36]

Anna was sometimes powerless to overrule her husband, but obviously she did not submit without protest, and she never gave up resisting. The historian Leeds Barroll has aptly referred to her 'relentless streak'.[37] She displayed these same qualities of defiance and tenacity in the long battle she waged with James over the custody of their first child, Prince Henry, who was born in 1594. (Anna gave birth to seven children altogether, but only three would survive infancy: Henry, Elizabeth and Charles.) During her first pregnancy, it was reported that Anna and James had made a pact: she promised 'to concur with and further his actions and courses', and he gave her 'the greatest part of his jewels' in return.[38] Like most married couples, Anna and James were trying to negotiate a working relationship, but if Anna ever truly made this promise of total submission, it was not one she could keep, no matter how many diamonds were involved. The pact broke down immediately upon Henry's birth. Anna wanted to raise her own children, but James insisted on putting Henry in the custody of the same guardians he himself had known (the Earl of Mar and his mother). Again Anna 'fell to tears'.[39] And again, although overpowered for the time being, she never gave up.

Anna waged a sustained campaign against James and Mar on this issue for nearly a decade, fighting with every weapon she had, both political and emotional. Anna was described as biding her time, waiting for the right opportunity.[40] In the summer of 1595, when she thought 'she had the King in a good humour', she plied him with fresh arguments, but again James refused.[41] Both the king and queen were described as unyielding in the matter. Anna tried to tip the balance by making allies, forming a 'Queen's faction', but the faction lost its nerve in the face of James's intractable opposition. Anna 'fell to tears' again and acted compliant. To complete his victory, James apparently arranged for a minister to preach a sermon before Anna about 'the duty of a woman to her husband', and she pretended to be persuaded. But her 'evil will', as one contemporary put it, was only waiting for another opportunity.[42]

The climax to this battle of wills occurred in 1603 when James travelled ahead of the rest of his family to England where he had just succeeded to the throne. Anna seized the opportunity to make a bold move. With her husband out of the country, Anna, although pregnant at the time, rode to Mar's castle accompanied by several sympathetic noblemen and demanded that her son be turned over to her. When Mar refused, Anna was so distraught that she experienced a miscarriage. Now in a sickened and weakened state, Anna still would not accept defeat. James tried to mediate the contest from England, but finally was forced – by the crisis Anna had created and her implacable resolve – to capitulate. Mar was relieved of his responsibility for Prince Henry, and Anna was allowed to bring him with her to England.[43]

England

Although they had their disagreements, there was also some degree of affection between Anna and James. She could not have played upon his feelings if he had not possessed such feelings for her in the first place. In the climactic events of 1603, James was no doubt anxious to quell the domestic rebellion in Scotland lest it undermine his assumption of power in England, but the documents also show him genuinely solicitous for the health and happiness of his wife.

After 1603 in England the feelings between Anna and James cooled. They conceived two more children, but both children died by the end of 1607. After that date the royal couple drifted increasingly apart. David M. Bergeron, the modern author who knows them best, detects an emotional dulling and 'growing chasm' between Anna and James at this point.[44] Simultaneously, James turned more and more to other males for his emotional and physical satisfaction. James's affection for other males had been less pronounced or visible in Scotland during the first thirteen years of his marriage than it would now become in England. He had two especially famous lovers in England: first Robert Carr, whom he elevated to the peerage as Earl of Somerset, and secondly, George Villiers whom he elevated even higher as Duke of Buckingham. These were definitely love affairs, and there is considerable reason to believe that they were also sexual affairs.[45]

Anna was powerless to prevent these extramarital affairs, but James did work out a strange accommodation with her: he gave Anna a right of prior approval. The Archbishop of Canterbury described the arrangement this way: 'James had a fashion, that he would never admit any to nearness about himself but such an one as the Queen should commend unto him.' The goal of this deal was more to shield James from criticism than to give Anna any real power in the matter. Again in the archbishop's words, 'if the Queen afterwards, being ill-treated, should complain of this dear one', James could reply that her complaint was unjust because 'you were the party that commended him unto me'. Aware of this arrangement, the archbishop and his allies sought Anna's support when they wanted to supplant Carr by replacing him in James's affections with Villiers. The archbishop succeeded in winning Anna's support, but she was not enthusiastic because she 'knew her husband well; and, having been bitten with Favorites both in England and Scotland, was very shie to adventure upon this request'.[46]

As this incident illustrates, Anna still retained a small residue of political influence, but it was nothing compared to what she had known in Scotland. More isolated politically in England, Anna turned to court culture as a way of promoting her agenda. What was that agenda? Of course she wanted to enhance her image and validate her own sense of self-worth, as Leeds Barroll has argued.[47] But Anna also used court culture in subtler ways, to counter the influence of her husband's 'dear ones' and cultivate an ethic of heroic manliness in opposition to these effeminate favourites.

James's personal behaviour here intersected with his foreign policy. One of his first accomplishments as King of England was to bring the protracted war with Spain to an end. He took pride in being called *Rex Pacificus* (the king of peace). He advocated ecumenical reconciliation instead of religious war in Europe.[48] But his critics interpreted this love of peace and aversion to war as yet another sign of softness. They made a connection between James's pacific foreign policy and his attraction to boyish favourites. Both seemed weak and effeminate.[49] Anna apparently sided with her husband's critics on these matters.

What happened in Jacobean England, therefore, was a surprising inversion of gender roles. The king stood for peace; the queen stood for war. The king advanced effeminate favourites at court; the queen allied herself with the hawks. The king wanted a softening, a redefinition of manliness, that elevated rationality and reflection over violent and impulsive behaviour.[50] The queen inclined toward a more conventional definition of manliness. She preferred men who favoured action over contemplation, men who were eager to prove their valour on the battlefield. Anna, as the Archbishop of Canterbury explained, had been bitten by favourites. And characteristically, she found ways to bite back.

From the outset of the reign in England, Anna openly joined the critics of her husband's conduct at court and in foreign affairs. In 1604 the French ambassador reported that James was being ridiculed on the London stage and his 'wife attends these representations in order to enjoy the laugh against her husband'.[51] Furthermore, Anna rebuffed the women James and his advisors recommended for her court, preferring instead women of her own choosing, several of whom were associated with the old Essex circle that had coalesced around the heroic figure of the second Earl of Essex under Queen Elizabeth.[52] She also befriended men from the Esssex circle, notably the Earl of Southampton who was a proponent of war and who got into trouble for complaining that there were too many 'boys and base fellows' at James's court. She also lobbied (unsuccessfully, as it turned out) for James to spare the life of Sir Walter Ralegh.[53]

Anna's most significant activity, however, was her role in helping to create the dramatic art form at court known as the masque. In contrast to the all-male acting companies of the day, Anna and the women of her court performed in these masques; and oftentimes they played assertive, militant, even martial women. In one of these Anna played 'War-like Pallas, in her Helmet drest'. Another masque featured a queen who led the women of her realm in the slaughter of their husbands.

Anna's masques are open to myriad interpretations. Most compelling for our purposes is the interpretation of Barbara Kiefer Lewalski. In her view, Anna reacted to 'the homosexual and patriarchal ethos' of her husband's court by establishing a vibrant court of her own that served as a locus for resistance. Unlike other interpreters, Lewalski does not evade the sexual motives for Anna's behaviour. She forthrightly declares that Anna was repelled by the 'attitudes, interests, and sexual proclivities' of her husband. Both 'the homosexual and patriarchal ethos of his court excluded her from any significant place in his personal or political life'. Thus, as Lewalski views it, 'James's homosexuality as well as other familial circumstances led to Queen Anne's progressive withdrawal to her own court and affairs'.[54]

At the very least, Anna's masques seem to express a desire to escape from the confines of the real world to an imaginary world where women could be strong, assertive, powerful figures. It is true that masques conventionally ended with some form of obeisance to the king, and this has prompted some scholars to minimize their subversive potential and emphasize their ultimate reaffirmation of patriarchy and the king. But it is difficult to believe that Anna and her fellow female performers did not feel at least momentarily empowered. Furthermore, if the masque did conclude by reaffirming male authority, it still came with a lesson. Anna seemed to be taunting her husband to act like a man. She paraded examples of militarism before his eyes and threatened that women would follow these examples if men did not. As a contemporary pamphlet expressed it, the women of England could only be expected to return to their sewing needles when the men of England took up their swords again.[55]

Anna would never be able to lead the men of England into war, but her son could. Masques were imaginary exercises in persuasion, but in Prince Henry lay Anna's best real chance of repudiating James and vindicating herself. Having regained control of Henry, it was reported that Anna now 'never lets him away from her side'.[56] If Anna could not make a man of her husband, then she was determined to make a man of her son. Most of all, he would have to become a warrior. The French ambassador reported that Anna 'says aloud, she hopes her son will one day overrun France as well as his ancestor Henry V' did.[57] The reputation of Henry V as a leader of men and a warrior-king was enhanced at this time in poetry and on the stage.[58] Anna was making a clearly political statement when she declared that her son 'is like that king'. She wanted her son to be like Henry V, not like his own father.

Prince Henry did become fervently militaristic. He developed a keen interest in all things military, especially the navy.[59] Like his mother, he used the vehicle of the court masque to express his oppositional values, casting himself in the role of an Arthurian knight on a mission to revive the nation's military glory.[60] There is no way of knowing how much Henry might have developed along these lines if he had been left to himself. Like many an adolescent male, he was creating an identity for himself in opposition to his father. But it is clear that Henry and his mother shared a revulsion against King James's values. The historian Roy Strong observed that even in his choice of clothing the prince was making 'a statement against the follies of his father's court', and 'he clearly abhorred the homosexuality of his father'.[61]

Henry's ostentatious repudiation of his father's values put him in an awkward position since it was imperative that he, like his mother, maintain an outward appearance of obedience and respect toward the king. James was visibly upset by the collusion of his wife and son. The French ambassador described him as 'perplexed by fear and jealousy respecting the alteration that is observable in the Prince of Wales, and produced by his mother'.[62] The Venetian ambassador reported that James was disturbed 'to see his son so beloved and of such promise that his subjects place all their hopes in him; and it would almost seem, to speak frankly, that the King was growing jealous'. James wanted his son to be a scholar, not a warrior, but Anna had other plans for him. The Venetian ambassador observed that Henry 'studies, but not with much delight, and chiefly under his father's spur, not of his own desire'. When James scolded Henry for neglecting his studies, Henry held his tongue but is supposed to have muttered afterward: 'I know what becomes a Prince. It is not necessary for me to be a professor, but a soldier and a man of the world.'[63] The queen's hand is particularly evident here because, as the French ambassador explained, she had endeavored 'hourly to corrupt the spirit and disposition' of the prince, 'diverting him from his lessons' on the grounds that they were 'unworthy of a great commander and conqueror'.[64]

Anna and many of her compatriots hoped that Prince Henry would lead England back into military glory, but those hopes were suddenly dashed when he died in 1612. Henry's unexpected death at the age of nineteen was a terrible blow for Anna, a loss compounded by James's diminishing concern for her in these final years. In 1618 the Venetian ambassador described her condition: 'She is unhappy because the king rarely sees her and many years have passed since he saw much of her.'[65]

Queen Anna died in 1619, King James in 1625. Whether or not it was through his mother's influence, her surviving son Charles, like his brother before him, tried to be different from James. This had its benefits: Charles had one of the most loving marriages that English royalty has ever known. And it had its liabilities: Charles was fatally determined to fulfil the role of 'commander and conqueror'. He spent nearly half his reign (1625–49) at war, ruining the careful work of his father and eventually provoking a civil war that culminated in his own public execution. As James had wisely understood, the price of manliness can run high.

QUEEN ANNA BITES BACK

Gender confusion

The marriage of Anna and James raises several perplexing questions for students of gender. In the first place, how did Anna manage to get away with so much defiant and disruptive behaviour? Anna's freedom of action was severely circumscribed, to be sure, and James certainly believed in patriarchy. Yet inside this blustering male's household, on closer examination, we discover that his wife was actually able to act in a surprisingly rebellious fashion. How is that possible? The wives of Henry VIII would never have dared to behave this way in the preceding century. Had society's expectations changed so drastically in the interim, or was James simply a more tolerant or caring husband? Were the very qualities of softness that Anna deplored in her husband responsible for the latitude he gave her? Or was James just afraid to treat Anna more brutally for fear of how Queen Elizabeth of England or King Christian IV of Denmark might react? Or does the problem lie with our stereotype of patriarchy in the early modern period? Have we drawn it too harshly?

Secondly, most historians today subscribe to the theory that concepts like masculinity are merely 'social constructs', malleable expectations about behaviour that vary throughout history. Yet the version of masculinity that prevailed in Jacobean England is very much the same as contemporary versions of masculinity that we are familiar with four hundred years later. In a word, people wanted James to act more 'macho'. Does this not support the dissenting view (of Lyndal Roper, for example) that masculinity stays pretty much the same from the sixteenth century to the present because it is more a function of biology than society?[66]

It is true, of course, that masculinities were 'contested' in Jacobean England, but in a strange way. It was the male James who wanted scholarly and conciliatory men. It was the female Anna who wanted heroic and aggressive men. Was Anna exceptional in this respect? Did she have more virile expectations of men because of her upbringing in Denmark, or because she was reacting against James's effeminate favourites? Or could it even be possible that Anna was expressing a more universal desire on the part of women regarding how men should behave?

When all is said and done, by the way, who was right in that contest over manliness? Was it Anna or James? England reentered Europe's religious wars against King James's better judgement. After five years of carnage, the badly beaten English retreated back into the blessed peace that James had originally bestowed on them. Yet King Charles, quick to stand on his honour and incapable of backing down in the face of a fight, soon abandoned that peace and rushed headlong into a bloody civil war that ended in his own decapitation. Was James's inglorious peace not preferable to Charles's costly heroics? Did Anna get her final vindication through her son, or was it James who was vindicated?

Finally, with whom should our sympathies lie? We have probably sympathized too much with Anna in this chapter. She seems an unfortunate woman trapped by circumstances beyond her control in a troublesome marriage with a man she did not respect whose deeper affections, she painfully knew, were reserved for his male lovers. But what about James? He did not desire women and would probably never have married one if his station in life had not required him to. He was forced into a marriage which he tried very hard to make work. Then he was ridiculed for his efforts to find a more personally satisfying relationship in a series of love affairs outside that marriage with other males. For a generation trained to empathize with the victim in history, who in this case was the victim?

Privileges of the soul, pains of the body: Teresa de Jesús, the mystic *beatas* and the Spanish Inquisition after Trent

JOAN CURBET SOLER

On 10 February 1577, in the presence of the authorities of the city of Seville, Doña Francisca Hernández, a 52-year Sevillan middle-class woman, stood publicly on the scaffold (*cadahalso*) that had been erected in the Plaza de San Francisco. She was holding a candle in her hands and had a rope tied around her neck. After being asked about the state of her soul, and about her willingness to repent, she immediately abjured all her previous errors as sinful, and was subsequently sentenced to receive one hundred lashes on the following day and to be expelled from the city for one whole year. The official *Relación* (account) of that *auto de fe*, based on information gathered from seven witnesses, explains the events that had brought her to public abjuration and punishment:

> Francisca Hernández, also known as López, a neighbour of Seville, of
> 52 years of age, was reported by six witnesses to have stated that, having
> been given a coat as an alm, she had a revelation that night, as she was at
> prayer, of what colour that coat had been; and that, wherever the state of
> contemplation took her, she stayed motionless and felt the burning of the
> Holy Spirit in her heart; and that, as the name of Jesus had been found
> written on the heart of a Saint, much more would be found written on
> hers, because God had decorated her heart with many beauties and
> blooming of flowers; and that our Lord had appeared to her in the image
> of *Ecce Homo*; and that, as a child, an angel had taken her to Hell and to
> Purgatory, and that afterwards they had climbed to Heaven, and the
> angel knocked on the gate and it would not open, and other visions and
> revelations, which were described as temerarious and deceptive, and which
> made her suspicious of being in the errors of the *Alumbrados* and the lost
> ones.
>
> Archivo de Historia Nacional: *Inquisición*, leg. 578, 368.[1]

The case of Francisca Hernández was not the only one that was publicly judged that day. María de Zúñiga and Francisca de Guzmán (the latter, a 90-year old woman) confessed themselves guilty of very similar doctrinal mistakes and transgressions, and were condemned to similar penalties. The account that has been extensively quoted above is not exceptional among the cases of female mysticism that were repressed by the Inquisition; on the contrary, it has been included here because of its representative quality. Among the most significant characteristics of this instance are the physical quality of the mystical experience, through the 'burning' that the accused experienced in the heart; the sense of a personal confrontation with Christ; the intermission of angels, and the notion of direct, unmediated revelation. Finally, it must be observed that the inquisitor himself notes that Francisca Hernández was suspected of being 'in the errors of the *Alumbrados*' (the illumined ones); that her situation, therefore, was not perceived by the inquisitors as a strictly individual case, but as being part of a widespread doctrinal disease. The term *alumbradismo* or any other of its derivations is not explicitly used in any of the other accounts of that day, but most of the same characteristics of this case reappear, in a far more spectacular and scandalous form, in the report on the above-mentioned Francisca de Guzmán:

> Francisca Guzman, a *beata* ('holy one'), a neighbour of Seville, of 90 years of age, was reported by six witnesses to have remained for a long time in bed, being perfectly well and healthy, and she said that God wanted her to remain there rejoicing with him, and not to hear Mass on Sundays or Holy days; and that when she complained of that spirit not letting her go to church nor get up from there, he answered to her: 'Is not God here, the same one whom you go to church to look for? What do you complain of?' And that spirit went to bed with her, and between the two occurred things that it would be shameful to report, as if a husband was with his wife; and he did not let her pray or think of any good thing, and she had it as a great privilege from God to be in the arms of that spirit.[2]

The spectacular quality of this report should not divert our attention away from the fact that the basic characteristics of this case are the same (though in a degree of heightened intensity) that we found in that of Francisca Hernández. There is here, as well, a sense of personal, direct intimacy with angelic entities, a pointed physicality, here turned into explicit eroticism. Once again there is also a very special sense of personal and unmediated revelation, which is verbalized by the spirit that Francisca Guzmán believed she had heard: 'Isn't God here, the same one that you go to Church to look for?' In Francisca's experience, the religious community has become superfluous: her very bed may become a place of sacred worship, and that worship may easily take the form of erotic stimulation. What is less unusual here is the term that the inquisitor uses to describe her case: she is not seen as an *alumbrada*, but, more specifically, as a *beata* (a 'holy one'). The meaning of this term became virtually interchangeable with that of *alumbrada*, which we have seen attributed to Francisca Hernández. The second term, however, is loaded with more significance, since it designates gender as well as heresy, and is never used, in this context, in its masculine inflection. The *beatas* are, especially, female mystics or religious leaders who may be, moreover, suspected of *alumbradismo*; representative cases, therefore, of the doctrinal disarray that was hinted at in the first quotation from the reports of this *auto de fe*.

Beatería and *alumbradismo* are two different but closely interrelated phenomena. Several of the females identified as *beatas* by the authorities had ties with, or belonged to, one of the groups of *alumbrados* that were active in the south of Spain throughout the second half of the seventeenth century. *Beata* is the Spanish translation (inflected to denote female gender) of the term *beatus*, used to refer to these dead individuals who have saved their souls and are acknowledged by the Church to have come close to sanctity. It is a category that, even today, is officially applied to specific figures before their canonization. The use of this term in official reports such as those quoted above obviously does not denote such a state of quasi-sanctity. When it is applied to female individuals accused by the Inquisition, it becomes derogatory and imbued with misogyny (there are no male *beatos* in the Inquisitorial reports) and, as Alastair Hamilton has shown, denotes the simulation of sanctity, a form of religious imposture practised by women.[3] The term *alumbradismo*, with which it is often linked in official reports, had suffered a similar devaluation by the 1770s.[4] At the start of the century, it had defined the Erasmian or Lutheran forms of religious practice, orientated toward inner spirituality rather than ritualism and ceremony. From the death of cardinal Cisneros onwards, it had come to denote the various forms of alternative religious discourse (whether influenced by Lutheranism, Antinomianism, or other tendencies perceived as heretical). But the *beatas* remain always identified in the documents of the Holy Office as a separate category, linked in various ways to *alumbrado* groups, seen as a different though equally subversive phenomenon.

There are two key cultural and historical causes that have been repeatedly proposed as explaining the impact and influence of female *beatería* on the popular strata of the centre and south of Spain at the end of the sixteenth century. On the one hand, there is the diffusion of Lutheran and Erasmian forms of spirituality through the south, which indirectly affected the female population through the act of preaching; on the other, there was a relative decrease of the male population in the cities, where the impact of the colonial enterprise had been particularly powerful.[5] These causes may contextualize the situation and explain the diffusion of illuminist or *alumbrado* forms of devotion among the female sectors of the population. However, what they do not explain is the particular form of the mystical visions that allowed some specific women to be perceived as *beatas*, nor the sustained desire to eradicate this phenomenon on the part of the authorities. I would suggest that the third and most important element that caused the emergence of mysticism among the *beatas* was the convergence of these factors with the renewed need for female models of sanctity that the Counter-Reformation itself was trying to promote. The aim of this chapter is to examine the cultural interaction and conflict that took place between the forms of female mysticism and the institutional discourse of the Spanish Catholic Church in the wake of the Council of Trent. This conflict, as I hope to prove, was motivated by the institutional need to repress and control the individual interpretation of some tendencies and forms of worship that Catholicism itself had put into circulation. In order to do so, I will try to contextualize the investigation carried out by the Inquisition against St Teresa de Jesús in the mid-1570s. I will do so not only because of the importance of her account of her own mystical experience, but because of her particularly ambiguous position within the Church at the time. She was perceived by the Holy Office both as a respected reformer and as a potential threat to doctrinal unification.

The particular political conditioning of the Council of Trent had set the stage in Spain for a renewed insistence on all those aspects of Catholic sacramental practice that differed from the Protestant concentration on interiority and austerity. The worship of saints and of the Virgin, the intense use of iconography in devotional practice, the authority of the clergy over the lay population in religious matters, were significantly intensified throughout the reign of Philip II, and the role of the Inquisition in this process was essential. It seems safe to assert, following the investigations of Henry Kamen and of Ángel Alcalá, that it was after the appointment of Fernando de Valdés as archbishop of Seville and general inquisitor in 1547 that the atmosphere of surveillance over religious non-conformists was increased.[6] The previous directors of the Holy Office had shown some tolerance for religious heterodoxy (especially Antonio de Cisneros, an Erasmist himself, and the author of the first trilingual version of the Bible to be published in Spain). However, Valdés worked hard toward defining the function of the Inquisition as an instrument of doctrinal control against non-Catholic or heretic forms of worship, especially through the commission of the *Compilación de las Instrucciones del Oficio de la Santa Inquisición* in 1561. This was preceded by a massive burning of Lutheran books in the previous three years, and of the sacrifice of twenty-four Protestant Spaniards in *autos de fe* throughout the kingdom between 1559 and 1560.[7] From that moment onward, and all through the seventies and nineties, the Spanish Inquisition would be used and perceived as an instrument of the state in defence of the rigorous principles approved by the Council of Trent, and of the doctrinal unification of the state. The need for this unification intensified the repression, not only of the several Christian doctrines that were perceived as heretical, but also of the individual voices that could be seen as opening a space of resistance to the established religious authority.

This doctrinal unification had immediate consequences in popular culture, reaching far beyond the limits of theological debate. Among the resolutions of Trent were some that had a direct and very purposeful incidence on forms of popular worship. Josse Clichtove's *Treatise on the Veneration of Saints* (1543) was revised, widely translated and applied by the Tridentine Church against the Lutheran disdain of iconography. The worship of images was insisted on as an important aid in prayer (especially, the contemplation of the Cross), and the authority of 2 Maccabees, on the use of images for the worship of the Lord, was used throughout in polemical writing. The contemplation of Christ on the Cross was a particularly favourite aspect of popular and ascetic poetry, and the iconographic aspects of Marian adoration became a central subject of Catholic art. Ignatius of Loyola, in the *Spiritual Exercices* (1526, translated into Spanish in 1541 and used as a handbook against Lutheran doctrine), had insisted particularly on the role of visual imagination in worship, encouraging the worshipper to build 'imaginative pictures' of Christ or of the sacred family. The Council of Trent had also stressed the need for a renewed emphasis on the mediating role of the Virgin, 'Mediatrix and companion of all humankind'. The insistence on Mariolatry, and especially on the theme of the *Mater Dolorosa*, gave rise to one of the richest and most expansive forms of iconography, constantly re-created in pictorial and sculptural form. The Marian brotherhoods proliferated throughout Andalusia and Extremadure, extending the cult among the lower strata of society. In Seville, the worship of the patrons of the city, St Rufina and St Justina, was intensely renewed: some fragments of their clothes and even bits of their fingers were exhibited in the cathedral and were offered to be kissed or worshipped at Christmas and Easter. The legend of their torture at the hands of the Romans, and of their having received the stigmata or wounds of Christ on their hands and feet, was popularized in the form of oral storytelling and ballads. The first *beatas*, operating in the thirties and forties, acquired some measure of prestige by letting their own clothes be used as relics, as if they were actual saints. Sor Magdalena de la Cruz, a Cordobese prioress who claimed to have the power to interact with angels, and who disciplined her body by constantly wearing a hair shirt, gave some of her vestments to be venerated. However, these vestments were used as evidence against her in the trial that brought about her banishment, in 1547. By the mid-seventies, when the Holy Office had intensified the repression of the *beatas*, their main identificative features were those that made them appear, in the eyes of the authorities, as a deformation of the Catholic hagiographic tradition. 'Little women', as Pedro de Ribadeneyra put it in 1576, 'who have appeared in our day in the most illustrious cities of Spain; women who with their revelations, ecstasies and stigmata have upset and fooled many people.'[8]

If we return now for a moment to the accounts above of the Sevillan *auto de fe*, it may be much easier to understand the particular form that the mystical experience of the accused *beatas* took. Through the inquisitorial reports in these cases, similar characteristics are repeated. These include a manifest sense of physicality on the part of the female subject who experiences the visions, an unshakeable conviction of preferment or of privilege being granted by God to her; and a tendency to concentrate on doctrinal aspects that are inherent to the Counter-Reformation. These include a vision of, or intercourse with, the souls of Purgatory, the desire to be given wounds on the palms of the hands, or to undergo the sufferings of St Rufina or St Justina. The very form that the mystical experience of the *beatas* often takes, then, is directly related to the cultural climate of the Counter-Reformation, and is thus manifestly Catholic in its conditioning. The cases of Francisca Hernández or Francisca Guzmán are very representative of the discursive complexity of the mystical discourse. This is a complexity that, as far as we can tell, must have manifested itself in a disorganized and incoherent form, but which is characterized both by an independence from official control and by a subjective re-adaptation of elements of worship that were promoted by the Spanish Church.

The form of the punishment that the mystic *beatas* received also fits firmly within that same cultural frame. Since it is in the physical, sensitive nature of the body that the mystical transports have been mainly experienced, it is the body that has to be punished so as to repress the transports of the soul. Only rarely were they actually executed (or, in the terminology of the period, *relajadas*, relaxed). The virulence the Inquisition showed against the Lutherans or Huguenots, who had to be physically destroyed, was substituted in the case of the *beatas* by the public lashes on the naked back of the accused. These varied between fifty and one hundred, and were followed by reclusion or expulsion from the cities where they had been operating, and, occasionally, by a period of imprisonment. The emphasis on the sensual nature of mystical experience is the key that authenticates that experience for the *beatas*, and that frees it from institutional and doctrinal bounds; in its turn, the repressive apparatus of the Inquisition must finally signal the re-inscription of the trespassers into the official dogma by placing the female body at the centre of the punishing process, just as it had been at the centre of the reported mystical experience.

Every attempt to reconstruct the personal experience of the mystic *beatas* from an early twenty-first century perspective, however, must remain incomplete: what we cannot obtain is any reliable information on their subjectivity, beyond the history of their confrontation with the institutions. All of the information that we have on them comes from the archives of the Inquisition, not from their own hands, and this mediatization is itself representative, not only of the rigour of the Holy Office, but also of these women's attitude toward writing. The *beatas* operated in the limits or fringes of fully established religious practice. They did not attach a particular importance to scholarship or writing, and the firm rooting of their work in popular culture, which directly contributed to their empowerment, also implied a relativization of the importance of written culture in their areas of influence. The lack of material authored by the *beatas* stands in stark contrast with the abundance of writings by Teresa de Jesús, the renowned mystic and reformer of the Discalced Carmelite order. This contrast becomes even more significant if we take into account the fact that Teresa herself was accused of *beatería* and underwent the scrutiny of the Inquisition. Beyond its literary value, Teresa's work allows a privileged perspective into the subjectivity of a female mystic within the cultural framework of the Spanish Counter-Reformation. By contextualizing the text that gave rise to the accusation against her in that particular cultural environment, and by examining the dynamics of the investigation itself, it is possible to chart both the cultural forces that informed the mystical female experience. We can also trace the institutional limits against which it defined itself and within which it could be allowed to exist.

We must be careful not to let our present perspective on Teresa de Jesús as a saint and Doctor of the Catholic Church mislead us when we attempt to interpret her early writings and the investigation against them. Her own position was quite uncertain until she underwent the interrogation by the Holy Office in the mid-1570s, and her early movements of reform toward a greater austerity within the Carmelite order had encountered a strong resistance from the start, coming from the male sections of the order. She had taken her vows in 1535, being twenty years old, in the Avilese monastery of Santa María de la Encarnación; from that moment and until 1542, she gained a remarkable reputation for her discipline and endurance under an ongoing illness that has been identified as a form of epilepsy. It is difficult to tell, from an early twenty-first century perspective, to what extent her constant relapses into epileptic attacks influenced her first mystical visions. We know for certain, however, that her mystical transports, which occurred in public, and her conviction of their transcendent nature brought her in her twenties and thirties into conflict with a series of confessors. These finally concluded with the supervision of Fr. García de Toledo, who encouraged her to write down her personal experience in detail; that account is the *Libro de la Vida* (*Book of Her Life*, 1562–67), which would be the main source of Teresa's confrontation with the Inquisition.

It is necessary to take into account from the start that the *Book of Her Life* poses an interesting problem in terms of textual authority. Even though the autobiographical perspective situates a female voice as its centre, the text must be seen as granting the final authority over its contents to its first readers. These readers are, on the one hand, Teresa's own confessor, García de Toledo (whom she often addresses directly) and, beyond him, the tribunal of the Holy Office, which might request the manuscript at any moment. Teresa's autobiography, then, owes its existence to the request of a superior male authority and was destined for a male readership. The text became a hybrid of autobiographical prose and religious treatise, loosely based on the model of St Augustine's *Confessions*, which Teresa had read in her early twenties. The essential difference lies in the deference toward higher authorities that the speaking subject explicitly adopts in this case. This is explained by her as caused by her female condition: 'It is perhaps convenient that little women like me, weak and devoid of all strength, should be given gifts, like God does to me; because in this way it will be easier for me to bear the great difficulties that his Majesty has desired me to endure.'[9] This acknowledgement of her personal weakness is at one with her submission to the institutional censorship of the Catholic Church, through the figure of the confessor:

> Whatever should go outside the simple discourse of my life, your honour should consider carefully (as you have repeatedly asked me to write about the privileges that God gives me in my prayers) whether it should conform to the truth of our holy Catholic faith, and, if it should not, then your honour may burn it, as I submit myself to this.[10]

This seeming self-depreciation should not be understood, however, as a rhetorical commonplace, and even less as an internalization of misogynistic commonplaces on the part of Teresa. On the contrary: it is a necessary part of her negotiation with the external authority that is going to judge her text, and one which is especially necessary if we consider the language which, from the very first passage, she uses to refer to her mystical experiences. This is the short preface she wrote for the autobiography:

> I would like, since I have been ordered and given licence to write the kinds of prayer and the privileges that God has granted to me, that it should be

granted me to state clearly and in great detail my great sins and unworthy life. It would give me great consolation, but they have not wanted it to be so, tying me strongly in this respect; and thus I ask, for the love of the Lord, everyone who should read this, to keep in mind that it [i.e. 'her life'] has been so worthless, and that I have found no Saint to console me, of all those who turned toward God. Because I think that, after he called them, they did not offend him any more: whereas I was not only worse, but seemed to study how to resist the privileges His Majesty granted me. . . . Let Him be for ever blessed, who ever waited for me, to whom I ask with all my heart to give me grace so that, with all clarity and truth I should make this account that my confessors have asked of me.[11]

Again and again, this text turns upon the speaker's sense of unworthiness, her scant education, her lack of merit as a woman. Such modesty may have been, judging from the testimonies we have about Teresa herself, quite genuine in her, but it was also necessary as a rhetorical means of securing the validity of her testimony.[12] The mystical experience that she is going to describe can only be conceived as *mercedes* (favours). These are a series of privileges that allow her direct access to sacred truth, and one that is granted directly by God, mirroring the privilege claimed by the *beatas*: a personal, unmediated access to revelation, and one that manifests itself outside the institutional structure of the Post-Tridentine Church. The precondition for any validation of such an experience is, as Teresa well knows, the official approval of the institution, within which, in the Catholic paradigm, lies the only valid access to sacred truth. As a consequence of this knowledge, Teresa's attitude toward external, male authority is dialectical. She starts by admitting that authority's power, by submitting her own text to its approval; but this very approval is necessary for her to secure her own claim to authority and to a personal privilege that, because of their very nature, operate independently of any institutional framework. Teresa never tried to disseminate her experiences without institutional support. She produced a written account of her experience at the request of male authority and she repeatedly invoked that authority as having the final word on the validity of her experience. She simultaneously asserted the transcendent nature of the privilege that had been given to her by a higher, supernatural power.

But the cultural framework of the Counter-Reformation is also at the centre of Teresa's text in other ways. The nature of her mystical experience, though described with a precision and detail that make it vain to search among the mediatized and brief accounts we have of the mystic *beatas*, seems to mirror several of the features that we have seen recurring in their cases. For Teresa, the transcendent nature of her experience manifests itself through physical as well as psychic effects; the initial sense of being in the power of transcendent forces, which originated in her twenties, never appeared without an accompanying sequence of physical sensations that can be described in very material terms:

> The Lord wanted me to see this vision: I saw an angel near my left side in corporeal form . . . not very tall, not small, very beautiful, the face burning, as it happens to the most elevated angels, who seem to be burning up; I saw in his hands a golden arrow, and at the end of the arrow I thought I saw some fire; this he seemed to put inside my heart several times, reaching my entrails; when he took it out, he seemed to take them away with it, and he left me all burning in love for God. It was such a strong pain, which made me complain, and it was such an extreme suavity that pain gave me, that there is no desiring to stop feeling it, nor does the soul satisfy itself any more, except with God.[13]

Of course, this was not only a merely personal sensation, but the result of a peculiar cultural climate. The erotic intensity of the transport, made evident in the key moment of the penetration of the angel's arrow into Teresa's heart, is particularly reminiscent of the superposition between spiritual and sexual ecstasy in the case of the *beatas*. This can be seen in the case already discussed of Francisca Guzmán. There is no attempt to present this experience as part of an allegorical or figural discourse. On the contrary, it is described in very immediate, physical terms ('I saw', 'He put (the arrow) inside my heart', 'He took it out', 'He left me burning with love'), erasing any possible differentiation between the sensitive and the spiritual nature of her perception. The initial fears that Teresa felt about these ecstasies and visions as the result of a possible demonic possession are presented as having been shared by her first confessor. He recommended her to respond with gestures of disdain (*dando higas*) whenever she saw the image of the crucified Christ appearing before her:

> When I saw this vision of the Lord, this refusal gave me the greatest pain; because, when I saw him present, I could not have believed him to be the devil even if I had been cut to pieces; and thus it was a great kind of penitence for me, and not to keep making the sign of the cross all day through, I took a cross in my hand. This I did quite often, the gestures of disdain not so often, because it made me very sorry. I remembered the injuries that the Jews had done to him, and I asked him to forgive me, since I did it to obey the one that was in his place (i.e. the confessor, who represents Christ in the sacrament), and not to blame me, for these were the ministers he had put in his Church. He told me not to worry, that I did well in obeying, but that he would make the truth well understood.[14]

A scene as powerful as this one is permeated through and through by the conflictive patterns of authority and power to which Teresa's writing responded from the start: in this case, the conflict is dramatically reproduced at the very heart of the mystical experience. Teresa is forced to refuse, with physical gestures of *dando higas* (that is, placing the thumbs between the other fingers and pointing them toward the vision) the presence of Christ. However, she also finds herself asking him for forgiveness at the same time, and reminding him of the fact that she is merely following the instructions of the ministers he has appointed in the 'Holy Mother our Church'. The conflict is defined, therefore, according to categories of gender (the male authority dictating the response of the young female novice) and of reception of the religious experience (institutional response versus spontaneous interior response). In itself, this double pattern of conflict mirrors the whole conflict of Counter-Reformation control over the interiorized, non-institutional forms of mysticism. The particular form of subjectivity that the text of Teresa exemplifies is entirely representative of its historical moment in its oscillation between the affirmation of a personal, unique experience and the framing of that experience within its proper institutional bounds.

Before Teresa asks for official authorization to found a convent, the reproaches of her confessor lead her to self-reproach and doubt:

> What greatly distressed me was that my confessor wrote to me on one occasion as if I had been acting against his instructions. . . . In his letter he told me that I ought to have realized by now the whole matter was just a dream. He advised me henceforth to lead a better life, and not to attempt anything more of the kind or even to talk about it, since I saw what scandal I had raised. He said some other things too, all of them most painful. This distressed me more than everything else put together, for I wondered whether I had been guilty of leading others into sin, whether these visions were illusory, whether all my prayers had been a deception, and whether I was not utterly lost and deceived. . . . For five or six months I kept quiet, making no move toward it [the foundation], and not even speaking about it, and the Lord did not give me a single command. I could not guess the reason for this, but was unable to rid myself of the belief that the foundation would eventually take place.[15]

The pressure exerted by institutional surveillance finds direct access to the conscience of the speaking subject; it informs her inner fears and generates self-doubt and mistrust of her own perception. But all through this time, and alongside this doubt, there remains an inner conviction set against these same tendencies, that encourages Teresa to persevere: an inner conviction, that cannot be adequately explained other than as a 'belief' of which the speaker is 'unable' to rid herself. This inner conviction, that is engendered within subjectivity, but which is just as real as the fears that are engendered in it from without, enabled her to carry on toward the permission for the foundation of a new monastery that finally was granted to her, in 1567, by the new rector of the Society of Jesus, Fr. Gaspar de Salazar. It would be inadequate, however, to see the interiority of the mystical experience as being directly opposed to an institutional and discursive pressure exerted from without on Teresa's subjectivity. The constant references to Mary or Joseph, to the community of Saints, or to specific figures from Catholic hagiography inform the whole discourse of the *Book of Her Life*. They are not only rhetorical features but elements that help her to process her subjective experience and the perception she has of her own work as a reformer of the order. The discourses and practices of the Counter-Reformation cannot be differentiated from the interiority of the speaker, or seen as external to it. Rather as in the case of the mystic *beatas*, though on a much more self-conscious and elaborate level, the sense of a direct, unmediated contact with transcendence takes a series of forms that mirror the representational and iconographic practices of the official Catholic discourse. These are based on its incarnational theology and its insistence on the use of contemplation and on the senses. It is precisely to the extent that Teresa's mystical discourse mirrors the dogmatic framework of the Catholic church while simultaneously asserting the subjective conviction of her own truth that it becomes most closely similar to the discourse of the *beatas*. Just as in their case, however, the sense of unmediated contact with the transcendent, the excessively sensual form of this contact and the superseding of the institutional limits set by male authority takes Teresa to a confrontation with authority. This took a particularly dangerous turn after the reception of the *Book of Her Life* by the Holy Office in the mid-1570s. For the remainder of this chapter, I will examine the ways in which the few references to the investigation that we can gather from the letters and works of Teresa are representative of the tension that the Counter-Reformation establishes between private subjectivity and institutional control. This is a tension that is both strongly gendered (created by male surveillance) and brought forth by the subject's appropriation of the very aesthetics and discursive forms that the institution puts in circulation.

On 26 July 1575, Teresa de Jesús entered the city of Seville, responding to the suggestions of her confessor, Fr. Gracián, in an attempt to negotiate the foundation of a new convent for the discalced nuns. To her astonishment, and against all expectations, she discovered that there was no building ready to receive the nuns, and that her community was placed in a rented house, left to subsist without any official support, and only through the reception of alms. In a few months, she learned of the active opposition of the male Carmelitas and asked for the official support of Fr. J.-B. Rubeo and of the king, Philip II, but to no avail; the community was left without any official economic support. Only by the end of the year could they move to a more commodious house left by a personal friend of Teresa, Lorenzo de Cepeda. The negotiations lengthened her stay in the city until the start of the following year, but by then the denunciations to the Inquisition had already started. In the month of January of 1576, the Consejo del Santo Oficio de Sevilla issued the following document:

> Several testimonies have been received in this Holy Office against
> Teresa de Jesús, the founder of some convents of the discalced nuns of
> the Carmen, and against Isabel de Santo Hierónimo, a nun of the same
> order, in a convent they have lately occupied in this city. And because it
> seems, according to the informations, a new doctrine, superstitious, false
> and similar to that of the Illuminists . . . we ask Your Honour to order
> the diligencies to be started and that they may be sent to us, since, as we
> have to proceed onwards on this cause, it will be necessary to have them,
> because they will contain all that can be charged against Teresa de Jesús,
> which, as we understand, are deceptions and falsehoods very dangerous for
> the Christian state.[16]

The source of the investigations were the rumours against a book: that book was obviously the *Book of Her Life*, unpublished at the moment, but which had already circulated in manuscript form, from García de Toledo to the Holy Office, where it had been requested. As for Teresa's initial reaction to this situation, it is impossible to document it closely, as several of the letters sent by her during this crucial year have been lost. Part of her correspondence on this subject must have been immediately destroyed by the addressees, and we must actively locate and identify the indirect though expressive references to it that she includes in her texts of this period. It is, nevertheless, clear that part of the danger inherent in this situation came not only from Teresa, whose sense of humility undoubtedly won the favour of the investigators, but from the other accused, Isabel de San Jerónimo. She insisted repeatedly on her capacity for undergoing visions and asserted her own mysticism in terms very close to those used by the *beatas*. Both cases seem to have been helped by Teresa's collaborative attitude and by her readiness to accept the authority of the Church, as she had already done in the *Book of Her Life*. However, Teresa's subjective response to the interrogations (only documented in a few references in her letters and in her later writings) betrays a different approach to the whole affair. Her own retrospective construction of the events of these months, in a brief fragment occurring in the *Book of the Foundations*, her late account of the process of reformation of the discalced order, written in the late 1570s, is most significant. Teresa does not mention the inquisition explicitly; she goes on to evoke the hardships she endured during her enforced stay in Seville:

> I do not know whether it was the very climate of that land – because
> I have heard that demons have greater ability there for temptation, which
> God must have given them – and there they oppressed me, who was never
> as pusillanimous and cowardly as I found myself to be then. I certainly did
> not know myself; though the confidence I have in Our Lord did not desert
> me; but my nature was so different from what I was since I have been
> involved in these matters, that I understood that the Lord was withdrawing
> his hand, so that I could see . . . that if I had had any will up to now, it
> had not been only mine.[17]

Such an expressive passage, even while conveying the bitterness and the sense of humiliation that Teresa felt, is based once more on the linguistic and symbolic network of references that the inquisitors and their accused shared, and which allowed the very conflict between the institution and the subject to occur. Teresa begins by representing her accusation as the work of demons, in front of whom she has felt nearly helpless. She goes on by conveying a sensation of deep despair and dejection that borders in self-reproach ('I was never as pusillanimous and cowardly as I found myself to be then'). She concludes with an implicit acknowledgement of the power of the inquisitors and of the strain through which she has been, where the situation is reinterpreted as a challenge brought about not by human institutions, but by God himself. The language of the accused and that of the accusers becomes almost interchangeable. The cultural frame of the Counter-Reformation brings about a circulation of terminology that may be suspect or beneficial depending on the gender of the speaker and on the circumstances, either officially sanctioned or extra-institutional, in which it is spoken. The whole episode of the investigation is read by Teresa as a test of her endurance. The aggression of the inquisitors is reinterpreted as the work of demons, and behind the whole episode appears the controlling will of God. The subjectivity of the female mystic is informed by a dialectical pattern that is particularly representative of its cultural moment and of its underlying power structures. The conflict between external authority and inner conviction creates the subjective perception of a painful, dramatic confrontation with forces that are beyond the speaker's control. The conviction of God's underlying control of the situation never deserts her. However, the form in which she recreates the conflict (a soul tempted and besieged by demonic forces, temporarily left to its own, but supervised by God) is in itself representative of the forms of spiritual conflict delineated by the institution within which, and against which, she struggles.

The last reference to the conflict in Teresa's correspondence occurs in a letter to Isabel de San Juan, another Carmelite, dated 29 April 1576, just after the interrogations had concluded:

> Tomorrow the post is leaving and I was not going to write to you, because there is no good thing to tell you. . . . This is much like hell. Oh, what a year have I had here! I confess that the people of this land are not for me, and that I desire to be in the promised one, if God desires so, though, if I understood that I was needed here, I would willingly remain, even though the abomination of sins about here are enough to cause great sorrow; they are to be greatly feared. May God put a remedy to it![18]

Teresa's own references to the investigation cease after 1577, but its influence continues to make itself present in her writing, and especially in *The Inner Castle* (*El Castillo Interior o Las Moradas*), her next major work, which she started in 1577 in Seville. *The Inner Castle* is one of the major didactic texts of the Spanish Counter-Reformation. This is a detailed account of the ways through which the individual soul can ascend through prayer and contemplation toward the contemplation of God. However, it is also a work that curiously manages to escape from the major intellectual currents of the time, not showing any serious influence of Neo-Platonism or Spanish Conceptism, and turning instead to older models of Catholic didacticism, most notably allegory. This shift in style has immediate consequences on the mode of representation of vital experience in the text. If the insistence on the sensitive nature of mysticism had established the major conflict between the subjective experience described in the *Book of Her Life* and the Holy Office, that emphasis is superseded in this new treatise through a new series of rhetorical devices. The most significant of these is a radical metaphorization of the body. For here the language of Teresa becomes filled with explicit comparisons and with explicit similes: verbs such as *parecer* (to seem) or prepositions such as *como* (like) recur again and again in the text, making explicit the figural, non-literal quality of the text. The culmination of the contemplative process is explained through an almost literal re-telling of the penetration of the angel's arrow into the heart as described in her autobiography (and quoted above). That absorbing experience, which was both physical and psychic in its origin, is carefully turned in *The Inner Castle* into a figure of speech, a 'coarse comparison' to express the highest level of transcendent consciousness reached in contemplation:

> Even though the comparison may be coarse, I do not find another one that can express what I mean than the sacrament of marriage. . . . It seems that the pain reaches toward the entrails, and that, when he who wounds them

draws out the arrow, it indeed seems in accord with the deep love the soul feels that God is drawing these very depths after Him. . . . The pain we seem to feel is great, though delightful and sweet.[19]

What are the effects of this shift toward the figural (a likening of the ecstasy of contemplation with the 'sacrament of marriage') in the description of an experience that had been presented not in comparative terms, but as a lived reality, in the *Book of Her Life*? The most obvious is the partial de-materialization of the mystical experience: its erotic quality is turned into a complex system of similes ('It is like', 'It indeed seems') and thus partly emptied of its immediate, physical reality. But this metaphorization of the body also implies the loss of the subjective quality of the text, which is written in the third person and which refers to the soul and to a shared perception ('we') rather than to the subjective sensations narrated in the *Life*. In that previous text, the female mystical subjectivity was directly created, as we have seen, by the sensitive nature of the experience, and the body was the site of the authentication of transcendent perception. In the allegorical system of the *Inner Castle*, that personal quality has been partly lost. Personal experience is turned into a model or a guide for progress in prayer.

Such a purposeful underlining of the figural and doctrinal nature of the description of ecstasy in contemplation allows the mystical experience to fit within the larger frame of the Catholic allegorical and didactic tradition. This textual strategy proved to be successful to the extent that, during the last years of her life, Teresa could go on to complete her reformation of the Discalced Order, founding eleven more convents. And it is in this specific aspect that Teresa's position can be clearly distinguished from that of the *beatas*. Unlike these women, Teresa's role as a member of a religious order led her to internalize notions of obedience and institutional control. The conflict between inner truth and the authority of the Church, which had been a key constitutive element of the subjectivity expressed in the *Book of Her Life*, was finally superseded in the *Inner Castle* by a form of figurative discourse that allowed the mystical experience to be reinterpreted within the *consensus fidelium*. For most of the mystic *beatas*, who operated outside the confines of nunneries and religious orders, that conflict took another, more threatening form: the struggle between an independent discourse that could empower women and the rigorous institutional and punishing discipline of the Holy Office. Even while Teresa's prestige was becoming more established, the repression of other female mystics was steadily progressing. Three *beatas* were publicly lashed in Seville in 1777, and the self-confessed mystic María González was ordered to do penance in 1579, a year after the publication of the *Inner Castle*. Five more would be ordered to do penance during the eighties, and one more would be executed in the *auto de fe* against *alumbradismo* in Llerena; in Seville alone, sixteen other cases would be investigated by the Holy Office between 1570 and 1649. From the Council of Trent and until the mid-seventeenth century, then, the attempts to build forms of independent female discourse were consistently repressed. It was the incapacity of the *beatas* to integrate their discourse into the institutional framework that brought about not only the dispersion of their influence, but the systematic elimination of any traces of their mystical discourse. On 3 October 1582, in a convent in Palencia, Teresa de Jesús received the Eucharist for the last time; just before receiving it, she thanked God for having been allowed to die as a 'daughter of the Holy Church'; it was the last time she spoke. She died the next day, holding a crucifix in her hands; on the morning of 15 October, the funeral ceremony took place, during which her body was exposed to the gaze of the public. In the month of July of the following year, her body was exhumed; and the documents on that exhumation represent her body as having remained wholesome and non-corrupted until that moment. As Diego de San José put it, 'this woman ceased to be a woman, restoring herself to the virile state, to greater glory than if she had been a man from the beginning. For she rectified nature's error with her virtue, transforming herself through virtue . . .'.[20] The physical, intimate dimension of the female mystical experience, which had been such an important part in the life experience of the *beatas*, and the potential subversiveness it entailed, had been re-absorbed by the official, male-dominated discourse. Teresa had become a saint *in spite of* being a woman and not because her mystical experience had had any material and gendered basis. Teresa was about to become an icon herself, a part of the official discourse of the Catholic Counter-Reformation.

CHAPTER NINE

Allarme to England!: Gender and militarism in early modern England

SIMON BARKER

This volume is concerned with issues of gender and power in early modern Europe. However, the relationship between gender and militarism, addressed in this chapter, also has a thoroughly contemporary relevance. In many places in the modern world, matters of gender and of sexual orientation have proved controversial in relation to the large and complex business of military organization. In the west in particular, there is a long history of excluding women from what is usually termed 'front-line action'. Alongside this has been a similar anxiety over including in the armed services individuals whose (overt) sexual orientation does not fit a seemingly 'natural' formula for the recruitment of volunteers or conscripts. Given the tenacity of such a defining formula, militarism provides an obvious and productive site for an examination of the historical connection between gender and power. It could be argued that the power of the state, or indeed the power of groups of individuals intent upon resisting the state, is at its most material (in its expression of ideological practice) when it is linked to military organization as the machinery of defence or change.

Armies recruit individuals, yet notions of individuality do not fit readily into the specialized human activity that is warfare: individual acts may be celebrated and awarded, but in the theatre of war their significance (as soliloquies) depends upon a collective 'troupe.' The controversy over sexuality and identity in modern military institutions is precisely predicated on the dialectical relationship between the individual body of the soldier (as a human resource) and the larger, corporate organization that shapes it, but which also relies on that individual resource. Militarism in the modern world, as in the early modern world, defines and conditions a highly specialized form of gendered subjectivity.

Women have always been involved in the business of war, usually as victims or guardians of the home front, rather than perpetrators. Non-fictional military narratives rarely dwell on the involvement of women in the extensive camp infrastructures that, for centuries, determined the success or failure of armies as they engaged (more 'heroically') at a little distance away on the field of battle itself. However, a new emphasis developed in the relationship between militarism and gender in the twentieth century. This was due in part to the increasing technical sophistication of warfare that led, for example, to women's direct involvement in wartime industrial production. Women were also more formally organized for nursing duties than they had been in the nineteenth century and were increasingly recruited for other kinds of uniformed operational duties. Similarly, the bombing of civilians, a tactic that evolved rapidly in line with developments in aviation, placed women at the heart of large-scale modern warfare.

There is, of course, a fundamental link between these strategic and technical initiatives and the struggle of women for equal rights and self-determination. Yet in the armed forces of the west, women were restricted, in theory if not in reality, to what were considered 'suitable' duties away from the front-line action. The ideal military subject, in terms of a perceived border between the actual front and the infrastructural hinterland remained irreducibly defined as masculine.

The controversy raised by recent challenges to this concept of the fighting soldier (as a certain kind of male heterosexual) shows just how entrenched the ideal of the soldier had become in the state armies of the west over the course of the twentieth century. The fact that the debate continues in a twenty-first century world of female firefighters, astronauts and political leaders (who themselves send men to war) shows something of the uniqueness and sensitivity of the ideological relations between gender and warfare. It also reveals the power and entrenched nature of the corporeal identity of the ideal military subject that has provided the reference point for this debate.

This chapter seeks to examine the basis of the naturalized soldier of modernity by suggesting that the history of the relationship between gender and militarism has, in fact, always been an inherently unstable one. Modern anxieties over women at the front, or gays in the ranks, echo the terms of a historical discourse which has sought, often with considerable difficulty, to construct and maintain an 'obvious' (and therefore naturalized) ideal of the masculine military soldier. At the same time, given the equation between the ('private') military subject and the larger military body (of the public or state army), it is a discourse that necessarily theorized the purpose of war itself; armies require an identity that is dictated by purpose. Theory translated into practice, across history, has had severe implications for those larger social formations that the military institutions claim to represent.

Some of the most resonant and decisive aspects of the unstable history of militarism and subjectivity are evident in late sixteenth- and early seventeenth-century England. If militarism can be thought of as a discourse governing the theory and practice of premeditated mass human conflict, then this was a period of considerable transformation throughout Europe. It was not, however, a period of tremendous involvement by the English in warfare abroad, or indeed at home until the civil conflict which dominated the middle years of the seventeenth century. Yet neither could this period be regarded strictly as a time of peace, or one free from considerable military ambition. It was more a period of minor military adventures, many of them at sea, together with a steady commitment to military activity in Ireland and the Low Countries. Yet it is precisely at this time of relative military inactivity that a widespread debate about the overall ideology of militarism was most determined. Indeed, it is possible to suggest that ideological debate in this period settled a range of existing uncertainties to do with militarism that were transformed into assumptions which were to underpin the more significant military establishment of the eighteenth and nineteenth centuries. This facilitated the constant sense of military engagement that characterized the growth and consolidation of the British Empire.

The early modern English debate over military matters, which led to the construction of what may be termed the gendered military subject, was part of a far larger discourse. Militarism is obviously linked, both literally and symbolically (since wars are sometimes 'cold'), to important issues of political change. Yet it is also connected to matters of day-to-day organization, identity and consent that seep from the walls of the institution (the military) into an ideally respectful civilian population. Examination of the paradigm that emerges of the gendered soldier (and the terms of his subjection to an overall military machine) reinforces the overall importance of matters of gender and power to the developing early modern notion of statehood. In the ideal emerging Renaissance proto-state the values of the military are seamlessly the values of the populous, hence the importance of military display to public ritual in succeeding centuries.

Much of this chapter is concerned with the abundant English prose writing of early modern military theorists. It is in this that the ideal of the military subject is problematized and finally constructed (with an increasing determination) into a recognizable model for empire and of the individual. However, this was also a period rich in theatrical representations of warfare, ranging from depictions of classical military conflict, through narratives of English civil and dynastic warfare, to telling topical commentaries on late Tudor and early Stuart military activity. The public theatre can be said to have foregrounded the more unsettling aspects of the debate about gender and militarism that was being conducted in the private military prose writing of the time. While the prose tended to contain anxieties and discontinuities in the discourse of militarism, the theatre (form against form) interrogated what some modern military historians have seen as a smooth progression towards the settled, naturalized male soldier-subject during the period known as the English Renaissance. This effect is more to do with the dynamic of theatrical representation rather than with political resistance. Had the plays of Shakespeare and his contemporaries and near-contemporaries offered a more formally politically aware (and credible) alternative to the inevitability of militarism as a determining source of identity for the emerging bourgeois state, warfare might have achieved less prominence or acceptance as part of the cultural condition of humanity. Yet the early modern theatre, like the agitprop political theatre of the late twentieth century, at least invites succeeding generations to glimpse a realm of difference and dissent.

The title of this chapter is drawn in part from a text that was published in 1578 in London by the prolific Barnabe Rich (*c.* 1540–1617). His many polemical writings constitute a general commentary on a variety of social and political ills that he saw as eroding the fabric of society in Tudor England. One of his complaints was the lamentable condition of the country's military resources, which he explored in a number of texts. Another was his perception that men and women were somehow losing their respective identities, or rather, that their identities, which should be distinct, were somehow merging together. Rich can be credited with an early (and frequent) use of the word 'emasculated'. His treatise, *Allarme to England, foreshewing what perilles are procured when people live without regarde to Martiall Lawe* (1578), allowed him to discuss these two preoccupations that begin to emerge as part of a single argument. For Rich, martial law (the codes by which war should be prosecuted) is where gender identity should be least ambiguous, and masculinity most clearly defined.

Rich's text is a good example of the abundant prose writing on military affairs which circulated in early modern England. However, it is especially noteworthy because in the process of arguing for the desirability of reform in England's military establishment (such as it was), it engages with a range of issues that may be encountered in similar texts from the period. These, however, appear sometimes only as single issues: small bullets of polemic, rather than Rich's all-embracing broadside. Like his fellow military writers, Rich swept aside any hesitation over the moral justification of warfare in order to begin to focus on its practicalities (training, organization, tactics), finally coming to settle on a main theme: the importance of issues of gender as the root cause of the present military decay. Rich's dismissal of any seeming discontinuity between Christian theology and contemporary pragmatics is therefore characteristic of a general view that can be found in a number of military texts from the period:

Christ hath especially commanded us unto peace: no doubt, that peace he hath commanded, which hee himselfe gave us, which does not consiste in pleasant reste and quietnesse, that man's nature is prone to [but the peace] which we may then especially enjoy when we most vehemently fight, either for safetie of our country, or maintainence of the faith of Christ and his religion.[1]

Rich offered, in fact, a dystopian and finally anthropocentric view of the military condition of the country. The emphasis is not upon the surety of God's hand in guaranteeing victory, but upon the decline of a general sense of awareness and purpose which he, and other writers, declared as coterminous with a seeming retreat from a sense of masculinity which had once defined the country and its military reputation. John Smythe, for example, reported in 1590 on the decline of the English longbow, a weapon both efficient in the field but also, clearly, symbolic of a military world which was slipping away. His claim was that men were simply no longer strong enough, or skilful enough, to deploy this old weapon: in other words, in his view, men were no longer as masculine as they once had been. He concluded that:

if through the negligence of the better sort of our nation, imitating and following the simple and ignorant opinions of our such unskilful men of war, it should come to pass [that the bow disappears] it doth in mine opinion argue nothing more than that God hath withdrawn His hand and all right judgment in matters military from us, and that in time to come, upon any war either offensive or defensive, we shall, when it is too late, report the same, greatly to the hazard and peril of our prince, country, and nation.[2]

Such writers idealized a past which was defined by clear masculine military skill and exemplified in the record of earlier military operations which had depended for their success on a culture which now appeared doomed. At the heart of the discourse was the body, objectified as a moral and political commodity, and problematized by appeals to an ideal of discipline and commitment. In *Allarme to England*, Rich suggests that the problem for contemporary militarism lay at the court of Elizabeth where 'carping cavaliers' had corrupted an English tradition of militarism and masculinity by:

growing lazy and greedy, wallowing in vice and wickenesse [and] neglecting those disciplines which had made them honourable and worshipful – whose magnamitie in the times of warre hath made them famous in forreine countries, and whose noblesse and vertues . . . in times of peace doe shine coequal with the best.[3]

So from within a general argument over the central question of the preparedness of the nation for war, a lament emerged over the general decline in standards in many and varied areas of military culture in which a common corporeal focus emerged concerning sexual identity and difference. This ranged from the sheer strength of individual military personnel (defining their masculinity), to their dress, demeanour, education and their overall lack of military awareness and discipline. Rich offered the view that:

> Gentlemen these days give themselves rather to become Battalus Knights
> (effeminate Men) rather that Martiall Knightes, and have better desire to
> be practised in the carpet trade than in real virtue. To be shorte, in
> England, Gentlemen have robbed our women of halfe their minds,
> and our women have robbed us of half our apparell.[4]

Outward effeminate dress codes for men implied an inner consciousness ill-equipped for war. Interestingly, this also announced a 'defeminization' of women, a concept that was endorsed for the military writers by the court's preoccupation with narratives of Amazons. What emerges for modern historians of sexual identity is that what might previously have been considered a constant of masculinity (against which femininity could be determined) was actually a construct. These early writers implied that a chivalric tradition had served an earlier England well, coupled with a smooth sense of hierarchy which had fed the values of that tradition down to the bowmen and foot soldiers in the field. This may seem a mythical piece of historiography, yet Rich laments the passing of an age of nobility when the tournament (as in the *Pas d'Armes*) was actually a display of military prowess. He scorned its transformation into the courtly jousting games and 'soft and silken wars' which Glynne Wickham confirms as having 'lingered as a Court prerogative . . . conducted in the tiltyard by day and in the banquet hall as a climax to a masquerade by night' well into the late years of the sixteenth century.[5] Although it is never stated outright that the monarchy itself had eroded this tradition, reducing it to display rather than substance, the increasing number of texts of this kind published in the last years of Elizabeth's reign points to an association between her regime and a gathering perception of a general decay in military preparedness and discipline.

It is important to note that the military writing of early modern England was not a specialized or limited discourse, or simply some bad-tempered voice from the margins. Military historians believe that these kinds of gender-orientated texts circulated widely and formed part of an overall philosophical debate about the purpose and justification of warfare. It might be said that the volume of such military writing expanded (with increasing practical concern for a sense of national preparedness for war), due to a settlement of any doubts that had been raised during the period of the Reformation concerning the justification of warfare. The theological anxiety over war found in the work of Thomas More, John Colet, and Desiderius Erasmus was swept aside in the military writing of the late Tudor and early Stuart period with increasing confidence.[6] Rich was more circumspect in 1578 than Thomas Digges, whose *Four Paradoxes, or Politique Discourses concerning Militarie Discipline*, published in 1604, dismissed Thomas More, along with several classical thinkers, as if to prove how outdated this kind of anxiety had now become. Digges announced that:

> to speake of peace perpetuall in this world of contention is but as
> ARISTOTLES FOELIX, XENOPHENS CYRUS, QUINTGIANS ORATOR, or
> Sir Thomas Moors *Utopia*, a matter of mere contemplation, the warre
> being in this iron age si bien enracinäe qu'il est impossible de l'en oster,
> si non avec la ruine de l'universe. So well engrafted it is impossible to
> take it away without a universal destruction.[7]

The extent of the post-Reformation writing on military matters can be seen in what remains the most comprehensive survey: M.J.D. Cockle's *A Bibliography of English Military Books up to 1642 and of Contemporary Foreign Works*.[8] Cockle gives details of over 150 English language books devoted exclusively to matters of warfare that were published in England from the late fifteenth century onward. He also lists many European texts that he believed circulated widely in their original languages, or were translated into English. Some of these foreign works were also incorporated into English-language volumes. The European military writing established itself as a paradoxical adjunct to the domestic writing; it represented an ideal of military culture abroad that was assumed to be superior to that at home. At the same time it established the clear threat from abroad and spoke of the necessity of urgent reform if the potential enemies across the water were to be matched in terms of military might and discipline. Of special interest to English readers of the late sixteenth century were those texts that described the perceived effectiveness of the Spanish military machine. In a curious contrast with the theatre's somewhat ambivalent presentation of Spanish (and Portuguese) masculinity, the contemporary military theorists recognized the Iberian peninsula as a reserve of chivalric masculinity which was no longer to be found at home.[9]

Having dealt with the theological questions, the military theorists proceeded toward the central question of gender by way of a range of practical issues. Some of these texts were essentially manuals, concerning the practical detail of warfare such as tactics, armaments and equipment. Yet the politics of organization, responsibility, expertise, training, morale and motivation ultimately had to be inscribed on the idealized body of the individual soldier rather than simply assumed as inherent to the military machine which deployed him. A list of titles offers a sense of these texts' overall concerns: *The Paithwaie to Martiall Discipline*; *The Defence of Militarie Profession*; *The Practice, Proceedings and Lawes of Armes*; *The Military Garden. Or Instructions For All Young Souldiers* and *The Bible-Battels Or The Sacred Art Military. For the Rightly Wageing of Warre According to Holy Writ.*[10]

The ideological certainty of these texts was quite formidable, not least because, having moved on from the doubts over the relationship between war and Christianity of earlier times, they insisted that war itself, the practical implication of the disciplines they proposed, was of great benefit to the well-governed nation. In his introduction to a 1560 translation of Machiavelli's *Libro dell'Arte della Guerra*, Peter Whitehorne claimed that domestic peace, and the sense of corporate identity and masculinity he espoused, were only ever guaranteed by war since, without it, earlier societies had surrendered to a condition figuratively defined as feminine. Such societies had:

> through long and continued peace, began to bee altogether given to
> pleasure and delicatenesse . . . warre is sometimes lesse hurtfull, and more
> to be wisht in a well-governed state than peace, since peace promoted Ease
> and Pleasure, two seducing Syrens in whose beastly servitude too many are
> intralled past recoveries. Forreine war is a sovereign medicine for
> domesticall inconveniences. Desire war rather than quietnesse, and
> therefore fall out at home if forreine foes the wanting.[11]

The imperative form of this kind of early modern English military writing should be seen in the context of the Tudor and early Stuart experiment in absolutist government. The preoccupation that many of the military writers reveal with symbols of an idealized chivalric past (such as 'Martiall Knights' and the longbow), which seemed to express a uniform sense of masculinity and power, can be measured against the contemporary political trend towards a form of centralized administration which distinctly lacked the vital ingredient of a trained and disciplined standing army. Few of the military writers really considered it possible to return to the military prestige associated with the battles of Crécy, Poitier or Agincourt. Nevertheless, they frequently cited these as examples of a lost England that could only be regained by urgent attention to the training, discipline and tactics of modern warfare. Looking abroad at the more sophisticated absolutist states where large armies were constantly on hand to suppress internal dissent or to wage war abroad, fewer still of the writers displayed much faith in a return to England's nobility as a vanguard of the military revival they recommended. In many places in Europe the professional soldier had taken over responsibility for the recruitment and training of armies. The English writers noted with approval a sense of evolution in these countries; the reputation and efficiency of the medieval nobility had inspired the codes of discipline that informed the modernizing armies of the absolutist states. In England, the situation was very different. As Perry Anderson has noted:

> In the isolationist context of the island kingdom there was an exceptionally early demilitarisation of the noble class itself. In 1500 every English peer bore arms; by Elizabeth's time, it has been calculated, only half the aristocracy had any fighting experience. On the eve of the Civil War in the seventeenth century, very few nobles had any military background.[12]

Without the ability to impose its will by force, English quasi-absolutism relied upon an extensive display of power in order to flood any channels through which discontent might flow towards the heart of the state. The limitation placed on the project of absolutism in England by the absence of anything like a modern military apparatus, and still less the medieval ideal espoused by the military writers, had effects well beyond an inability to suppress any acts of unrest. The crucial display of sovereign power was an expensive spectacle that required a concerted and coherent foreign policy (including a commitment to the Reformation) that would have to be seen to be effective. This unfortunately necessitated the raising of a conscripted army. By the early Stuart years a series of parliaments as increasingly unwilling to finance what proved to be a series of mismanaged adventures as they were to fund domestic extravagance contributed to the overthrow of the monarchy by an army which finally put in place the modernizing 'new model' practices which, ironically, the military writers had thought necessary to keep rebellion at bay.

The English attempt to conjure a sense of absolutism let to the contradictory situation in which, lacking a repressive apparatus for internal policing (and thus the enforcing of consent) it nonetheless attempted a foreign policy which required parliamentary approval. This highlighted the importance of the relationship between domestic stability and foreign policy which many of the military writers brought into focus. In *The Politicke and Militarie Discourses*, a text published in London in 1587, François de La Noue sets out a philosophy concerning the relationship between foreign war and domestic stability which was repeated by a good number of the English military writers:

> [A] great estate replenished with warlike people, ought still to have some foreine warre wherewith to keepe it occupied, least being at quiet they convert their weapons against each other.[13]

The absence in England of the kind of military establishment found abroad not only fuelled the polemic of those military writers who perceived the symbolic effect of foreign wars for domestic policy. Many also recognized the strategic importance of militarism for the expanding realm of trade and colonialism. Thus the constitution of the body of the 'soldier-subject' in early modern military writing comes close to Michel Foucault's sense of a body totally imprinted by history and the process of history. This is partly because of the sheer range of metaphorical and institutional inscription the body has to bear but also because of the quite literal implication of the body of the soldier in the obliteration of others. The vitality of the ideal masculine military body speaks only through the mortality of its counter-image. Its subjectivity is focused only through the atomization of its other, and the realm of colonial activity was to provide a perfect scope for a reinforcement of the preferred ideal against the 'feminine' bodies of those who were to be colonized.

Before turning to examples of drama texts which foreground and problematize this inscription on the military body of codes of state and civil power, it is worth considering just how powerful and detailed this inscription appears in the military prose. Foucault wrote of the precision of military discipline as:

> a meticulous observation of detail and a political awareness of these small things for the control and use of men, bearing with them a whole set of techniques, a whole corpus of methods and knowledges, descriptions, plans and data.[14]

In the military texts of the mid-seventeenth century, by which time their authors had moved on from philosophical questions about the nature and justification of war to deal almost exclusively with its practice, a major preoccupation was with the transformation of recruits (or pressed men) into the ideal soldier-subject in the face of a seeming propensity for recruits to 'return' somehow to their origins. In practice, English footsoldiers had for many years been taken from the prisons and the streets. Elizabeth had complained that soldiers were the 'very scomme of the earth', a point also made, in rather more detail, by Barnabe Rich in *Allarme to England* where he noted that:

> When they set forth soldiers, either they scoure their prisons of thives, or their streets of rogues and vagabonds . . . the name of soldier is become so odious to the common people . . . God grant us that we never be given to trie the service of such people.[15]

Given the nature of the raw recruit, the prescription for the ideal soldier in seventeenth-century military writing is tellingly overdetermined; it is a response to the idea that any recruit is likely to lapse back into the condition from which he has been drawn. Thomas Smith's *The Art of Gunnerie* is a good example of this genre. In a summary of the qualities of a soldier which seems very close to Foucault's point about expertise, Smith remarked that;

> He may well be called a soldier . . . that knows by the sound of drum
> and trumpet, without any voice, when to march, fight, retire, etc.; that
> has some some in the mathematicals and in geometrical instruments,
> for the conveying of mines under the ground, to plant and manage great
> ordnance, to batter or beat down the walles of any town or castle; that can
> measure altitude, latitudes and longitudes, etc. Such a one may well be
> termed an expert soldier.[16]

By anyone's standards this is a demanding profile but, without such con-straints, it was thought, the soldier would surely slide back into ill discipline. What is implied here is not simply the ideal of latter-day militarist historio-graphy, that the soldier fights better if he has a cause (a knowledge of arms but also a knowledge of why he must use them), but a scourging of the recruit's clear inclination to resist the transforming power of discipline in favour of some natural state which must necessarily be occluded.

The sense of overdetermination in the presentation of the ideal soldier, totally removed from the conditions from which he has been recruited, can be found in William Neade's extraordinary book, *The Double-armed Man* of 1625. A frontispiece illustrates a pikeman who stands 'croucht and charged for the horse with his sword drawne'. This is the experienced, valued, expert soldier, and in many ways the figure represents everything that could be desired in the contemporary ideal. The figure is strong in body, for how else could he maintain the unnatural crouch with one knee bent toward the enemy, his other leg stretched out behind him, and his sword raised above his head? He is alert and ready for an oncoming cavalry charge, with his long pike set against his rear foot and extending through his left hand. In this sense he is the ideal masculine figure, embodying a sense of strength and diligence that proves that training has distanced him from some more primitive state. The figure also contains an imprint of the ideal of earlier times since he is also the medieval knight. His helmet is plumed, his armour is heavy and protects his thigh, and he is wearing spurs. The figure is anachronistic and impractical since it seems that his pike is somehow also a longbow (that other potent symbol of a lost ideal of masculinity). Neverthe-less, this fantastic soldier is symbolically resonant with the values of both the old and the new: a restored masculinity, a modernized chivalry and the beard and ruff of the contemporary gentleman.

A second example shows that the masculinity espoused by this ideal was balanced by the feminine nature of the lands and peoples that were to be subdued. The gendering of military and geopolitical concerns in this writing is nowhere more shockingly supplied than in an account of Ireland produced in the 1620s by the retired solider Luke Gernon:

> This Nymph of Ireland is at all points like a young wench that hath the green sickness for want of occupying. She is very fair of visage and hath a smooth skin of tender grass. Indeed, she is somewhat freckled (as the Irish are) – some parts darker than others. Her flesh is of a soft and delicate mold of earth, and her blue veins trailing through every part of her like rivulets. She hath one master vein called the Shannon, which passeth quite through her, and if it were not for one knot (one main rock), it were navigable from head to foot. She hath three other veins called the sisters – the Suir, the Nore, and the Barrow, which, rising at one spring, trail through her middle parts and join together in their going out. Her bones are of polished marble, the grey houses show like colleges, and being polished is most embellished. Her breasts are round hillocks of milk-yielding grass and that so fertile that they contend with the valleys. And betwixt her legs (for Ireland is full of havens) she hath an open harbor, but not much frequented. It is now since she was drawn out of rebellion some sixteen years and yet she wants a husband: she is not embraced; she is not hedged and ditched; there is no quickset put into her.[17]

Such erotic descriptions were calculated to reinforce the masculinity of the colonial project and to seduce the post-rebellion colonizers who were to be 'planted' in Ireland. Yet they also guaranteed the masculinity of the military enterprise that was to secure that project. Yet in texts like this it is also possible to read that the soldier-subject was to be drawn away from any tendency toward domestic rebellion at home as well as to the business of maintaining and planting post-rebellion Ireland. The threat of unrest at home was altogether associated with the process of raising troops for the quasi-absolutist regimes of the late Tudors and early Stuarts. Yet state documents from the period are also full of embarrassed accounts of colonizers adopting the supposedly feminine trappings and language of the colonized. Edmund Spenser's *A View of the Present State of Ireland*, written in the last decade of the sixteenth century, reported on this phenomenon among those populations planted in Ireland in order to introduce Protestant politics and values, but who succumbed to the 'feminine' Irish language and the social mores of the culture they were supposed to eradicate.[18]

In England, the business of raising troops brought riot and mutiny, an active and popular resistance to the emerging ideal of the military subject. Evidence of popular disturbances associated with raising armies in the late sixteenth and seventeenth centuries has proved a contentious area of investigation for scholars. For some these events seem to determine a class-consciousness, which might be said to prefigure later combinations and popular politic movements. In the work of the historian Keith Wrightson, it is clear that in whatever fashion history interprets these events it was also the case that the system of raising men for domestic and foreign military duty was not only one of the causes of the widespread rioting which worried the Elizabethan and early Stuart administrations, but actually offered a pattern and model for what Wrightson has called 'a series of controlled and remarkably disciplined demonstrations rather than an abandonment of restraint on the part of the people'.[19]

This collective resistance was matched by a more individual undermining of the military ideal found in non-military prose works. Contemporary descriptions of the many phoney soldiers to be observed in the streets of London record general alarm (and sometimes amusement), not only because of their threat to the civilian population but because of their corrupting duplicity. Thomas Dekker and Robert Greene in *The High Way to the Spittal House* describe in detail the science of self-mutilation that involved plates of copper, bandages and arrested gangrene, which wrote onto the bodies of pretend soldiers a seemingly authentic message of self-sacrifice in the name of national identity.[20] Thus the streets of London were full of individuals who could claim to have fought on behalf of the military idealism of the soldier-subject, but whose integrity could not be proved.

The drama of the period provided a carnivalesque inversion of the codes of propriety which were written for both the body of the soldier-subject and for the larger body of the military institution. There had been a long medieval tradition of literary resistance to the institutionalization of warfare. For example, general scepticism abounded in the reign of Edward III, which saw the production of such cryptic and playful texts as *The Alliterative Morte Arthure* and the parodic *Wynnere and Wastoure*. Some late twentieth-century criticism has controversially questioned Chaucer's presentation of the medieval knight as anything but heroic.[21]

Early modern drama could be said to have inherited this tradition of mocking a heroic interpretation of warfare by inviting its audiences to consider an inversion of an ideological hierarchy which disguised the realities of war by elevating a discourse of masculine rhetoric. For example, the phenomenon of self-mutilation on which Dekker and Greene reported from the streets of London invites a reading of Shakespeare's *Coriolanus* that is quite at odds with orthodox understandings of a heroic corporeal paradigm.

Coriolanus's 'speaking wounds' speech contests a Plebeian desire for the body to utter its own meaning in terms of civic duty. In Shakespeare's play, Caius Martius Coriolanus is persuaded that in order to be an acceptable leader of Rome he has to display his wounds to the citizens:

CORIOLANUS:
Most sweet voices!
Better it is to die, better to starve,
Than crave the hire which first we do deserve.
Why in this womanish toge should I stand here
To beg of Hob and Dick that does appear
Their needless vouches? Custom calls me to't.
What custom wills, in all things should we do't,
The dust on antique time would lie unswept,
And mountainous error be too highly heaped
For truth to o'erpeer. Rather than fool it so,
Let the high office and the honour go
To one that would do thus. I am half through.
The one part suffered, the other will I do.
                    Enter three Citizens more
Here come more voices.
Your voices! For your voices I have fought,
Watched for your voices, for your voices bear
Of wounds two dozen odd; battles thrice six
I have seen and heard of for your voices, have
Done many things, some less, some more. Your voices![22]

In the streets of London it was being daily proved that a wounded body could only speak of its own artificiality, or, at best, its ambiguity. The inscription on the body of 'service' demanded a civic response (in the form of alms), but the problematizing of its authenticity demanded, in fact, a more clearly determined provenance. It may even be that this widespread and spectacular disruption of the chain of meaning from battlefield to charity registered an instability that led to a more humane treatment of returned soldiers in the later decades of the seventeenth century. Shakespeare seems to invite scepticism of the heroic values invested in the discourse of the individual classical warrior so widely rehearsed in the military writing, which he may have had on his bookshelf. The relationship between Coriolanus's masculine (anti-womanish) appeal and the Roman state is shown to depend upon a militarism which is self-fulfilling and bound by its own ideological limits: it is finally transferable (to the enemy Volsces to whom Coriolanus defects) rather than grounded in the particularities of the Roman state.

This sense of a defined discourse of masculine militarism had earlier been undermined in Shakespeare's presentation of Richard of Gloucester.

No figure on the English stage speaks more contemptuously of the decadence of peace:

RICHARD GLOUCESTER:
Now is the winter of our discontent
Made glorious summer by this son of York:
And all the clouds that loured upon our house
In the deep bosom of the ocean buried.
Now are our brows bound with victorious wreaths,
Our bruisèd arms hung up for monuments,
Our stern alarums changed to merry meetings,
Our dreadful marches to delightful measures.
Grim-visaged war hath smoothed his wrinkled front,
And now – instead of mounting barbèd steeds
To fright the souls of fearful adversaries –
He capers nimbly in a lady's chamber
To the lascivious pleasing of a lute.[23]

Richard's 'glorious summer' could have come straight from one of the contemporary military theorists. In one of the most fulsome sneers in the whole of English drama, 'Piping peace' has given way to 'merry meetings' and 'delightful measures' that clearly threaten the fabric of the state's ascendancy. Richard denounces the feminizing of the state in much the same way as the contemporary writers of military theory were to do. The play invites its audience to regard Richard's ambition (recorded as simultaneously military and misogynist) as the very essence of the world which the Tudors had swept aside, an unsettling ideological stance for contemporary advocates of English remilitarization.

Shakespeare invites a similar scepticism about heroic militarism in *The Life of Henry the Fifth*. The figure of Henry has traditionally been regarded as an embodiment of heroic militarism or, at worst, a pragmatic leader, yet it has taken several plays to get him to this position. Earlier in the cycle Prince Hal was more bound to codes of drinking and civilian licence than warlike pursuits. When, as king, he comes to the battlefield, Shakespeare questions the righteousness of warlike pursuits through their juxtaposition with the world the prince has left behind, represented by the 'absent-presence' of Falstaff. The war in France is won through divine support and the power of rhetoric rather than the positive codes of masculinity recommended by the contemporary military theorists.

A central scene in the play resists the heroic masculinity that has removed him from the condition of the inn. 'May I with right and conscience make this claim?' he had asked the Archbishop of Canterbury in the debate about

Salic Law at the beginning of the play. Yet it is with 'conscience wide as hell' that he signals the consequences for the citizens of Harfleur if they refuse to give in to his siege.

KING HARRY:
How yet resolves the Governor of the town?
This is the latest parle we will admit.
Therefore to our best mercy give yourselves,
Or like to men proud of destruction
Defy us to our worst. For as I am a soldier,
A name that in my thoughts becomes me best,
If I begin the batt'ry once again
I will not leave the half-achievèd Harfleur
Till in her ashes she lie burièd.
The gates of mercy shall be all shut up,
And the fleshed soldier, rough and hard of heart,
In liberty of bloody hand shall range
With conscience wide as hell, mowing like grass
Your fresh fair virgins and your flow'ring infants.
What is it then to me if impious war
Arrayed in flames like to the prince of fiends
Do with his smirched complexion all fell feats
Enlinked to waste and desolation?
What is't to me, when you yourselves are cause,
If your pure maidens fall into the hand
Of hot and forcing violation?
What rein can hold licentious wickedness
When down the hill he holds his fierce career?
We may as bootless spend our vain command
Upon th'enragèd soldiers in their spoil
As send precepts to the leviathan
To come ashore. Therefore, you men of Harfleur,
Take pity of your town and of your people
Whiles yet my soldiers are in my command,
Whiles yet the cool and temperate wind of grace
O'erblows the filthy and contagious clouds
Of heady murder, spoil, and villainy.
If not – why, in a moment look to see
The blind and bloody soldier with foul hand
Defile the locks of your shrill-shrieking beards,
And their most reverend heads dashed to the walls;
Your naked infants spitted upon pikes,
Whiles the mad mothers with their howls confused
Do break the clouds, as did the wives of Jewry
At Herod's bloody-hunting slaughtermen.[24]

155

Shakespeare invites us to consider the distance between war and civilian ethics. The idea that in his thoughts he is a soldier, mirrors the recommendations of the military writers (that a soldier should have a knowledge of his status and purpose), but the outcome is an anti-civic mayhem in which the unrestrained behaviour of his soldiers will show the contradiction between their cause and their nature as soldiers. Henry's thoughts extend to self-identification as Herod, a figure with significant resonance as the pursuer of the infant Christ. It is a scene that sits uncomfortably with a rationale that contrasts the figure of 'Hal' with 'Henry' (and the carnivalesque and feminine realm of the Boar's Head against the battlefields of France) and unquestioningly sees the former as the epitome of militarized kingship.

Shakespeare is the most accommodating of writers. Critics as historically distant from each other as Samuel Johnson and E.M.W. Tillyard have assessed those plays that foreground issues of war as showing the inevitability of military solutions to ethical dilemmas. This humanist approach, while it shows disquiet in the critical response over the brutality of the solutions on offer, has nonetheless privileged a distinct relationship between militarism and masculinity. Henry rides to war with a maturity based on his denial of the lure of the Boar's Head. Coriolanus is torn between private and public duty because he is driven by a discourse of masculinity that has shaped him from birth, his mother having declared:

> To a cruel war I sent him, from whence he returned his brows bound with oak. I tell thee, daughter, I sprang not more in joy at first hearing he was a man-child than now in first seeing he had proved himself a man.[25]

Less accommodating is the complex of lesser-known plays from the period that invites a sharper critique of the connections between military codes (as masculine) and a discourse of peace, often associated with femininity. What can be traced in these is a counter-blast to the military idealists, either in terms of a rescuing of a late-medieval quasi-pacifism, or an outright celebration of the vitality of civil life in response to the inevitability of death as a consequence of military duty. Thomas Preston's *Cambises* (1569) and Thomas Lodge's *The Wounds of Civil War* (1588) presented a severe critique of the long-term consequences of supporting a male ruler who seeks foreign engagements to support unity at home. Such plays privilege domestic harmony, which is to be achieved by responding to the lessons drawn from the irrationality of a pursuit of military aims. Robert Wilson's *The Three Lords and the three Ladies of London*, staged first in 1588, called simply for complete trust in divine protection above military preparation. London is seen as a feminine entity, protected by the hand of God and, if this seems absurd in the year of the Spanish Armada, it neatly coincided with the official Tudor propaganda of the time that saw that same God's hand at

156

work in the meteorological phenomena which helped repulse the Spanish threat. George Peele's *The Battle of Alcazar* (1589) similarly celebrated Britain's natural defences and the intellectual superiority of Venus over Mars.

At the end of the sixteenth century, *The Life and Death of Jack Straw* (*c.* 1590) openly challenged the audience to debate the relationship between the absolutist codes of the military leadership of the past and modern civil codes of responsibility. This play foregrounded the idea of knowing citizens, of both sexes, as a repository of ideas of rebellion and a site for democratic debate.

Examples of plays which celebrate 'feminized' civil life above military duty are fairly common, including some from the early part of the seventeenth century which make conscious reference to Shakespeare's occasionally heroic interpretation of the militarized state. Examples would include Thomas Dekker's celebration of civil life in *The Shoemaker's Holiday*.[26] Francis Beaumont's *The Knight of the Burning Pestle* (*c.* 1607) is particularly mischievous in its mockery both of Shakespeare's militarized protagonists and of the contemporary exercises of the militia in the Mile End Road.

RAFE: 'Tis a fault, my friend: put it in again. You want a nose, and you a stone. Sergeant, take a note on't, for I mean to stop it in the pay. Remove, and march! Soft and fair, gentlemen, soft and fair! Double your files! As you were! Faces about! Now, you with the sodden face, keep it there! Look to your match, sirrah; it will be in your fellow's flask anon! So, make a crescent now! Advance your pikes! Stand and give ear! Gentlemen, countrymen, friends, and my fellow soldiers, I have brought you this day from the shops of security and the counters of content to measure out in these furious fields honour by the ell and prowess by the pound. Let it not, O, let it not, I say, be told hereafter the noble issue of this city fainted; but bear yourselves in this fair action like men, valiant men and free men! Fear not the face of the enemy nor the noise of the guns; for believe me, brethren, the rude rumbling of a brewer's car is far more terrible, of which you have daily experience; neither let the stink of powder offend you since a more valiant stink is nightly with you. To a resolved mind, his home is everywhere: I speak not this to take away the hope of your return, for you shall see (I do not doubt it), and that very shortly, your loving wives again and your sweet children, whose care doth bear you company in baskets. Remember then, whose cause you have in hand and, like a sort of true-born scavengers, scour me this famous realm of enemies. I have no more to say but this: stand to your tacklings, lads, and show to the world you can as well brandish a sword as shake an apron. Saint George, and on, my hearts.[27]

This play parodies the rhetoric of Shakespeare's military heroes and privileges home and hearth, sex and society, above the call to arms.

This celebration of civilian life was, perhaps, the clearest endorsement in the popular theatre of a resistance to the developing sense of the modern military state and the codes of masculinity that became a 'naturalized' component of its regimes. Early modern English culture shows that this component had to be carefully constructed, in the face of parody and opposition, and that it is not natural at all. Modern political regimes that inherit this ideal of military subjectivity have carefully to occlude these historical discontinuities and hesitations. They are, however, at risk of resurfacing as an alternative history that liberates both men and woman from the 'natural' discipline of war.

CHAPTER TEN

The Guise women:
Politics, war and peace

PENNY RICHARDS

'Tis no less unbecoming [in] a Woman to levy Forces, to conduct an
Army, to give a Signal to the Battle, than it is for a Man to tease Wool,
to handle the Distaff, to Spin or Card, and to perform the other
Services of the weaker Sex.

George Buchanan[1]

Making war and playing
politics – women's work?

George Buchanan's sentiments are typical of the patriarchal ruling ideology
of the sixteenth and seventeenth centuries and we are familiar with them
from many contemporary sources. In Shakespeare's *Henry V*, for instance,
the French princess Katherine asks her lady in waiting to teach her English
as she knows that marriage to the invading English king, Henry V, will be
part of any peace treaty with England. Katherine's role seems quite clear,
she is (along with land) a negotiable entity: the actual fighting is for men.
In the *Henry VI* plays, on the other hand, Shakespeare presents a militant,
fighting queen, Margaret of Anjou, who fights on while her timid husband
prays. Such representations of women's involvement in war, as passive or
active, shrinking virgin or fierce virago, have long historical antecedents and
descendants.

I should like to take this opportunity to thank Jessica Munns, the members of Women's Study
Group, 1600–1830 and my students at the University of Gloucestershire for helpful discussions.

159

In actuality, however, this was a period that saw a large number of elite women wielding and aspiring to political and military power. As Lisa Hopkins has pointed out, 'the chances of birth, marriage, and death amongst its royal families brought to sixteenth-century Europe a rash of countries ruled not by Kings but by Queens'.[2] In England for instance, Mary Tudor's brief reign (1553–58) was followed by the far longer reign of her sister, Elizabeth I (1558–1603) – eulogized after her death as 'a Deborah, a Judith, a Susanna, a Virgin, a Virago, a Diana'.[3] In Scotland, Mary of Guise was active as Queen dowager following the death of her husband James V in 1542, assuming the regency of Scotland in 1554. Her daughter's troubled reign lasted from 1561 to 1568. In France two mothers acted as regents for their sons at appropriate moments, Louise of Savoy for Francis 1,[4] and Catherine de' Medici for her son Charles IX, and at either end of the sixteenth century Anne of Brittany and Jeanne d'Albret, Dowager Queen of Navarre, exercised the power and prerogatives of rulers. Moreover, to characterize these female rulers as 'passing' as or standing in for men would be inaccurate. Many of them not only governed but also fulfilled traditional female roles as wives and mothers – indeed governing as a consequence of their sons' minorities. Elizabeth I, who lived a non-traditional 'female' life as a 'virgin' queen, was also surrounded by courtiers who participated in the renowned cult of 'Gloriana' emphasizing her femininity and beauty. In fact, women who ruled negotiated a range of positions across the gender spectrum. In other words, the notion that women either fulfil traditional female roles or are monstrous, does not accord with contemporary actuality at either the highest levels, where women had to function in the public and political realms, or at lower levels where women toiled alongside men. As is often the case, ideology presents us with an outline of the way people thought about the world they lived in, but not necessarily the way that world functioned.

It was not only women within the royal circles who sought or exercised political power in the public realm. Elite women in particular had a direct investment in supporting action, including wars, which affected property and status. The mothers, wives and daughters of great magnates could, in fact, rarely enjoy a quiet life during turbulent times, or perhaps wish to enjoy one. The early modern magnate family was a powerful and ruthless unit. Women as well as men were deployed to serve family interests – through marriage, warfare and public protest, as well as through the skills of the courtier – tact, charm, the giving of tasteful gifts and dispensation of favours – to secure patronage and extend the family's power.

Times of extended violence and unrest, such as the civil wars in France over the period 1560–98, certainly called on 'male' skills in direct fighting, but also involved women who participated in war efforts in a variety of ways. It has long been recognized that the management of very considerable estates was often undertaken by noblewomen; indeed, how to run a house-hold was a major part of their training before marriage and subsequently a life-long activity.[5] Such an activity was not simply 'domestic', as Kristen B. Neuschel points out, 'managing military resources was a dimension of property management'. Indeed, Neuschel remarks that 'the content of the culture of violence, as well as material support for violence, involved the work of women as well as men'.[6]

This chapter will first briefly describe the French civil wars, and will then look at the roles played during this turbulent period by a number of women related by blood and marriage within the powerful Guise family and their affinity.[7] Two generations of the Guise family were deeply involved in these wars: they were aggressors, and also victims of assassinations. They offered a continual threat to the authority of the Valois rulers of France, and from the 1580s waged war against Henry of Navarre, the Protestant heir to the French throne. Behind, beside and in front of the generations of warlike and ambitious Guise men, were their mothers, sisters, and wives – every bit as dedicated to the Guise war machine as the men in the clan.

1562–98: Civil war, religion and magnate power

In the second half of the sixteenth century France experienced a protracted period of civil conflict, often known as the Wars of Religion since the major contestants divided up along the lines of Catholics and Huguenots (Protest-ants). However, as R.J. Knecht has pointed out, 'the wars may also be seen as struggles for power between rival families of noblemen'.[8] Although the different religious adherences were doubtless sincerely followed, they also provided rallying points, established group allegiances and represented family traditions and character. The event usually credited with provoking this period of turmoil and civil conflict is the massacre at Vassy in March 1562 when François, second duc de Guise and his retainers and servants attacked a congregation of Huguenots worshipping in a barn in the town of Vassy inside Guise territory. With 30 worshippers left dead and over 100 wounded, the massacre provoked strong reactions; while Guise and his Catholic allies took control of Paris, the Protestant Prince de Condé successfully marched on and captured the city of Orléans. Clearly however, this advanced and rapidly armed state of conflict had its roots further back in the past. The rise and spread of Huguenot belief, and the growing rivalry of the great families of Guise and Navarre/Bourbon coincided with and were enabled by the weakness of the French monarchy following the death of Henry II in 1559. The death of his sickly eldest son Francis II in late 1560, was followed by the minority of Charles IX (1561–63), who was, however, only thirteen when declared of age to rule. Charles IX died without heirs in 1574, and the throne passed to Henry III, who was rapidly recalled from his recently acquired throne in Poland. Henry III's political judgement was certainly insufficient to control the tempestuous mixture of religion and ambition that destabilized France at this time.

Catherine de' Medici can be seen constantly working both to stem the rise of Huguenot power, curb the power of her Catholic 'supporters' and retain the French throne for her Valois sons. As she wrote to her daughter, 'my principle aim is to have the honour of God before my eyes in all things, and to preserve my authority, not for myself, but for the conservation of this kingdom and for the good of all your brothers'.[9] Nevertheless, the weakness at the power centre provided opportunities for violent magnate rivalries, and political assassinations, such as that of François, duc de Guise in 1563. Civil dissension and violence spread over urban and rural areas and, perhaps, most famously led to the St Bartholomew Night massacres of 1572.

On that occasion – the marriage of the Valois princess, Marguerite to the Huguenot and Bourbon Prince, Henry of Navarre – the attempt, probably stemming from Catherine de' Medici, to unite the warring factions was violently terminated.[10] There is a large literature on the reasons and responsibility for these horrific massacres.[11] There is, however, little doubt but that the Guise were heavily involved, and quite possibly provoked its inception by inciting the murder of the Huguenot war leader, Admiral Coligny, thereafter moving into the offensive against the angry and alarmed Huguenots gathered in Paris for the wedding. The massacres were the prelude to a period of even greater dissension and violence than before. Nicola M. Sutherland writes of this event that 'the extensive consequences of the massacres of 1572 . . . disposed of no problems but created a leadership vacuum. The result was a degree of disintegration, the unleashing of a revolutionary element and the emergence of ephemeral political liaisons.'[12]

During the 1560s and 1570s Catholics formed themselves into a variety of organizations, usually called leagues, to defend their notion of Christianity and nation against that of Protestants. By 1584 the death of the heir apparent to the throne, François, duc d'Anjou, led to increased Catholic fears. Henry III and his wife, Louise of Lorraine, seemed unlikely to produce any children and (by Salic Law) that left the Huguenot Henry of Navarre (the future Henry IV) as the direct heir to the throne. In the face of this threat, the Guise reanimated Catholic league politics forming the second League in 1584, dedicated to excluding Henry of Navarre from the throne, if necessary by war, an initiative that was subsidized by Philip II of Spain.[13] Henri, duc de

Guise and his brother, Louis, Cardinal de Guise were assassinated at the Château de Blois on the night of 23/24 December 1588 on the orders of Henry III. The king clearly hoped that by removing two of the leading figures in the Guise family and in League politics he would regain control of his throne.[14] However, the results of this action – which included the imprisonment of other members of the Guise family – were merely to harden the lines of conflict, enrage the survivors, and, as we shall see, provide the League with powerful anti-Valois propaganda.

Paris became a Guise and League stronghold, enduring the terrible siege of 1590, culminating eventually in a truce and the triumphal entry of Henry of Navarre, now Henry IV in 1594. Retrospectively, the late 1580s and the early 1590s can be seen as the Guise 'endgame' as they struggled to hold on to Paris and other centres of power in the face of the warlike Henry of Navarre's increasingly successful conquests.[15]

The Guise women and the family network of power

As this brief outline indicates, although the civil wars spread out over French territories and involved and depended on the widespread participation (willing and forced) of thousands of urban and country dwellers, the ambition, religious affiliation and power of great magnates turned religious division into organized and violent warfare. Throughout the long years of civil war, few families were as directly involved and significant to the events and outcomes as the Guise. During the sixteenth century, the Guise family, who held lands largely in the north and centre of France (and originated as a cadet line of the house of Lorraine), rose to extreme power. The sixteenth century in France was very much the Guise century – a time when they sought to control at various times, through warfare and networks of alliances, the thrones of Scotland and France.[16]

Notably, the Guise were both blessed and cursed by producing or allying themselves with very remarkable women who undoubtedly helped to shape the family's fortunes. The family's meteoric rise to power was accelerated by Claude de Guise's friendship with Francis I. He made an excellent marriage to Antoinette de Bourbon, who was an extremely able woman, estate manager and became a powerful matriarch.[17] At the main family seat at Joinville, Antoinette brought up and educated several generations of Guise children, together with children from the Guise affinity within her well-regulated catholic household.[18] As Stuart Carroll has noted, Joinville was the location for the largest and most important family conferences until Antoinette's death in 1583.[19] Antoinette kept up a regular correspondence with family, friends and clients, her concerns ranging from issues of family aggrandizement, religion, estate management and health.

Undoubtedly Claude and Antoinette laid the foundations for the family's fortunes, both in material and visionary terms. Not least, they produced a large and able family of sons and daughters, who provided ecclesiastical and military leaders and, with their eldest daughter Mary (1515–60), as we have seen, the coup of marriage to King James V of Scotland in 1538.[20] Mary Stuart was brought up in France, and in 1558 married the dauphin of France, Francis. Briefly, from 1559 to1560, Francis and Mary were king and queen of France: this period represents the high point of Guise successful ambition – achieved directly through the deployment and participation of Guise women. Indeed, a flow of letters between Scotland and France shows Guise concern with the reception and deportment of the little queen of Scotland in France. Mary of Guise wrote regularly to her Guise family, especially her mother, Antoinette de Bourbon, as she kept up to date with family activities, marriages and births. When Mary of Guise initially sent her daughter to France in 1548, Antoinette de Bourbon wrote to her confirming the child's safe arrival. She assured her that she would stay with the child at the royal palace of Saint-Germain 'until she has settled down with the Dauphin and the princesses'.[21] The future of this very important royal and half Guise child, and the development of her court skills were of prime significance not only on the familial but also on the political level. Mary of Guise also received letters from her son (by her first marriage), and her brother François, duc d'Aumale (the future duke of Guise), as well as his wife, Anne d'Este. These letters assured her that the little Queen of Scotland was thought to be very pretty and of their loyalty to her daughter's interests.[22] These assurances were sincerely made: Mary Stuart was potentially the most successful and fully royal member of the Guise. Indeed, during her years in Scotland and then her subsequent years of imprisonment in England, her Guise relatives looked after her French lands and revenues.[23] Mary Stuart continued to look to her Guise relatives for help, and in 1581 commissioned the duc de Guise to form an association in her name hoping this would lead to her freedom.[24] Indeed, between 1581 and 1583 there were real attempts made by Henri de Guise to come to his cousin's assistance[25]. As John Bossy notes 'the forces of political Catholicism in Western Europe were extremely strong in 1583 and 1584'.[26] A rescue, on the one hand, and/or gaining control for Catholics of the boy king James VI on the other, must have seemed both plausible and imperative.[27]

Mary Stuart was not, however, the only Guise with royal connections. The marriage arranged between François d'Aumale (soon to be second duc de Guise) and Anne d'Este was described in glowing terms to Mary of Guise by her son. He waxed lyrical about Anne d'Este's beauty and demeanour – 'one of the most beautiful and proper princesses one could hope to see'.[28] This match was also another major Guise coup since Anne d'Este, the daughter of the duke and duchess of Ferrara, was through her mother the granddaughter of Louis XII, King of France. The Este marriage was immensely prestigious for the Guise and provided them with *another* direct connection to Valois rulers of France. This match also provided them with a highly educated Renaissance princess, a renowned beauty who became a great courtier, a fertile and devoted mother, and a very loyal member of the Guise family who, in time, succeeded and surpassed her mother-in-law, Antoinette de Bourbon, as matriarch of the clan.

The Guise women and war

How did these Guise women engage in war? Not as directly as did their fathers, brothers and husbands by riding into battles, but without any doubt they actively enabled and supported their family's political role as initiators and participants in Catholic and League politics and war. One can see that on the material level Guise women made considerable contributions: they all looked after their family estates competently, and they vigilantly guarded the patrimony. There is ample evidence that both Anne d'Este and her daughter-in-law, Catherine de Clèves, wife of Anne's eldest son Henry of Guise, dealt with estate management and financial business throughout their lives.[29] Other Guise wives were similarly occupied; as Stuart Carroll has pointed out, while Charles of Lorraine, duc d'Aumale, campaigned in the Guise/League wars, his wife took charge of the finances.[30] Guise male confidence in raising troops, forming the League, confronting armed Huguenot resistance and implicitly challenging the crown must in some measure have been based on their assurance that their formidable mothers and wives were in charge on the home front.

The women were also very active on the political front – indeed, as we have seen, domestic and public, familial and political did not represent very different spheres for the male and female members of elite families. The crisis of the assassination of François, duc de Guise in 1563 provoked strong responses in which his widow and his mother figured centrally. Anne d'Este and Anoinette de Bourbon brilliantly *staged themselves*, that is, they used their gender, family and status to construct a political theatre following the assassination. On this occasion the grieving mother and widow, 'formally dressed . . . and rending the air with their groans', led a procession to the church at Meulan where King Charles IX was worshipping to present him with a petition requesting redress.[31] The massive Guise participation the following year in the young Charles IX's famous royal tour of France – his two-year-long progress through his realm – represents less their forgiveness, than the determination of the Guise and their affinity to remain at the centre. Guise men took part in various pageants in roles and robes that flattered and privileged themselves as much as the monarch, and the women took part in the various and many ceremonial processions.[32]

Anne d'Este did not remain a widow for very long and, far from reject-ing the mores of the violent family into which she had married, now married Jacques de Savoie, duc de Nemours in 1566. Nemours was a notable soldier, related to the ruling house of Savoy, who functioned entirely within the Guise affinity as a major Catholic magnate. The marriage is certainly indicative of the ongoing Guise policy of using their women to tie in useful allies (as did all great families) and, if it were to come to fighting, then Nemours was a good choice. Indeed their children were in time to provide support for the Guise half-brothers during the tumult of the 1580s. The family anger at the assassination of François, duc de Guise had remained unassuaged; indeed, they were convinced that the Huguenot Admiral de Coligny, a favourite of Charles IX, was behind the assassination. How directly Anne d'Este was involved in the assassination of Coligny – the event that sparked off the St Bartholomew massacre – is open to speculation.[33] It is, however, known that the assassin, Maurevert, a Guise servant stayed in the lodgings granted to Anne d'Este (now Madame de Nemours) by the court.[34]

If the Guise thought they had been successful overall in 1572, this was not the case by 1588. During the intervening years, their incessant pressure on the crown had certainly placed them at the centre of power, but had deeply alienated them from Henry III whose every move they checked. The second major crisis that faced the Guise clan was that of the assassinations of Madame de Nemours's sons, Henri, duc de Guise and his brother Louis, Cardinal of Guise. This assassination, definitely instigated by Henry III, took place on the night of 23/24 December 1588 during a meeting of the Estates General at the Château of Blois. During this ultimate crisis for the Guise, the female voice was articulated and utilized in the political and military arenas. Madame de Nemours, her daughter and her bereaved daughter-in-law became the rallying points for opposition to the crown.

Madame de Nemours and Catherine de' Medici, the Queen mother, were regular correspondents, perhaps in part as fellow Italians in France, as well as due to the courteous exchanges expected of monarch and magnate wife. Hence it was to Catherine as Queen Mother that Anne wrote following the murder of her sons asking to be given back the duke's body and for protection for her children.[35] Vatican sources describe Catherine de' Medici as responding that she had lost any influence over her son.[36] Not only did Anne not get her son's body back, she was herself briefly arrested and taken from Blois to Amboise. Indeed, Pierre de L' Estoile, the invaluable memorialist of this period, described the extent of the king's attempt to erase the Guise bodies which were burnt, the ashes thrown to the winds, in order, as he notes that they should not remain as 'relics' or 'memorials'.[37] Destroying the bodies, however, failed to destroy the Guise and League faction. On hearing the news, Paris, already in revolt against the king, was further enraged, enabling the surviving Guise to make that city their stronghold.

The arrest of Madame de Nemours, far from neutralizing her, placed her centre stage. The words attributed to her on this occasion indicate her sense of her status – not as a Guise or Nemours, but more grandly as a member of the royal family of France. A Catholic League propaganda pamphlet, *Le martire des deux freres* (The Martyrdom of the two Brothers) (1589), describes her arrest at the Château of Blois. As she left, she gazed at a statue of her grandfather Louis XII and remarked that he would never have allowed her to be treated in this way.[38] Indeed, the bereavement and mistreatment of Madame de Nemours provided excellent copy for numerous Catholic League pamphlets: one of them, the *Remonstrance faicte au Roy par Madame de Nemours*, 1588, may well be based on a letter she wrote to Henry III.[39] Clearly this tragic mother, who had lost first her husband and now her sons by assassination, had every 'right' not merely to grieve but to be angry, and this pamphlet specifically accuses Henry III of tyranny. This was a very strong term and accusation in relation to sixteenth- and seventeenth-century theories of monarchy, government and conditions under which revolt were justified. Madame de Nemours's position as matriarch of the leading oppositional magnate family, and her royal blood, allowed grief and anger to elide the maternal, familial and private with the political and public – without any loss of femininity. Indeed, the gender of the narrating voice gives power and veracity to the complaint.

A similarly strong pamphlet of 1588 is the *Pleurs et soupirs de Madame de Guyse* (Tears and sighs of Madame de Guyse) published and circulated in the name of Catherine de Clèves, the widow of the assassinated duc de Guise. This pamphlet assured the readers that a just God would not allow her to die before she had avenged the sad and cruel death of her husband.[40] Catherine de Clèves was not merely deployed as a pamphlet voice, for as Richard Cooper has noted she organized 'her own campaign of protest'. In early January [1589] she appealed for justice to the *Parlement* of Paris, which appointed a commissioner to investigate' the murders. As he notes, she also enlisted support from her brother-in-law Charles de Mayenne, from the Sorbonne, and from the Paris city fathers in an appeal to Pope Sixtus V – to whom she also sent an ambassador.[41] On her release from her brief imprisonment, Madame de Nemours went to Paris, held by the League, where she and her daughter, Catherine, duchesse de Montpensier, and her daughter-in-law, Catherine de Clèves, were rallying points for those loyal to the League. As such, the women played roles both symbolic and actual in the defence of Paris. As Diefendorf notes, when Catherine de Clèves, who was pregnant at the time of her husband's murder, gave birth to their son in Paris this provided the opportunity for public processions and 'an elaborate reception'.[42] The Guise women's activity in Paris was a public indication that their cause was not defeated, and they were also more than figures of symbolic and political significance.

On 1 August 1589 Henry III was assassinated by a friar, Jacques Clément, very probably at the instigation of the duchesse de Montpensier. Certainly when Madame de Montpensier was told the news she is reputed to have exclaimed: 'God! but you give me pleasure. It is marred by only one thing, that is he did not know before he died that it was I who had it done.'[43] The monarchist and anti-League writer, Etienne Pasquier also regarded the Guise women as instrumental in the assassination. In his pamphlet *Le Anti-Martyr de Jacques Clément* (1590) he claimed that 'everybody knows that the mother, daughter, and daughter-in-law spared neither their means nor their honour to bring about this coup, promising to give the damoiselle de Guise to whoever would do the deed'.[44] In a famous and frequently cited description of this event, the diarist Pierre de L'Estoile recorded that Madame de Nemours and her daughter drove through Paris in their carriages announcing the 'good news' of the 'tyrant's' death.[45] Both L'Estoile and Pasquier were hostile to the Guise and their faction, and clearly they were particularly offended by the activity and leadership displayed by the Guise women. While the language of their remarks may be attributed to the writers' politics and misogyny, there is little reason to doubt but that these three powerful women of the Guise family, Madame de Nemours, her daughter and daughter-in-law, were very active, and very involved, helping to hold Paris for the League during the long and terrible siege the city endured.

The Guise women's involvement was not unique; as recent scholarship has demonstrated, female activity in pro- or anti-League politics was widespread.[46] Chrétienne d'Aguerre, comtesse de Sault, for instance, led an exciting life at the centre of Southern French League politics.[47] The comtesse was brought up within the Lorraine–Guise ambit into which she also married in 1571. With the death of her husband in 1586, her major concern at this time of instability and civil war was to safeguard the considerable patrimony of her three children. From her main chateau and base at Aix-en-Provence, she gathered around her political, legal and military allies, and exercised both civil and military authority. The comtesse was undoubtedly extremely pro-active, welcoming her near and powerful neighbour the duke of Savoy in 1590. However, in the same year she also undertook secret negotiations with Philip II of Spain, a reliable supporter of League nobles, to establish Provence as a free state under the protection of Spain. In return Spain would gain access to a Mediterranean port in Provence. However, by 1592 she accepted the inevitable – the triumph of Henry IV. It is notable that at the same time, in the summer of 1592, the Guise women took a similar route to that of the comtesse de Sault.[48] The female leaders of the League read the situation more accurately than the male leaders and were perhaps more able to move from defiant militarism to tactful and skilful negotiation for peace.

It took time for the League to disintegrate as Henry IV defeated or bribed the leaders and, with the withering away of their power-base within the League, the Guise had to negotiate or, as in the case of the defiant duc d'Aumale, move into exile. The Guise women were prominent throughout this process, Catherine de Clèves, for instance, was asked by the comtesse de Sault in 1592 to intervene with the duc de Mayenne on behalf of some of her Provençal adherents. Catherine de Clèves was also involved in the negotiations for the loyalty of her son, the young duc de Guise, helping to secure for him a large financial settlement and the governorship of Provence in 1595.[49] Madame de Nemours similarly negotiated between her surviving sons and Henry IV, adroitly exchanging gifts. Indeed, the mother of the Guise was able to reassume her role as a prominent courtier and between 1601 and 1608 she was *superintendente* of the household of Marie de Médicis, Henry IV's second wife.[50]

Pierre Brantôme famously remarked that Madame de Nemours was as lovely in her autumn as in her spring – that she had had two good husbands and could have had a third.[51] This is a masculinist perspective on a prominent political figure, though indeed, her fabled beauty was surely never a disadvantage. However, as has been demonstrated, it would be more accurate to say that Madame de Nemours, and the other women within the Guise family and affinity, were never simply lovely and passive spectators of the play of war and peace. Nor, however much they suffered as their male kin died in battle or assassination, were they simply victims. They were active and militant participants in their families' ambitious and violent activities. They were as engaged in defeat as in victory, and as essential to the cohesion of their faction and survival of their family interests in their middle and later years as in their youth. Indeed, it was their positions as mothers, wives and widows, daughters and sisters that gave them motivation and authority. War may not have been women's *business* in the sixteenth century, but it gave them plenty of work to do. More specifically, it was work natural to these women of the nobility, given their status and lines of affiliation. Supporting, and enabling warfare and negotiating for peace, was work for which their upbringing trained them, and which their gender made them supremely well-equipped to carry out. Noblewomen belonging to anti-League families were also engaged in the processes of materially and morally supporting their faction, and there can be little doubt but that lower down the social scale, the religious and political issues involved and invoked affected women – as well as cruelly disrupting their lives.

Women were always involved in warfare in early modern Europe. Sometimes they were direct participants, sometimes they were part of treaty negotiations. They were always part of the baggage train of any army, and were often victims of carnage. They provided material and psychological support for active combatants, and not least, as mothers they produced those combatants. Civil wars are, perhaps, wars that most directly involve women. In an era before aerial bombing, an international conflict might pass most women and indeed, most civilians, by. In civil wars, however, when region and town pit themselves against each other, and when the breakdown of order offers opportunities for ambitious families to rise, or the necessity for others to defend themselves, war takes on a strongly familial aspect and women become directly involved. They defended family domains, made alliances and provisioned forces. The women of the Guise, however, stand out in their active adherence to the ambitions of their widespread, militant and very powerful family. The wars that tore France apart in the latter half of the sixteenth century were wars of religion and magnate ambition and – for better or for worse – these competent and politically motivated women were an integral part of the war machine.

NOTES

Introduction

1. Jacob Burckhardt, *The Age of the Renaissance*.

2. Joan Kelly, 'Did Women have a Renaissance?' first published in Renate Bridenthan and Claudia Koonz (eds), *Becoming Visible: Women in European History* (New York, 1977).

3. Alan Bray, *Homosexuality in Renaissance England* (London, 1982); Michael Rourke, *Forbidden Friendships: Homosexuality and Male Culture in Renaissance Florence* (Oxford, 1996).

4. For a discussion of this term see Lynn Hunt's introduction to Lynn Hunt (ed.), *The New Cultural History* (Berkeley, CA, 1989).

5. See, for instance, Gordon Kipling's *The Triumph of Honour: Burgundian Origins of the Elizabethan Renaissance* (Leyden, 1977); Graeme Small, 'Centre and Periphery in Late Medieval France: Tournai 1384–1477', in Christopher Allmand (ed.), *War, Government, and Power in Late medieval France* (Liverpool, 2000).

Chapter One   Gender and sexuality in early modern England

1. Joan Kelly, 'Did Women Have a Renaissance?', *Women, History, and Theory: The Essays of Joan Kelly* (Chicago, IL, 1984), pp. 19–50. See also Judith M. Bennett, 'Medieval Women, Modern Women: Across the Great Divide', in Ann-Louise Shapiro (ed.), *Feminists Revision History* (New Brunswick, NJ, 1994), pp. 47–72; and Margaret W. Ferguson, Maureen Quilligan and Nancy J. Vickers, 'Introduction', in *Rewriting the Renaissance: The Discourses of Sexual Difference in Early Modern Europe* (Chicago, IL, 1986), pp. xv–xxiii.

2. Merry Weisner's *Women and Gender in Early Modern Europe* (Cambridge, 1993) begins with 'Ideas and Laws'; Sara Mendelson and Patricia Crawford's *Women in Early Modern England* (Oxford, 1998) with 'Contexts'; and Olwen Hufton's

The Prospect Before Her: A History of Women in Western Europe, 1500–1800 (New York, 1995) with 'Constructing Woman'. See also Ian Mclean, *The Renaissance Notion of Woman: A Study in the Fortunes of Scholasticism and Medical Science in European Intellectual Life* (Cambridge, 1980) and Constance Jordan, *Renaissance Feminism: Literary Texts and Political Models* (Ithaca, NY, 1990), especially ch. 3.

3. Judith Butler has been enormously influential on gender studies in the early modern period and on my own arguments here. See her *Gender Trouble: Feminism and the Subversion of Identity* (New York, 1990) and *Bodies That Matter: On the Discursive Limits of Sex* (New York, 1993). See also Gayle Greene and Coppelia Kahn, 'Feminist Scholarship and the Social Construction of Woman', in Greene and Kahn (eds), *Making a Difference: Feminist Literary Criticism* (London, 1985), pp. 1–36; Jean E. Howard, 'Towards a Postmodern, Politically Committed, Historical Practice', in Francis Barker, Peter Hulme and Margaret Iversen (eds), *Uses of History: Marxism, Postmodernism and the Renaissance* (Manchester and New York, 1991), pp. 101–22; Denise Riley, *Am I That Name? Feminism and the Category of 'Women' in History* (Minneapolis, MN, 1988); and Joan W. Scott, 'Gender: A Useful Category of Historical Analysis', in *Gender and the Politics of History* (New York, 1988), pp. 28–50.

4. Frances E. Dolan (ed.), William Shakespeare, *The Taming of the Shrew: Texts and Contexts* (Boston, MA, 1996).

5. Peter Stallybrass, 'Transvestism and the "Body Beneath": Speculating on the Boy Actor', in Susan Zimmerman (ed.), *Erotic Politics: Desire on the Renaissance Stage* (New York, 1992), pp. 64–83, especially pp. 74–5.

6. Dympna C. Callaghan, *Shakespeare without Women: Representing Gender and Race on the Renaissance Stage* (London, 2000); Will Fisher, 'The Renaissance Beard: Masculinity in Early Modern England', *Renaissance Quarterly* 54 (2001), pp. 155–87, especially p. 180; Marjorie Garber, *Vested Interests: Cross-Dressing and Cultural Anxiety* (New York, 1992); Jean E. Howard, *The Stage and Social Struggle in Early Modern England* (London, 1994); Mary Beth Rose, *The Expense of Spirit: Love and Sexuality in English Renaissance Drama* (Ithaca, NY, 1988), ch. 2; and Peter Stallybrass, 'Transvestism and the "Body Beneath"'.

7. Teresa de Lauretis, 'Eccentric Subjects: Feminist Theory and Historical Consciousness', *Signs* 16 (1) (Spring 1990), pp. 115–50; Joan W. Scott, 'The Evidence of Experience', *Critical Inquiry* 17 (Summer 1991), pp. 773–97.

8. Foucault's theories of power have been especially influential. See, for instance, Colin Gordon (ed.), *Power/Knowledge* (New York, 1980). For a critique of the utility of Foucault's theory of power for gender analysis, see Nancy Hartsock, 'Foucault on Power: A Theory for Women?', in Linda J. Nicholson (ed.), *Feminism/Postmodernism* (New York, 1990), pp. 157–75.

9. This was Elizabeth Cary's motto.

10. Paula McDowell, *Women of Grub Street: Press, Politics, and Gender in the London Literary Marketplace, 1678–1730* (Oxford, 1998), pp. 15, 19, 22. See also Phyllis Mack, *Visionary Women: Ecstatic Prophecy in Seventeenth-Century England* (Berkeley and Los Angeles, CA, 1989).

11. For an introduction to early women writers, see: Elaine Beilin, *Redeeming Eve: Women Writers of the English Renaissance* (Princeton, NJ, 1987); Helen Wilcox (ed.), *Women and Literature in Britain, 1500–1700* (Cambridge, 1996); and Susanne Woods and Margaret P. Hannay (eds), *Teaching Tudor and Stuart Women Writers* (New York, 2000).

12. David E. Underdown, *A Freeborn People: Politics and the Nation in Seventeenth-Century England* (Oxford, 1996), p. 62; Kim F. Hall, *Things of Darkness: Economies of Race and Gender in Early Modern England* (Ithaca, NY, 1995), p. 28; Natalie Zemon Davis, 'Women on Top', in *Society and Culture in Early Modern France* (Stanford, CA, 1975), pp. 124–51; Peter Stallybrass, 'The World Turned Upside Down: Inversion, Gender, and the State', in Valerie Wayne (ed.), *The Matter of Difference: Materialist Feminist Criticism of Shakespeare* (Ithaca, NY, 1991), pp. 201–20.

13. Frances E. Dolan, *Whores of Babylon: Catholicism, Gender, and Seventeenth-Century Print Culture* (Ithaca, NY, 1999); Claire McEachern, *The Poetics of English Nationhood, 1590–1612* (Cambridge, 1996); Jodi Mikalachki, *The Legacy of Boadicea: Gender and Nation in Early Modern England* (London, 1998).

14. Susan Amussen, *An Ordered Society: Gender and Class in Early Modern England* (Oxford, 1988); David E. Underdown, 'The Taming of the Scold: The Enforcement of Patriarchal Authority in Early Modern England', in Anthony Fletcher and John Stevenson (eds), *Order and Disorder in Early Modern England* (Cambridge, 1985), pp. 116–36.

15. David Cressy, 'Gender Trouble and Cross-Dressing in Early Modern England', *Journal of British Studies* 35.4 (October 1996), pp. 438–65, especially p. 464; Martin Ingram, ' "Scolding women cucked or washed": A Crisis in Gender Relations in Early Modern England?' in Jenny Kermode and Garthine Walker (eds), *Women, Crime, and the Courts in Early Modern England* (London, 1994), pp. 48–80.

16. Lynda E. Boose, '*The Taming of the Shrew*, Good Husbandry, and Enclosure', in Russ McDonald (ed.), *Shakespeare Reread: The Texts in New Contexts* (Ithaca, NY, 1994), pp. 193–225; Lisa Jardine, 'Companionate Marriage Versus Male Friendship: Anxiety for the Lineal Family in Jacobean Drama', in Susan D. Amussen and Mark A. Kishlansky (eds), *Political Culture and Cultural Politics in Early Modern England: Essays Presented to David Underdown* (Manchester, 1995), pp. 234–54; Linda A. Pollock, 'Rethinking Patriarchy and the Family in Seventeenth-Century England', *Journal of Family History* 23 (1) (1998), pp. 3–27. Eve Sedgwick's formulation of the 'homosocial' has been enormously influential in discussions of early modern English culture. See *Between Men: English Literature and Male Homosocial Desire* (New York, 1985).

17. Fisher, 'The Renaissance Beard'.

18. Gail Kern Paster, *The Body Embarrassed: Drama and the Disciplines of Shame in Early Modern England* (Ithaca, NY, 1993), p. 8 and 'The Unbearable Coldness of Female Being: Women's Imperfection and the Humoral Economy', *English Literary Renaissance* 28 (3) (1998), pp. 416–40, especially p. 430. See also Norbert Elias, *The Civilizing Process*, vol. 1: *The History of Manners*, trans. Edmund Jephcott (New York, 1978); Margaret Pelling, 'Appearance and Reality: Barber-Surgeons, the Body, and Disease', in A.L. Beier and Roger Finlay (eds), *London, 1500–1700: The Making of the Metropolis* (London, 1986), pp. 82–112, and *The Common Lot: Sickness, Medical Occupations, and the Urban Poor in Early Modern England* (London, 1998).

19. Thomas Laqueur, *Making Sex: Body and Gender from the Greeks to Freud* (Cambridge, MA, 1990).

20. Ann Rosalind Jones and Peter Stallybrass, 'Fetishizing Gender: Constructing the Hermaphrodite in Renaissance Europe', in Julia Epstein and Kristina Straub (eds), *Body Guards: The Cultural Politics of Gender Ambiguity* (New York, 1991), pp. 80–111.

21. Laura Levine, *Men in Women's Clothing: Anti-Theatricality and Effeminization, 1579–1642* (Cambridge, 1994), p. 8.

22. Scott C. Shershow, *Puppets and 'Popular' Culture* (Ithaca, NY, 1995), and 'New Life: Cultural Studies and the Problem of the "Popular"', *Textual Practice* 12 (1) (1998), pp. 23–47.

23. Mary Fissell, 'Gender and Generation: Representing Reproduction in Early Modern England', *Gender & History* 7 (3) (1995), pp. 433–56.

24. Garthine Walker, 'Rereading Rape and Sexual Violence in Early Modern England', *Gender & History* 10 (1) (1998), pp. 1–25.

25. Mark Breitenberg, *Anxious Masculinity in Early Modern England* (Cambridge, 1996); Anthony Fletcher, *Gender, Sex, and Subordination in England, 1500–1800* (New Haven, CT, 1995); Stephen Orgel, *Impersonations: The Performance of Gender in Shakespeare's England* (Cambridge, 1996), p. 153. See also Bernard Capp, 'The Double Standard Revisited: Plebeian Women and Male Sexual Reputation in Early Modern England', *Past and Present* 162 (February, 1999), pp. 70–100; and Elizabeth Foyster, *Manhood in Early Modern England* (London, 1999).

26. Martin Ingram, 'Ridings, Rough Music, and the "Reform of Popular Culture" in Early Modern England', *Past and Present* 105 (1984), pp. 79–113.

27. Frances E. Dolan (ed.), William Shakespeare, *As You Like It* (New York, 2000), II, vii, ll. 138–65.

28. Susan D. Amussen, '"The part of a Christian man": the Cultural Politics of Manhood in Early Modern England', in *Political Culture and Cultural Politics,*

pp. 213–33 (223). See also Alexandra Shepard, 'Manhood, Credit, and Patriarchy in Early Modern England, *c.* 1580–1640', *Past and Present* 167 (May
2000), pp. 75–106.

29. Caroline Walker Bynum, *Jesus as Mother: Studies in the Spirituality of the High
Middle Ages* (Berkeley, CA, 1982); Paster, *The Body Embarrassed*; and James
Shapiro, *Shakespeare and the Jews* (New York, 1996); Richard Rambuss,
'Pleasure and Devotion: The Body of Jesus and Seventeenth-Century Religious
Lyric', in Jonathan Goldberg (ed.), *Queering the Renaissance* (Durham, NC, 1994),
pp. 253–79.

30. Michael McKeon, 'Historicizing Patriarchy: The Emergence of Gender
Difference in England, 1660–1760', *Eighteenth-Century Studies* 28 (3) (1995),
pp. 295–322; Gary Spear, 'Shakespeare's "Manly" Parts: Masculinity and
Effeminacy in *Troilus and Cressida*', *Shakespeare Quarterly* 44 (4) (Winter 1993),
pp. 409–22; and Stephen Orgel, *Impersonations*, p. 124.

31. Jonathan Goldberg, *Sodometries: Renaissance Texts, Modern Sexualities* (Stanford,
CA, 1992), p. 8. See also Gregory W. Bredbeck, *Sodomy and Interpretation:
Marlowe to Milton* (Ithaca, NY, 1991).

32. The phrase 'proximate others' is from Jonathan Z. Smith, 'Differential Equa-
tions: On Constructing the "Other"', Thirteenth Annual University Lecture
in Religion, Arizona State University, 5 March 1992. See also Claire
McEachern, '"A whore at the first blush seemeth only a woman": John Bale's
Image of Both Churches and the Terms of Religious Difference in the Early
English Reformation', *Journal of Medieval and Renaissance Studies* 25 (2) (1995),
pp. 245–69; Frances E. Dolan, *Dangerous Familiars: Representations of Domestic
Crime in England, 1550–1700* (Ithaca, NY, 1994), and *Whores of Babylon*; Cynthia
Herrup, 'The Patriarch at Home: The Trial of the 2nd Earl of Castlehaven
for Rape and Sodomy', *History Workshop Journal* 41 (1996), pp. 1–18; and
Valerie Traub, 'The Perversion of "Lesbian" Desire', *History Workshop Journal*
41 (1996), pp. 23–49.

33. David Halperin, *One Hundred Years of Homosexuality and Other Essays on Greek Love*
(New York, 1990); Bruce Smith, *Homosexual Desire in Shakespeare's England: A
Cultural Poetics* (Chicago, IL, 1991), pp. 193–7. See also Alan Bray, *Homosexual-
ity in Renaissance England* (New York, 1982, 1995); and Mario di Gangi, *The
Homoerotics of Early Modern Drama* (Cambridge, 1997).

34. Henry Abelove, 'Some Speculations on the History of Sexual Intercourse
during the Long Eighteenth Century in England', *Genders* 6 (Fall 1989),
pp. 125–30.

35. Alan Stewart, *Close Readers: Humanism and Sodomy in Early Modern England*
(Princeton, NJ, 1997; Jeffrey Masten, *Textual Intercourse: Collaboration, Author-
ship, and Sexualities in Renaissance Drama* (Cambridge, 1997).

36. Katharine Park, 'The Rediscovery of the Clitoris', in David Hillman and Carla Mazzio (eds), *The Body in Parts: Fantasies of Corporeality in Early Modern Europe* (London, 1997), pp. 171–93.

37. 'The scornful damsel's overthrow' (*c.* 1685), in Hyder E. Rollins (ed.), *The Pepys Ballads* (Cambridge, MA, 1930), vol. 3 (1666–88), no. 138.

38. John Lyly, *Gallathea*, in Russell A. Fraser and Norman Rabkin (eds), *Drama of the English Renaissance I: The Tudor Period* (New York, 1976), V, iii, ll. 141–59.

39. Valerie Traub, 'The (In)Significance of "Lesbian" Desire in Early Modern England', in *Queering the Renaissance*, pp. 62–83, especially p. 64. On women's alliances, see Susan Frye and Karen Robertson (eds), *Maids and Mistresses, Cousins and Queens: Women's Alliances in Early Modern England* (New York, 1999; and Bernard Capp, 'Separate Domains? Women and Authority in Early Modern England', in Paul Griffiths, Adam Fox and Steve Hindle (eds), *The Experience of Authority in Early Modern England* (Macmillan, 1996), pp. 117–45.

40. Laura Gowing, *Domestic Dangers: Women, Words, and Sex in Early Modern London* (Oxford, 1996), and 'Secret Births and Infanticide in Seventeenth-Century England', *Past and Present* 156 (August 1997), pp. 87–115; and J.A. Sharpe, 'Women, Witchcraft, and the Legal Process', in *Women, Crime, and the Courts*, pp. 106–24.

41. Judith M. Bennett and Amy M. Froide, *Singlewomen in the European Past, 1250–1800* (Philadelphia, PA, 1999).

Chapter Two Gender and early emancipation in the Low Countries in the late Middle Ages and early modern period

1. Gabriel Le Bras, 'Mariage', *Dictionnaire de Théologie catholique* 9 (1926), col. 2044–2317; Charles Donahue, 'The Canon Law on the Formation of Marriage and Social Practice in the Later Middle Ages', *Journal of Family History* 8 (1983), pp. 144–58; Thérèse de Hemptinne and Walter Prevenier, 'Ehe in der Gesellschaft des Mittelalters', *Lexikon des Mittelalters* III, Lief. 52 (1986), col. 1635–40.

2. Jeremy Boulton, 'Clandestine Marriages in London: Examination of a neglected Urban Variable', *Urban History* 20 (2) (1993), pp. 191–210; Monique Vleeschouwers-Van Melkebeek, 'Bina matrimonia: matrimonium praesumptum versus matrimonium manifestum', in Serge Dauchy *et al.* (eds), *Auctoritates xenia R.C. Van Caenegem oblata, Iuris scripta historica* 13 (1997), pp. 245–55; Monique Vleeschouwers-Van Melkebeek, 'Aspects du lien matrimonial dans le Liber Sentenciarum de Bruxelles (1448–1459)', *Revue de l'histoire du*

Droit 53 (1985), pp. 49–67; Walter Prevenier, 'Les réseaux familiaux', in Walter Prevenier *et al.*, *Le prince et le peuple. Images de la société du temps des ducs de Bourgogne, 1384–1530* (Anvers, 1998), pp. 185–92.

3. Eric Bousmar, 'Des alliances liées à la procréation: les fonctions du mariage dans les Pays-Bas bourguignons', *Mediaevistik* 7 (1994), pp. 11–69.

4. Anne Marie De Vocht, 'Het Gentse antwoord op de armoede: de sociale instellingen van wevers en volders te Gent in de late middeleeuwen', *Annalen van de Belgische Vereniging voor Hospitaalgeschiedenis* 19 (1981), pp. 3–32.

5. Henri Pirenne, 'Les dénombrements de la population d'Ypres au XVe siècle', *Vierteljahrschrift für Social und Wirtschaftsgeschichte* 1 (1903), pp. 1–32; on Florence: David Herlihy and Christiane Klapisch-Zuber, *Tuscans and their Families* (New Haven, CT and London, 1985), pp. 215–18.

6. P.J.E. de Smyttere, *Essai historique sur Yolande de Flandre, comtesse de Bar* (Lille, 1877), p. 245.

7. Martha Howell, 'Citizenship and Gender: Women's Political Status in Northern Medieval Cities', in M. Erler and M. Kowaleski (eds), *Women and Power in the Middle Ages* (London, 1988), pp. 37–60; Martha Howell, *Women, Production, and Patriarchy in Late Medieval Cities* (Chicago, IL, 1986), pp. 9–26, 70–94.

8. David Nicholas, 'Child and Adolescent Labour in the Late Medieval City: A Flemish Model in Regional Perspective', *English Historical Review* 110 (1995), pp. 1105–31; David Herlihy, *Medieval Households* (Cambridge, MA, 1985), pp. 153–5.

9. Alain Derville, 'L'alphabétisation du peuple à la fin du moyen âge', *Revue du Nord* 66 (1984), pp. 761–76.

10. Herlihy and Klapisch-Zuber, *Tuscans*, p. 301.

11. Peter Stabel, 'Women at the Market. Gender and Retail in the Towns of Late Medieval Flanders', in Willem P. Blockmans, Marc Boone and Thérèse de Hemptinne (eds), *Secretum scriptorum. Liber alumnorum Walter Prevenier* (Leuven–Apeldoorn, 1999), pp. 259–76.

12. M.W. Labarge, 'Three Medieval Widows and a Second Career', in Michael M. Sheehan (ed.), *Aging and the Aged in Medieval Europe* (Toronto, Pontifical Institute of Medieval Studies, 1990), pp. 159–72; Prevenier, 'Les réseaux familiaux', pp. 194–6.

13. Martha Howell, *The Marriage Exchange. Property, Social Place, and Gender in Cities of the Low Countries, 1300–1550* (Chicago, IL, 1998), pp. 27–46, 229–33.

14. J.F. Niermeyer, *Mediae Latinitatis Lexicon Minus* (Leiden, 1954), p. 4.

15. Henriette Benveniste, 'Les enlèvements: stratégies matrimoniales, discours juridique et discours politique en France à la fin du moyen age', *Revue Historique* 283 (1990), pp. 13–35; Claude Gauvard, *De grâce especial. Crime, état et société en France à la fin du moyen âge* (Paris, 1991), II, pp. 813–22.

16. Frans de Potter, *Petit cartulaire de Gand* (Gand, 1885), pp. 66–9.

17. Frans de Potter, ibid., pp. 66–9.

18. Walter Prevenier, 'Quelques réflexions sur la situation de l'individu face au pouvoir dans les Pays-Bas de l'Ancien Régime', in John Gilissen (ed.), *L'individu face au pouvoir, Man versus Political Power* (Bruxelles, Recueils de la Société Jean Bodin, 48, 3° partie, Europe Occidentale, 1989), pp. 349–65.

19. Walter Prevenier, 'Violence against Women in Fifteenth-Century France and the Burgundian State', in Barbara A. Hanawalt and David Wallace (eds), *Medieval Crime and Social Control* (Minneapolis, MN, 1999), p. 194, and note 44.

20. Myriam Greilsammer, 'Rapts de séduction et rapts violents en Flandre et en Brabant à la fin du Moyen Age', *Revue de l'Histoire du Droit* 56 (1988), pp. 49–84.

21. Prevenier, 'Violence against Women in Fifteenth-Century France', pp. 193–4; Walter Prevenier, 'Les réseaux en action', in Walter Prevenier *et al.*, *Le prince et le peuple. Images de la société du temps des ducs de Bourgogne, 1384–1530* (Anvers, 1998), pp. 297–301. Another case of clientage by both parties in a conflict: Walter Prevenier, 'Violence against Women in a Medieval Metropolis: Paris around 1400', in Bernard S. Bachrach and David Nicholas (eds), *Law, Custom, and the Social Fabric in Medieval Europe, Essays in Honor of Bryce Lyon* (Kalamazoo, MI, Western Michigan University, 1990), pp. 262–84.

22. A discussion on the double standard and legal inconsistencies can be found in Prevenier, 'Violence against Women in Fifteenth-Century France', pp. 190–5; case of de Pottere: note 53; case of Thuisy: note 30.

23. Prevenier, 'Violence against Women in Fifteenth-Century France, pp. 189–90; text of 1297: A.E. Gheldolf, *Coutumes de la ville de Gand* (Bruxelles, 1868), 1, p. 450.

24. Walter Prevenier, 'La stratégie et le discours politique des ducs de Bourgogne concernant les rapts et les enlèvements de femmes parmi les élites des Pays-Bas au XVe siècle', in Jan Hirschbiegel and Walter Paravicini (eds), *Das Frauenzimmer. Die Frau bei Hofe in Spätmittelalter und früher Neuzeit* (Stuttgart, 2000), p. 431.

25. Vleeschouwers-Van Melkebeek, 'Aspects du lien matrimonial', pp. 43–97.

26. Eric Bousmar, 'Du marché aux bordiaulx. Hommes, femmes et rapports de sexe dans les villes des Pays-Bas au moyen âge', in Myriam Carlier *et al.* (eds), *Core and Periphery in Late Medieval Society* (Leuven–Apeldoorn, 1997), pp. 51–70; there is also an excellent study (in Dutch) by Guy Dupont, *Maagdenverleidsters, hoeren en speculanten. Prostitutie in Brugge tijdens de Bourgondische periode (1385–1515)* (Brugge, 1996) which has an English summary on pp. 233–6.

27. Marc Boone, 'State power and illicit sexuality: the persecution of sodomy in late medieval Bruges', *Journal of Medieval History* 22 (1996), pp. 135–53.

28. Gheldolf, *Coutume de la ville de Gand*, 1, p. 672 (art. 1); L. Gilliodts-van Severen, *Coutume de la ville d'Ypres* (Bruxelles, 1908), 1, p. 489 (art. 1).

29. Marc Boone, 'Les gens de métiers à l'époque corporative à Gand et les litiges professionnels (1350–1450)', in Marc Boone and Maarten Prak (eds), *Individual, corporate and judicial status in European cities (late middle ages and early modern period)* (Leuven–Apeldoorn, 1996), pp. 23–47.

30. On gender discrimination see Prevenier, 'Violence against Women in Fifteenth-Century France', p. 189; Prevenier, 'Les réseaux familiaux', p. 210; W. Prevenier, 'Les divertissements à la ville et à la campagne', in Walter Prevenier *et al.*, *Le prince et le peuple. Images de la société du temps des ducs de Bourgogne, 1384–1530* (Anvers, 1998), pp. 138–9.

31. Walter Prevenier and Willem P. Blockmans, *The Burgundian Netherlands* (Cambridge, 1986), p. 224; this drawing is part of a series sold by H.P. Kraus, New York; a description of this collection from the 'French Netherlands', *c.* 1470, in: H.P. Kraus, *Catalogue 108, The Illustrated Book* (New York, s.d.), p. 23.

32. Prevenier and Blockmans, ibid., p. 87. *The Burgundian Netherlands*, p. 87 (a bronze aquamanile from *c.* 1400).

33. In the extraordinary woodcut 'The wise man and the wise wife', attributed to Cornelis Anthonisz., commented on by Yvonne Bleyerveld, *Hoe bedriechlijk dat die vrouwen zijn. Vrouwenlisten in de beeldende kunsten in de Nederlanden, 1350–1650* (Leiden, 1999), the wise wife, holding a mirror in front of her face, sees Jesus Christ on his cross. On the contrary in Hieronymus Bosch's *Garden of Pleasure* (1475) the devil appears in the mirror, a theme Bosch borrowed from the 'Livre de l'enseignement de ses filles' of the Chevalier de la Tour Landry (1370): cf. John B. Friedman, 'L'iconographie de Vénus', in B. Roy (ed.), *L'érotisme au moyen âge* (Montréal, Institut d'Etudes médiévales, 1977), pp. 70–1.

34. On strong women and weak men, see Walter Prevenier, 'Imitation et comportements spécifiques', in Walter Prevenier *et al.*, *Le prince et le peuple. Images de la société du temps des ducs de Bourgogne, 1384–1530* (Anvers, 1998), pp. 173–6.

35. Myriam Carlier, 'Paternity in Late Medieval Flanders', in Willem P. Blockmans, Marc Boone and Thérèse de Hemptinne (eds), *Secretum scriptorum*, pp. 235–58.

36. Robert Jacob, *Les époux, le seigneur et la cité. Coutumes et pratiques matrimoniales des bourgeois et paysans de France du Nord au moyen âge* (Bruxelles, 1990).

37. John Gilissen, 'Le statut de la femme dans l'ancien droit belge', in John Gilissen (ed.), *La femme* (Bruxelles, Recueil Société Jean Bodin, 12, Bruxelles, 1962), pp. 255–321.

38. Marianne Danneel, 'Gender and the Life Course in the Late Medieval Flemish Town', in Willem P. Blockmans, Marc Boone and Thérèse de Hemptinne (eds), *Secretum scriptorum.*, pp. 225–33; Herlihy and Klapisch-Zuber, *Tuscans*, pp. 203–11; Philippe Godding, *Le droit privé dans les Pays-Bas méridionaux du 12e au 18e siècle* (Bruxelles, 1987), pp. 70–1.

39. Philippe Godding, 'La pratique testamentaire en Flandre au 13e siècle', *Tijdschrift voor Rechtsgeschiedenis* 58 (1990), pp. 281–300.

40. David Nicholas, *The Domestic Life of a Medieval City. Women, Children and the Family in Fourteenth-Century Ghent* (Lincoln, 1985), pp. 13–132.

41. Marianne Danneel, 'Orphanhood and marriage in fifteenth-century Ghent', in Walter Prevenier (ed.), *Marriage and Social Mobility in the Middle Ages*, Studia Historica Gandensia 274 (Gent, 1992), pp. 123–39.

42. Prevenier, 'Les réseaux familiaux', pp. 201–2.

43. John Gilissen, 'Puissance paternelle et majorité émancipatrice dans l'ancien droit de la Belgique et du Nord de la France', *Revue d'Histoire du Droit français et étranger* 38 (1960), pp. 5–57.

44. Anthony Molho, *Marriage Alliance in late Medieval Florence* (Cambridge, MA, 1994), pp. 193, 274–97; Walter Prevenier (ed.), *Marriage and Social Mobility in the Middle Ages*, Studia Historica Gandensia 274, 2nd edn (Gent, 1992).

45. Myriam Greilsammer, *L'envers du tableau. Mariage et Maternité en Flandre Mediévale* (Paris, 1990); Myriam Carlier and Tim Soens (eds), *The Household in Late Medieval Cities. Italy and Northwestern Europe Compared* (Leuven-Apeldoorn, 2001); Prevenier, 'Les réseaux familiaux', pp. 185–231.

46. Werner Paravicini, 'The court of the dukes of Burgundy. A model for Europe?', in R.G. Asch and A.M. Birke (eds), *Princes, patronage and the nobility. The court at the beginning of the Modern Age, ca. 1450–1650* (Oxford, 1991), pp. 69–102 (esp. 90–102).

47. Robert Muchembled (ed.), *Cultural Transfers in Europe, 1400–1700* (forthcoming book in an ESF-program).

Chapter Three   'So was thys castell layd wyde open': Battles for the phallus in the early modern responses to Chaucer's Pardoner

1. Robert S. Sturges, *Chaucer's Pardoner and Gender Theory: Bodies of Discourse* (New York, 2000), pp. 152–68.

2. David Herlihy, *The Black Death and the Transformation of the West*, Samuel K. Cohn Jr (ed.), (Cambridge, MA, 1997). Herlihy's book as a whole provides a recent assessment of the Black Death as the major cause of late medieval demographic and cultural transformations. See also Philip Ziegler, *The Black Death* (New York, 1969), pp. 232–51. On the plague's short-term effects and attempts at repression, see Paul Freedman, *Images of the Medieval Peasant* (Stanford, CA, 1999), pp. 262, 287.

3. See, for example, the following documents: 'The Statute of Labourers, 1351', in A.R. Myers (ed.), *English Historical Documents, 1327–1485*, vol. 4 of *English Historical Documents*, gen. ed. David C. Douglas (London, 1969), p. 993; and 'The lower orders are not to be allowed to hunt, 1390', in Myers, p. 1004.

4. See P.J.P. Goldberg's influential *Women, Work, and Life Cycle in a Medieval Economy: Women in York and Yorkshire c. 1300–1520* (Oxford, 1992), pp. 280–304.

5. The Prologue to *The Tale of Beryn* can be found in John M. Bowers (ed.), *The Canterbury Tales: Fifteenth-Century Continuations and Additions* (Kalamazoo, MI, 1992), pp. 60–78, where it is entitled 'The Canterbury Interlude'. Quotations from this edition will be cited by line number in the text.

6. Bowers, p. 165.

7. On women in trade and in the guilds, see Judith M. Bennett, *Ale, Beer, and Brewsters in England: Women's Work in a Changing World, 1300–1600* (Oxford, 1996), pp. 37–76; Helen Jewell, *Women in Medieval England* (Manchester, 1996), pp. 88–95; Mavis E. Mate, *Women in Medieval English Society* (Cambridge, 1999), pp. 46–56.

8. On these developments in late medieval queenship, see John Carmi Parsons, *Medieval Queenship* (New York, 1993), and a cluster of essays in Jennifer Carpenter and Sally-Beth MacLean (eds), *Power of the Weak: Studies on Medieval Women* (Urbana, IL, 1995); Lois L. Huneycutt, 'Intercession and the High-Medieval Queen: The Esther Topos', pp. 126–46; John Carmi Parsons, 'The Queen's Intercession in Thirteenth-Century England', pp. 147–77; and Elizabeth McCartney, 'Ceremonies and Privileges of Office: Queenship in Late Medieval France', pp. 178–219.

9. On the social position of the whore, see Ruth Mazo Karras, *Common Women: Prostitution and Sexuality in Medieval England* (Oxford, 1996).

10. John Guy, *Tudor England* (Oxford, 1988), p. 44.

11. Jewell, p. 114, citing Goldberg, *Women, Work, and Life-Cycle*, p. 347.

12. Ian Maclean, *The Renaissance Notion of Woman: A Study in the Fortunes of Scholasticism and Medical Science in European Intellectual Life* (Cambridge, 1980), pp. 6–27 and 28–46.

13. Ibid., p. 66.

14. See, for example, Margaret R. Sommerville, *Sex and Subjection: Attitudes to Women in Early-Modern Society* (London, 1995).

15. See Linda Woodbridge, *Women and the English Renaissance: Literature and the Nature of Womankind, 1540–1620* (Urbana, IL, 1984) and – more helpfully for the 1520s and 1530s – Pamela Joseph Benson, *The Invention of the Renaissance Woman: The Challenge of Female Independence in the Literature and Thought of Italy and England* (University Park, PA, 1992), especially pp. 157–81.

16. Richard Axton and Peter Happé (eds), *The Plays of John Heywood* (Cambridge, 1991), pp. xiv, 42.

17. John Heywood, *A Mery Play Betwene the Pardoner and the Frere, the Curate and Neybour Pratte*, in Axton and Happé, pp. 93–109; for Chaucer's influence on Heywood, see John S. Farmer (ed.), *The Dramatic Writings of John Heywood* (London, 1905; rpt. New York, 1977), pp. 236–7; Axton and Happé, pp. 38–45; and Sturges, pp. 156, 208 n. 52.

18. John Heywood, *The Foure PP*, in Axton and Happé, pp. 111–42. All quotations are from this edition and will be cited by line numbers in the text. For a reading of the Pardoner's earlier speeches in terms of gender, see Sturges, pp. 156–8.

19. Margery's name may also be reminiscent of St Margaret of Antioch, who like Margery defeated and indeed humiliated the devil in specifically gendered terms: 'The demon cried out: "O blessed Margaret, I'm beaten! If I'd been beaten by a young man I wouldn't mind, but by a tender girl . . . !"' See Jacobus de Voragine, *The Golden Legend: Readings on the Saints*, trans. William Granger Ryan, 2 vols (Princeton, NJ, 1993), vol. 1, p. 369. A different St Margaret is also transgendered; see vol. 2, pp. 232–3.

20. Axton and Happé, p. 260.

21. Theodora A. Jankowski, *Women in Power in the Early Modern Drama* (Urbana, IL, 1992), suggests that, in the transition from the late Middle Ages to the early modern period, most young women's options narrowed to include little beyond marriage, pp. 22–49.

22. Ibid., p. 260.

23. Guy, p. 116.

24. For Heywood's Catholicism and position in Henry VIII's court (and in Thomas More's domestic circle), see the biographical study by Robert W. Bolwell, *The Life and Works of John Heywood* (New York, 1921), pp. 1–41, and, more briefly, Greg Walker, 'John Heywood and the Politics of Contentment', in his *The Politics of Performance in Early Renaissance Drama* (Cambridge, 1998), pp. 76–116, at 76–8. The only full-length study of Heywood other than Bolwell's is Robert Carl Johnson, *John Heywood* (New York, 1970), which is heavily dependent on Bolwell. It is not clear just where *The Foure PP* would have been performed,

but Bolwell speculates that it might have been privately performed at the home of Heywood's father-in-law John Rastell (p. 22), and/or at a court dinner, where '[t]he satire of the churchmen would have been relished; the pious conclusion tolerated' (p. 105). Walker understands the play as encouraging compromise and pluralism in religious and political views (pp. 91–100), and sees all Heywood's interludes as advice to the king, pleading for reconciliation (pp. 100–16).

25. Maclean, pp. 40, 41.

26. Axton and Happé, p. 258.

27. Ibid., p. 258.

28. David Cressy, *Birth, Marriage, and Death: Ritual, Religion, and the Life-Cycle in Tudor and Stuart England* (Oxford, 1997), p. 15.

29. Axton and Happé, p. 258. Cressy points out that herbal 'glisters' were commonly used in prenatal care (p. 47). The link between guns and wombs may also be supported by certain early modern visual images of the womb in which it is imagined as being shaped like a late medieval cannon: see, for example, the illustration of the uterus from Eucharius Roesslin, *The Birth of Mankynde* (1560), in Cressy, p. 142; and compare the very similar cannon depicted in a 1327 manuscript, in DeVries, *Technology*, p. 144. A later early modern poem that also makes this connection is John Donne's 'Elegy XVIII: The Comparison', ll. 39–42.

30. On guns as 'virility symbols', see DeVries, *Technology*, p. 163, and an essay cited there: J.R. Hale, 'Gunpowder and the Renaissance: An Essay in the History of Ideas', in C.H. Carter (ed.), *From Renaissance to Counter-Reformation: Essays in Honour of Garrett Mattingly* (London, 1966), pp. 113–44.

31. See Cressy, pp. 55–94, and Gail Kern Paster, *The Body Embarrassed: Drama and the Disciplines of Shame in Early Modern England* (Ithaca, NY, 1993), pp. 163–6.

32. On childbirth as an exclusively female province, see Cressy, pp. 55–94.

33. J.J. Scarisbrick, *Henry VIII* (Berkeley, CA, 1968), p. 149. My account of Henry VIII's relations with Katherine of Aragon and Anne Boleyn follows Scarisbrick throughout.

34. Axton and Happé, p. 260.

35. Maclean, pp. 73–5, 77. Jankowski also surveys this controversy and concludes that the negative assessment of women's ability to rule was more influential, pp. 54–74.

36. For Henry's building projects at Windsor in the 1520s, see Charles Oman, *Castles* (New York, 1978), pp. 34–5, and Patrick Cormack, *Castles of Britain* (New York, 1982), p. 181.

37. Christopher Hibbert, *The Court at Windsor: A Domestic History* (New York, 1964), pp. 38–42.

38. *Regent* had been sunk in 1512. See Axton and Happé, p. 258.

39. Oman, p. 29. The photograph facing p. 26 clearly shows both the chalk cliff and the river.

40. See Bolwell, pp. 15–18, 28–30, 42–63. On 'the Queen's Two Bodies', see Marie Axton, *The Queen's Two Bodies: Drama and the Elizabethan Succession* (London, 1977), pp. 11–25.

41. See Jankowski, pp. 60–74.

42. See two essays in David Cressy, *Travesties and Transgressions in Tudor and Stuart England: Tales of Discord and Dissension* (Oxford, 2000): 'Agnes Bowker's Cat: Childbirth, Seduction, Bestiality, and Lies', pp. 9–28 and 'Monstrous Births and Credible Reports: Portents, Texts, and Testimonies', pp. 29–50; Paster, pp. 23–63, 163–214; Jeffrey Masten, 'Is the Fundament a Grave?', in David Hillman and Carla Mazzio (eds), *The Body in Parts: Fantasies of Corporeality in Early Modern Europe* (New York, 1997), pp. 129–45.

Chapter Four   The importance of a name: Gender, power and the strategy of naming a child in a noble Italian family: the Martinengo of Brescia

1. A first approach to the history of Italian names can be found in C. Maestrelli, 'La recherche onomastique en Italie', in AA.VV. [autori varii], *Namenforschung/ Name Studies* vol. I (Berlin and New York, 1995), pp. 163–70, and in a paper by E. Baldetti, 'La recherche anthroponymique et historique en Italie: problèmes et perspectives', in *Atti in corso di stampa del XVIII Congresso Internazionale di Scienze Onomastiche di Treviri, aprile 1993.*

2. O. Guyotjeannin, J. Pycke and B.M. Tocke, *Diplomatique médiévale* (Paris, 1993); see especially the papers 'L'identification des lieux/L'identification des établissements religieux/L'identification des personnes', pp. 34–46. See also J.M. Martin and F. Menant (eds), *Genèse médiévale de l'anthroiponymie moderne: l'espace italien*, Acte de la table ronde de Milan avril 1994; *Mélanges de l'Ecole Française de Rome, Moyen Age* 107 (1995), 2 vols.

3. Good introductions to noble families of Venice can be found in G. Borelli, 'Patriziato della Dominante e Patriziato di Terraferma', in A. Tagliaferrii (ed.), *Venezia e la Terraferma* (Milan, 1981), pp. 79–95. For the public authorities see G. Cozzi, 'Authority and law in Renaissance Venice', in J.R. Hale (ed.),

Renaissance Venice (London, 1983), pp. 293–345. See also J.C. Davis, *The decline of the Venetian Nobility as a Ruling Class* (Baltimore, MD, 1962) and B. Pullan, 'Service to the Venetian State: Aspects of Myth and Reality in the Early Seventeenth Century', *Studi secenteschi* 5 (1964), pp. 95–148.

4. For a first introduction to the history of the Martinengo see G. Bonomi, *Il castello di Cavenago e i conti Martinengo Colleoni, memorie storiche* (Bergamo, 1884); L. Fè D'Ostiani, *Delle illustri famiglie bresciane recentemente estintesi*, fasc. I: Martinengo da Barco e Martinengo Colleoni (Brescia, 1890); P. Guerrini, *I conti Martinengo e il feudo di Urago d'Oglio* (Brescia, 1924); id., *Una celebre famiglia lombarda. I conti di Martinengo* (Brescia, 1930); F. Nardini, 'I signori della pianura: potenza, proprietà, imprese dei Martinengo', in AA.VV., *Atlante della Bassa* (Brescia, 1984), pp. 85–100.

5. A bibliographical approach can be found in M.A. Cortellazzo, *Nomi propri: bibliografia veneta* (Padua, 1981) and E. De Felice, *Dizionario dei nomi italiani: origine, etimologia, storia, diffusione e frequenza di oltre 18,000 nomi* (Milan, 1997).

6. A. Sala, *Fra Bergamo e Brescia: una famiglia capitaneale nei secoli XI e XII, i De Martinengo* (Brescia, 1990). See also M. Aymard, 'Pour une histoire des élites dans l'Italie Moderne', in AA.VV., *La famiglia e la vita quotidiana in Europa dal Quattrocento al Seicento* (Rome, 1986), pp. 207–19.

7. For the other Martinengo surname, see P. Guerrini, 'Una celebre famiglia', pp.133–76, 196–8, and D. Parzini, 'Il territorio di Brescia intorno alla metà del Quattrocento', *Studi bresciani* 12 (1983), pp. 49–75.

8. A. Monti della Corte, *Le famiglie del patriziato bresciano* (Brescia, 1960); id., *Fonti araldiche e blasoniche bresciane.. Il registro veneto dei nobili detti rurali o agresti estimati nel territorio bresciano fra il 1496 e il 1948* (Brescia, 1962). See also A. Ventura, *Nobiltà e popolo nella società veneta del Quattrocento e Cinquecento* (Bari, 1964); B. Pullan, 'The occupations and investments of the Venetian nobility in the middle and late sixteenth century', in J.R. Hale (ed.), *Renaissance Venice*, pp. 379–408; J. Ferraro, 'Feudal patrician investments in the Bresciano and the politics of the *estimo*', in *Studi veneziani* 7 (1983), pp. 31–57; id., 'Proprietà terriera e potere nello stato veneto: la nobiltà bresciana del Quattrocento e Cinquecento', in G. Gracco and M. Knapton, *Dentro lo 'stato italico'. Venezia e la Terraferma fra Quattrocento e Seicento* (Trento, 1984), pp. 159–82.

9. A good analysis of the French cases can be found in M. Noally (ed.), 'Nom propre et nomination', *Actes du colloque de Brest*, avril 1994 (Paris, 1995), and in K. Jonasson, *Le nom propre: Constructions et interprétations* (Louvaine-la-Neuve, 1994). See also B. Garnot, 'Les prénoms populaires à Chartres au XVIII siècle', *Revue historique* 227 (1) (1988). For different names with the same meaning M.C. Casper, 'Hans, Jean et Joannes ou les langues du prénom', *Langage et Société* 66 (1993), pp. 77–97. See also E.D. Lawson's bibliography, 'Personal names: 100 years of social science contributions', *Names* 3 (London,

1984), pp. 45–73; also, *More names and naming. An Annotated Bibliography* (London, 1995).

10. For the world of the Venetian women, see S.Chojnacki, 'Patrician women in early Renaissance Venice', *Studies in the Renaissance* 21 (1974), pp. 176–203.

11. For Brescian examples see G. Bonfiglio Dosio, 'Vicende di donne, vicende di archivi: Camilla Fenaroli, Veronica Porcellaga e gli archivi Martinengo da Barco e Porcellaga', in AA.VV., *Studi in onore di Ugo Vaglia* (Brescia, 1989), pp. 301–8; E. Selmi, *La scrittura femminile a Brescia fra il Quattrocento e l'Ottocento* (Brescia, 2001).

12. G. Duby and E. Goff, *Famille et parentèle dans l'Occident médiéval* (Roma, 1977); F. Zonabend, 'Perchè dar nomi? I nomi di persona in un villaggio francese', in C. Levi-Strauss (ed.), *L'Identità* (Palermo, 1980); the papers concerning 'Le nom de personne', *L'Homme* 20 (1980), and 'I sistemi di denominazione', in *L'Uomo* 1 (2) (1983); P. Niles, 'Baptism and the naming of children in late medieval England', *Medieval Prosopography* 1 (1982), pp. 63–94; Agnès Fine, *Le prénom. Mode et histoire* (Paris, 1984); also, *Léonard, Marie, Jean et les autres. Les prénoms en Limousine depuis un millénaire* (Paris, 1984).

13. *Memoria delli figlioli et figliole dell'Ill.mo Conte Silla Martinengo Cesaresco et Co: Domicilla Gambara Martinenga Cesaresca in cui si vede l'anno et il giorno della di loro natività*, Manuscript in Biblioteca Queriniana Brescia, Raccolta Fè d'Ostiani, 34/misc.2.

14. In 60 cases where the name of the godparent is known, the Martinengo give the child a different name. For other European regions (with over 90 per cent of cases with the same name) see F. Zonabend, 'La parenté baptismale à Minot', *Annales ESC* 3 (1978), pp. 663–75; A. Burguière, *Prénoms et parenté*, pp. 113–20; A. Fine, 'L'Héritage du nom de Baptême', *Annales ESC* 4 (1987), pp. 853–77.

15. For the church in Brescia, see M. Pegari, 'I giochi del potere. Presenza e incidenza del patriziato nella Brescia del Cinquecento', in AA.VV., *Arte, economia, cultura e religione nella Brescia del XVI secolo* (Brescia, 1988), pp. 219–37. See also B. Pullan, *Rich and poor in Renaissance Venice. The social foundation of a Catholic State* (Oxford, 1971).

16. *Enciclopedia cattolica*, vol. VIII, 'nome' (Firenze, 1952), and V. Larock, 'Essai sur la valeur sacrée et la valeur sociale des noms de personnes dans les sociétés', in *Revue de l'Histoire des religions* 101/102 (1930). 13.8 per cent of Martinengo family names are multiple: in other Italian families the figure is over 70 per cent.

17. For the demography of Brescia, see C. Pasero, 'Dati statistici e notizie intorno al movimento della popolazione bresciana durante il dominio veneto', *Archivio Storico Lombardo* 9 (1961), pp. 71–97 and J. Ferraro, *Family and public life in Brescia 1580–1650: the foundation of power in the Venetian State* (Cambridge, 1993),

pp. 50–5. For the demography of Venetian nobility, see G.M. Weiner, 'Statistical aspect of the decline of the Venetian nobility', *Genius* 1 (1970), pp. 59–72.

18. L. Ercolani, *Mamme e bambini nelle tradizioni popolari romagnole* (Ravenna, 1975); C. Klapish-Zuber, 'Le nom refait: la transmission des noms à Florence', *L'Homme* 4 (1980).

19. On re-marriage in Italian society see M. Buonanno (ed.), *Le funzioni sociali del matrimonio: modelli e regole nella scelta del coniuge dal IV al XX secolo* (Milan, 1980).

20. D. Zanetti, *La demogafia del patriziato milanese nei secoli XVII–XIX* (Pavia, 1972), pp. 19–57; D.O. Hughes, 'Strutture famigliari e sistemi di successione ereditaria nei testamenti dell'Europa medievale', in *Quaderni storici* 33 (1976), pp. 929–52. For Brescia see also J. Ferraro, 'Feudal patrician investments in the Bresciano and the politics of *estimo*', *Studi veneziani* 7 (1983), pp. 31–57.

21. See a famous example in J.C. Davis, *A Venetian family and its fortune* (Philadelphia, PA, 1975).

22. For the Martinengo possessions see F. Bettoni Cazzago, 'La nobiltà bresciana', in AA.VV., *Brixia 1882* (Brescia, 1882), pp. 91–113; C. Poni, 'Accumulation primitive et agronomie capitaliste: le cas de Brescia', *Studia Historiae Oeconomicae* 10 (1975), pp. 17–38; J. Ferraro, 'Proprietà terriera e potere nello stato veneto: la nobiltà bresciana del Quattrocento e Cinquecento', in AA.VV., *Dentro lo stato italico* (Trento, 1984), pp. 159–82.

23. P. Guerrini, *Una celebre famiglia*, p. 471.

24. Ibid., p. 216.

25. Ibid., p. 445. See also P. Perancini, *Il palazzo di Barbarano* (Salò, 1864).

26. B. di vesme, 'Dai Supponidi agli Obertenghi', *Bollettino Storico Bibliografico Subalpino* 22 (1920); C. Klapish-Zuber, 'Le choix du prénom dans la Florence de la Renaissance', *L'Uomo* 1 (2) (1983), pp. 51–64.

27. M. Zane, 'Nomi per un cognome: Strategie dell'identità e scelte onomastica della nobile famiglia Martinengo di Brescia (XV–XIX secolo)', *Rivista Italiana di Onomastica* 2 (1996), pp. 234–62.

28. For the case of Florence see C. Klapish-Zuber, 'Le choix du prénom dans la Florence de la Renaissance', p. 57. In France this rate reaches 43 per cent: see A. Burguière, 'Prénoms et parenté', *L'Uomo* 1 (2) (1983) p. 117.

29. P. Guerrini, *Una celebre famiglia*, pp. 501–3.

30. P. Guerrini, 'L'amore di Ortensia Martinengo', in *Figure della storia e della cronaca* (Brescia, 1986), pp. 548–50. See also F. Lane, 'Family partnership and joint ventures in Venice and history', in *The collected papers of Frederick C. Lane* (Baltimore, MD, 1966).

31. A vision of Brescian female nobility can be found in J. Ferraro, *Family and public life in Brescia 1580–1650: the foundation of the power in the Venetian State* (Cambridge, 1993). Another example is the biography of Maria Maddalena Martinengo da Barco (1687–1737), in G. Pozzi and C. Leonardi, *Scrittrici mistiche italiane* (Genoa, 1988), pp. 552–63.

Chapter Five 'Our Trinity!': Francis I, Louise of Savoy and Marguerite d'Angoulême

1. R.J. Knecht, '"Born between two women . . .", Jules Michelet and Francis I', *Renaissance Studies* 19 (2000), pp. 329–43.

2. Jules Michelet, *Renaissance et Réforme. Histoire de France au XVIe siècle* (Paris, 1982), p. 191.

3. Ibid., p. 192.

4. Ibid.

5. Cited by A. Mitzman, *Michelet, Historian. Rebirth and Romanticism in Nineteenth-Century France* (New Haven, CT, 1990), p. 60; P. Viallaneix, *Michelet, les travaux et les jours, 1798–1874* (Paris, 1998), pp. 31, 37.

6. Michelet, *Renaissance et Réforme*, p. 208.

7. Ibid.

8. Ibid.

9. Ibid., p. 192.

10. Ibid., p. 193.

11. L. Febvre, *Michelet et la Renaissance* (Paris, 1992), p. 183.

12. Elizabeth McCartney, 'The King's mother and Royal Prerogative in early sixteenth-century France', in J. Carmi Parsons (ed.), *Medieval Queenship* (New York, 1993), pp. 117–217.

13. R. de Maulde La Clavière (ed.), *Procédures politiques du règne de Louis XII* (Paris, 1885), pp. xiii–cxxxi.

14. A.-M. Lecoq, *François Ier imaginaire: symbolique et politique à l'aube de la Renaissance française* (Paris, 1987), pp. 77–101; Myra D. Orth, 'Louise de Savoie et le pouvoir du livre', in Kathleen Wilson-Chevalier and Éliane Viennot (eds), *Royaume de féyminie: pouvoirs, contraintes, espaces de liberté des femmes de la Renaissance à la Fronde* (Paris, 1999), pp. 71–90; R. de Maulde La Clavière, *Louise de Savoie et François Ier* (Paris, 1895), pp. 233–41.

15. J.-F. Michaud and J.-J.F. Poujoulat, *Nouvelle collection de mémoires*, 1st ser., vol. v (1836), p. 7; B. Castiglione, *The Book of the Courtier*, tr. G. Bull (Harmondsworth, 1967), p. 88.

16. M.H. Smith, 'François Ier, l'Italie et le Château de Blois: nouveaux documents, nouvelles dates', *Bulletin monumental* 147 (4), p. 309.

17. Evelyne Berriot-Salvadore, *Les femmes dans la société française de la Renaissance* (Geneva, 1990), pp. 391–4, 406. For the *Journal de Louise de Savoie* see *Nouvelle collection des Mémoires pour servir à l'histoire de France*, ed. Michaud et Poujoulat (Paris, 1838), v, 83–93.

18. F. Génin (ed.), *Lettres de Marguerite d'Angoulême* (Paris, 1841), i, 145.

19. P. Jourda, *Marguerite d'Angoulême* (Paris, 1930), i, 27.

20. Michaud et Poujoulat, v, 88.

21. P. de Vaissière (ed.), *Le Journal de Jean Barrillon* (Paris, 1897–99), i, 4, 16; *Ordonnances des rois de France: règne de François Ier* (Paris, 1902–75), i, nos 20–1.

22. A. Buisson, *Le Chancelier Antoine Duprat* (Paris, 1935), pp. 17–68.

23. A. Champollion-Figeac (ed.), *Captivité du Roi François Ier* (Paris, 1847), p. 129.

24. R.J. Knecht, 'Francis I and Fontainebleau', *The Court Historian*, iv (1999), pp. 100–1.

25. J.R. Hale (ed.), *The Travel Journal of Antonio de Beatis* (London: Hakluyt Society, 1979), pp. 107–8.

26. *Ordonnances des rois de France: règne de François Ier*, i, 262–8. See also Simone Bertière, 'Régence et pouvoir féminin', in *Royaume de fémynie*, pp. 63–70; Elizabeth McCartney, 'The King's Mother and Royal Prerogative in Early-Sixteenth-Century France', in John Carmi Parsons (ed.), *Medieval Queenship* (New York, 1998), pp. 117–217.

27. V.-L. Bourrilly and F. Vindry (eds), *Mémoires de Martin et Guillaume du Bellay* (Paris, 1908–19), ii, 2; R. Doucet, *Étude sur le gouvernement de François Ier dans ses rapports avec le Parlement de Paris* (Paris, 1921–26), ii, 30, n. 4; V.-L. Bourrilly (ed.), *Le Journal d'un Bourgeois de Paris sous le règne de François Ier (1515–36)* (Paris, 1910), p. 195.

28. R.J. Knecht, *Renaissance Warrior and Patron*, pp. 227–31.

29. R.J. Knecht, 'Francis I and the *Lit de Justice*: a "Legend" defended', *French History* vii (1993), pp. 53–83.

30. J.S. Brewer, J. Gairdner and R.H. Brodie (eds), *Letters and Papers, Foreign and Domestic, of the Reign of Henry VIII*, 21 vols (London, 1862–1910), iii, no. 1656.

31. *L. & P.*, iii, nos 416, 514.

32. *L.& P.*, iii, no. 1402.

33. *L. & P.*, iii, no. 1441. Florimond Robertet was secretary of state. See C.A. Mayer and D. Bentley-Cranch, *Florimond Robertet (?–1527), Homme d'état français* (Paris, 1994).

34. *L. & P.*, Appendix, no. 29.

35. *L.& P.*, iii, no. 1651.

36. *L. & P.*, iii, no. 1971.

37. *L. & P.*, iii, no. 2059.

38. *L. & P.*, iii, no. 2522.

39. On the Bourbon treason see A. Lebey, *Le Connétable de Bourbon, 1490–1527* (Paris, 1904), *passim*, and R. Doucet, *Étude sur le gouvernement de François Ier dans ses rapports avec le Parlement de Paris*, pt.1 (Paris, 1921), pp. 203–317.

40. A. Lebey, pp. 119–20; R. Doucet, pp. 215–17.

41. Michaud et Poujoulat, v, 90.

42. *Mémoires de Martin et Guillaume du Bellay*, i, 233–4.

43. Michelet, *Histoire de France au seizième siècle*, x, La Réforme (Paris, n.d.), p. 163.

44. A. Spont, *Semblançay* (Paris, 1895), p. 188.

45. R. Doucet, *Étude sur le gouvernement de François Ier*, i, pp. 186–201; Spont, *Semblançay*, pp. 208–28.

46. P. Hamon, *L'Argent du roi. Les finances sous François Ier* (Paris, 1994), pp. 344–52.

47. Various dates are given for her death. Bryan and Foxe, writing from Senlis on 30 September, give it as 23 September, *L.& P.*, v, no. 454. It is often said that Louise died of the plague that was raging in her neighbourhood at the time. If so, we may wonder how Marguerite avoided catching it!

48. A. Tuetey (ed.), *Registres des délibérations du Bureau de la Ville de Paris* (Paris: Imprimerie nationale, 1886), ii, 127–8.

49. The funeral of Claude in 1524 was modelled on that of Anne of Brittany in 1514. No other queen of France was given a state funeral thereafter, not even Catherine de' Medici who was buried without ceremony at Blois in 1589 and only transferred to Saint-Denis in 1610. See Fanny Cosandey, *La Reine de France. Symbole et pouvoir* (Paris, 2000), pp. 206–7. She overlooks the funeral of Louise of Savoy, presumably because she was not officially a queen.

50. *Journal d'un bourgeois de Paris*, p. 353.

51. C. Marot, *Oeuvres lyriques*, ed. C.A. Mayer (London, 1964), pp. 321–37.

52 P. de Gayangos (ed.), *Cal. of State Papers, Venetian* (London, 1882), v, no. 1024.

53. By far the best biography of Marguerite is P. Jourda, *Marguerite d'Angoulême* (Paris, 1930). For a shorter, more popular treatment see Jean-Luc Déjean, *Marguerite de Navarre* (Paris, 1987).

54. P. Jourda, *Marguerite d'Angoulême*, ii, pp. 1009–10.

55. R.J. Knecht, *Renaissance Warrior and Patron*, pp. 245–6.

56. *L.& P.*, iii, no. 1581.

57. F. Decrue, *Anne de Montmorency, Grand Maître et Connétable de France, à la cour, aux armées et au conseil du roi François Ier* (Paris, 1885), pp. 174 ff.

58. See the many letters which she wrote to him in F. Génin (ed.), *Lettres de Marguerite d'Angoulême*.

59. P. Jourda, i, 205–6.

60. *L. & P.*, xv, no. 223.

61. E. Desjardins, *Les favorites des rois. Anne de Pisseleu, duchesse d'Étampes et François Ier* (Paris, 1904).

62. *L.& P.*, vi, no. 692.

63. M. François, *Le cardinal François de Tournon* (Paris, 1951), p. 179 n.1.

64. *Calendar of State Papers Spanish*, vi (pt.1), 117.

65. F. Decrue, *Anne de Montmorency, grand maître et connétable de France* (Paris, 1885), i, 402.

66. J. Lestocquoy (ed.), *Correspondance des nonces . . . Carpi et Ferrerio, 1535–40* (Rome and Paris, 1961), p. 220.

67. P. Jourda, *Marguerite d'Angoulême*, i, 215–24, 228–30, 234.

68. Ibid., i, 153.

69. Ibid., i, 251–66.

70. G. Briçonnet and Marguerite d'Angoulême, *Correspondance (1521–1524)*, ed. C. Martineau and M. Veissière (Geneva, 1975–79), 2 vols.

71. L. Febvre, *Autour de l'Heptaméron* (Paris, 1944), pp. 106–22.

72. Archives nationales, Xla 1529, fos. 198–9, 316, 442–3.

73. Archives nationales, Xla 1530, fos. 33b–34a.

74. J.K. Farge, *Orthodoxy and Reform in Early Reformation France* (Leiden, 1985), pp. 201–3.

75. Ibid., p. 204.

76. R.J. Knecht, *Renaissance Warrior and Patron*, pp. 313–21.

77. P. Jourda, *Marguerite d'Angoulême*, ii, 1028.

78. *L.& P.*, xvii, 128; *State Papers of Henry VIII*, viii, 660.

79. Jourda, *Marguerite d'Angoulême*, i, 272.

80. D. Potter, *War and Government in the French provinces: Picardy 1470–1560* (Cambridge, 1993), pp. 135–6.

81. P. Jourda, *Marguerite d'Angoulême*, i, 275–98.

82. *Registres des délibérations du Bureau de la Ville de Paris*, ii, 129.

83. Eliane Viennot, 'Des "femmes d'Etat" au XVIe siècle: les princesses de la Ligue et l'écriture de l'histoire', in Danielle Haase Dubosc and Eliane Viennot (eds), *Femmes et pouvoirs sous l'ancien régime* (Paris, 1991), pp. 77–97.

Chapter Six   Elizabeth I as Deborah: Biblical typology, prophecy and political power

1. James M. Osborn (ed.), *The Quenes Maiesties Passage through the Citie of London to Westminster the Day before her Coronacion* (New Haven, CT, 1960) p. 28 (hereafter *The Quenes Maiesties Passage*). See also Sidney Anglo in *Spectacle, Pageantry and Early Tudor Policy* (Oxford, 1969); David Bergeron in *English Civic Pageantry* (London, 1971); J.N. King in 'The Godly Woman in Elizabethan Iconography', *Renaissance Quarterly* 38 (1985), pp. 41–84; David Bergeron, 'Elizabeth's Coronation Entry (1559): New Manuscript Evidence', *English Literary Renaissance* viii (1978), pp. 3–8.

2. *Calendar of State Papers Venetian 1558–1580* (London, 1890), vii, p. 15; cited in David Bergeron, *English Civic Pageantry*, p. 18.

3. Patrick Collinson, 'Puritans, Men of Business and Elizabethan Parliaments', *Parliamentary History* 7 (2) (1988), pp. 187–211 (esp. p. 190).

4. 'Deborah' may have been wearing a costume designed to be similar to Elizabeth's costume on the day, in which case, as David Bergeron notes, symbol and reality would have fused. David Bergeron, 'Elizabeth's Coronation Entry 1559: New Manuscript Evidence', p. 7.

5. The description of Deborah given in the 1578 Norwich civic pageant. See J.N. King, 'The Godly Woman in Elizabethan Iconography'.

6. *The Quenes Maiesties Passage*, p. 65.

7. John Strype makes the identification in his *Annals of the Reformation and Establishment of Religion and other various occurrences in the Church of England during Queen Elizabeth's Happy Reign; together with an appendix of original papers of state, records and letters*, 7 vols (Oxford, 1824), vol. II, ii, p. 75.

The Compact Edition of the Oxford English Dictionary, 2 vols (Oxford, 1971), vol. I, p. 1473.

9. See, for example, J.A. Guy, *Tudor England* (Oxford, 1998), p. 265.

10. David Laing (ed.), *The Works of John Knox*, 6 vols (Edinburgh: 1846–64), vi, pp. 50–1.

11. J.N. King, 'The Godly Woman in Elizabethan Iconography', p. 57.

12. Throughout the chapter I use 'councillors' to refer to Elizabeth's official advisers, normally members of the Privy Council, and 'counsellors' to refer to that wider constituency who saw themselves as called upon – by birth, position or vocation – to advise the queen. See A.N. McLaren, *Political Culture in the Reign of Elizabeth I: Queen and Commonwealth 1558–1585* (Cambridge, 1999), p. 10.

13. See, for example, Laurence Humphrey's *apologia* for Elizabeth's accession, *The Nobles or of Nobility* (London, 1563), fols. Aii.r–Bii.v.

14. For the insistently male character of the Protestant Reformation and its implication in political thought, see Donald R. Kelley, *The Beginning of Ideology: Consciousness and Society in the French Reformation* (Cambridge, 1981).

15. Merry E. Weisner, *Women and Gender in Early Modern Europe* (Cambridge, 1993), p. 241.

16. Sarah Hanley, 'The Monarchic State in Early Modern France: Marital Regime Government and Male Right', in Adrianna E. Bakos (ed.), *Politics, Ideology and the Law in Early Modern Europe: Essays in Honour of J.H.M. Salmon* (Rochester, NY, 1994).

17. James E. Phillips, 'The Background of Spenser's Attitude Toward Women Rulers', *Huntington Library Quarterly* v (1941), pp. 5–32, (8).

18. See John Knox's interpretation of Genesis in the *Blast*: 'As God should say: forasmuch as thou hast abused thy former condition, and because thy free will hath brought thy self and mankind into the bondage of Satan, I therefore will bring thee in bondage to man. For where before, thy obedience should have been voluntary, now it shall be by constraint and by necessity: and that because thou hast deceived thy man, thou shalt therefore be no longer mistress over thine own appetites, over thine own will nor desires. For in thee there is neither reason nor discretion, which be able to moderate thy affections.' Marvin Breslow (ed.), *The Political Writings of John Knox* (Washington, DC, 1985), pp. 42–3.

19. Merry Weisner, *Women and Gender in Early Modern Europe*, pp. 23, 27.

20. H.G. Koenigsberger, George L. Mosse and G.Q. Bowler, *Europe in the Sixteenth Century* (London, 1989), pp. 303–4.

21. See Anne McLaren, 'The Quest for a King: Gender, Marriage and Succession in Elizabethan England', *Journal of British Studies* 41 (2002), pp. 259–90.

22. Quoted in J.A. Guy, *Christopher St German on Chancery and Statute* (London, 1985), p. 44.

23. Margaret Aston, *The King's Bedpost: Reformation and Iconography in a Tudor Group Portrait* (Cambridge, 1993).

24. J.A. Guy, *Christopher St German on Chancery and Statute*, p. 44. St Paul's often-quoted injunction prohibiting women from speaking in the congregation was read as both confirming their relative spiritual incapacity and denying them such authority.

25. For the concept of the 'king's two bodies' in the context of Elizabeth's reign, see Marie Axton, *The Queen's Two Bodies: Drama and the Elizabethan Succession* (London, 1977).

26. For the debate and its significance see A.N. McLaren, *Political Culture in the Reign of Elizabeth I*, esp. pp. 12–23.

27. See, for example, Louis Montrose's seminal article, '"Shaping Fantasies": Figurations of Gender and Power in Elizabethan Culture', in Stephen Greenblatt (ed.), *Representing the English Renaissance* (Berkeley, CA, 1988), pp. 31–64.

28. D.M. Loades, *Politics and the Nation, 1450–1660* (Oxford, 1974), p. 235.

29. Robert M. Healey, 'Waiting for Deborah: John Knox and Four Ruling Queens', *Sixteenth Century Journal* 25 (2) (1994), pp. 371–86 and Carole Levin, 'John Foxe and the Responsibilities of Queenship', in Mary Beth Rose (ed.), *Women in the Middle Ages and Renaissance: Literary and Historical Perspectives* (Syracuse, NY, 1986), pp. 113–33.

30. Heinrich Bullinger, 'An Answer Given to a Certain Scotsman', in David Laing (ed.), *The Works of John Knox*, iii, pp. 217–26.

31. T.E. Hartley, *Elizabeth's Parliaments: Queen, Lords and Commons, 1559–1601* (Manchester, 1992), pp. 63–7, 74.

32. John Strype, *Annals of the Reformation*, III, i, p. 537.

33. J.E. Neale, *The Elizabethan House of Commons* (London, 1949; revised edn., 1963); Wallace Notestein, *The Winning of the Initiative by the House of Commons* (London, 1924).

34. David Starkey, *The English Court: From the War of the Roses to the Civil War* (London, 1987), Introduction, p. 21.

35. For this theorization of political activity, see Quentin Skinner, 'Meaning and Understanding in the History of Ideas', in James Tully (ed.), *Meaning and Context: Quentin Skinner and His Critics* (Cambridge, 1988), pp. 29–67.

36. F.W. Conrad, 'A Preservative Against Tyranny: The Political Theology of Sir Thomas Elyot', PhD thesis, Johns Hopkins University, Baltimore, MD, 1988.

37. John Aylmer, *An harborowe for faithfull and trewe subjects, agaynst the late blowne Blaste, concernings the Government of Wemen* (Strasbourg, 1559), fol. O2.

38. 'I am Richard II, know ye not that?', Elizabeth is reported to have said to the antiquarian William Lambarde. For the comment, and the play's contemporary popularity, see E.K. Chambers, *William Shakespeare*, 2 vols (Oxford, 1930), vol. 2, pp. 320–1.

39. John Strype, *Annals of the Reformation*, II, ii, pp. 662–5.

40. Lawrence Stone, *Crisis of the Aristocracy 1558–1641* (Oxford, 1967; 1977), pp. 340–1. More generally see Patrick Collinson, *The Elizabethan Puritan Movement* (London, 1967).

41. T.E. Hartley (ed.), *Proceedings in the Parliaments of Elizabeth I*, 3 vols (Leicester, 1981–1995) vol. I, pp. 294–5.

42. Patrick Collinson, 'The Downfall of Archbishop Grindal and its Place in Elizabethan Political and Ecclesiastical History', in Patrick Collinson (ed.), *Godly People: Essays on English Protestantism and Puritanism* (London, 1983), pp. 371–98.

43. Quoted in Patrick Collinson, 'The Downfall of Archbishop Grindal', p. 376.

44. A.N. McLaren, *Political Culture in the Reign of Elizabeth I*, Introduction.

45. Albert Feuillerat (ed.), *The Prose Works of Sir Philip Sidney*, 3 vols (Cambridge, 1968), iii, Letter lxxxix, p. 167.

46. J.E. Neale, *Elizabeth I and Her Parliaments 1584–1601* (London, 1957), pp. 150–1.

47. William Haller, *Foxe's Book of Martyrs and the Elect Nation* (London, 1963). Haller's thesis has withstood the battering it received in the 1970s and 1980s. It has now emerged in a more nuanced form in part due to the work of scholars associated with the John Foxe Project. See especially the essays by Susan Felch, Tom Betteridge, and Margaret Aston and Elizabeth Ingram in David Loades (ed.), *John Foxe and the English Reformation* (Aldershot, 1997).

48. See Anne McLaren, 'Gender, Religion and Early Modern Nationalism: Elizabeth I, Mary Queen of Scots and the Genesis of English Anti-Catholicism', *American Historical Review* 107 (2002), pp. 739–67.

49. See, for example, Lucy Hutchinson's characterization of Charles's regime: 'Wherever male princes are so effeminate as to suffer women of foreign birth and different religions to intermeddle with affairs of state, it is always found to produce sad desolulations.' James Sutherland (ed.), *Memoirs of the life of Colonel Hutchinson [by] Lucy Hutchinson* (London, 1973).

50. 'These answers were made by Mr Richard Bertie . . . against the book of John Knox 1558', given as an appendix to Amanda Shephard's valuable dissertation, 'Gender and Authority in Sixteenth Century England', PhD dissertation, University of Lancaster (Lancaster, 1990), pp. 409–10.

51.　Frances Yates, *Astraea: The Imperial Theme in the Sixteenth Century* (London, 1975), p. 43.

52.　For the first modern recognition of its significance, see Patrick Collinson, 'The Monarchical Republic of Queen Elizabeth I', *Bulletin of the John Rylands University of Manchester* 69 (1986–7), pp. 394–424.

Chapter Seven　Queen Anna bites back: Protest, effeminacy and manliness at the Jacobean court

1.　J. Bain *et al.* (eds), *Calendar of the State Papers Relating to Scotland and Mary, Queen of Scots 1547–1603*, 13 vols (Edinburgh:1898–1969), ix, p. 655. Hereafter *CSP Scotland.*

2.　David Bergeron, author of the most insightful full-length study of Anna and James, observed, 'James's personal desires and interests clearly interfered with political judgement; in part James paid the political price of his desire for love'. *Royal Family, Royal Lovers: King James of England and Scotland* (Columbia, MO, 1991), p. 35. See also Michael B. Young, *King James and the History of Homosexuality* (New York, 2000), p. 136 (published in Britain as *James VI and I and the History of Homosexuality*).

3.　The Frenchman was Monsieur de Fontenay, an agent sent by Mary Queen of Scots to size up her son. Robert Ashton (ed.), *James I by His Contemporaries* (London, 1969), p. 3. Ashton explained in a footnote: 'Fontenay is almost certainly referring to James's affection for male favourites.'

4.　Recent reappraisals of various aspects of James's reign in Scotland can be found in Julian Goodare and Michael Lynch (eds), *The Reign of James VI* (East Linton, Scotland, 2000).

5.　James's life up to the age of seventeen is related in Caroline Bingham, *The Making of a King: The Early Years of James VI and I* (London, 1968).

6.　G.P.V. Akrigg (ed.), *Letters of King James VI & I* (Berkeley, CA, 1984), p. 98.

7.　*CSP Scotland*, x, p. 87.

8.　There is only one full biography of Anna, and it has serious limitations. Ethel Carleton Williams, *Anna of Denmark: Wife of James VI of Scotland: James I of England* (London, 1970). For Anna's life prior to her marriage, see chapters 1 and 2.

9.　There is now a whole book devoted to the period of courtship and marriage, including the translation of a contemporary Danish account. David Stevenson, *Scotland's Last Royal Wedding: The Marriage of James VI and Anne of Denmark*

(Edinburgh, 1997). The marriage negotiations can also be followed in chapter 2 of Williams, *Anna of Denmark*, or chapter 6 of David H. Willson, *King James VI and I* (New York, 1967).

10. Williams, *Anna of Denmark*, p. 14.

11. *CSP Scotland*, x, 124, 130.

12. *CSP Scotland*, x, 122, 124.

13. David Moysie, *Memoirs of the Affairs of Scotland* (Edinburgh, 1830), pp. 80–1. I have modernized spelling.

14. There are two modern editions of these works: Charles Howard McIlwain (ed.), *The Political Works of James I* (New York, 1965) and Johann P. Sommerville (ed.), *King James VI and I: Political Writings* (Cambridge, 1994).

15. From James's *Basilikon Doron* in Sommerville, *Political Writings*, p. 42.

16. Frederick von Raumer, *History of the Sixteenth and Seventeenth Centuries, Illustrated by Original Sources*, trans. H.E. Lloyd, 2 vols (London, 1835), ii, 196.

17. Maurice Lee Jr, *Great Britain's Solomon: James VI and I in His Three Kingdoms* (Urbana, IL, 1990), p. 32.

18. Willson, *James VI & I*, pp. 94–5.

19. A.L. Rowse, *Homosexuals in History: A Study of Ambivalence in Society, Literature and the Arts* (New York, 1977), p. 54.

20. Lee, *Great Britain's Solomon*, p. 74.

21. Maurice Ashley, *The House of Stuart: Its Rise and Fall* (London, 1980), p. 116.

22. See, for example, Leeds Barroll, *Anna of Denmark, Queen of England: A Cultural Biography* (Philadelphia, PA, 2001) and 'The Court of the First Stuart Queen', in Linda Levy Peck (ed.), *The Mental World of the Jacobean Court* (Cambridge, 1991), pp. 191–208; David M. Bergeron, 'Francis Bacon's *Henry VII*: Commentary on King James I', *Albion* 24 (Spring 1992), pp. 17–26; David M. Bergeron, 'Masculine Interpretation of Queen Anna, Wife of James I', *Biography* 18 (1) (1995), pp. 42–54; and Maureen Meikle, 'A Meddlesome Princess: Anna of Denmark and Scottish Court Politics, 1589–1603', in Goodare and Lynch, *Reign of James VI*, pp. 126–40.

23. Stevenson, *Scotland's Last Royal Wedding*, p. vii.

24. The best accounts of Anna's political activities in Scotland are Barroll, *Anna of Denmark*, ch. 2 and Meikle, 'Meddlesome Princess', in Goodare and Lynch, *Reign of James VI*, pp. 126–40.

25. These early efforts are discussed in Meikle, 'Meddlesome Princess', pp. 130–2. Anna's first interventions appear in *CSP Scotland*, x, 507, 533, 536 and continue frequently thereafter.

26. Meikle, 'Meddlesome Princess', p. 133 and Barroll, *Anna of Denmark*, pp. 18–20.

27. *CSP Scotland*, xi, 100, 234, 237.

28. From James's *Basilikon Doron* in Sommerville, *Political Writings*, p. 42.

29. Bergeron, *Royal Family*, p. 52.

30. *CSP Scotland*, xiii, part i, 133, 264.

31. Meikle, 'Meddlesome Princess', p. 140; Barroll, *Anna of Denmark*, p. 24.

32. *CSP Scotland*, x, 722.

33. *CSP Scotland*, x, 755.

34. *CSP Scotland*, xiii, part ii, 721.

35. *CSP Scotland*, xiii, part ii, 1092.

36. Ethel Carleton Williams, writing more than thirty years ago, gave more attention to Anna's histrionics in this episode than more recent accounts do. See her *Anne of Denmark*, pp. 61–5. Compare Barroll, *Anna of Denmark*, pp. 25–7. *CSP Scotland*, xiii, part ii, 1095–6, 1110; William Arbuckle, 'The "Gowrie Conspiracy" – Part II', *Scottish Historical Review* 36 (October 1957), 96–7; Alexandre Teulet (ed.), *Relations Politiques de la France et de L'Espagne avec L'Ecosse au XVI Siècle*, 5 vols (Paris, 1862), iv, 234–5.

37. Barroll, *Anna of Denmark*, p. 23.

38. *CSP Scotland*, xi, 237.

39. *CSP Scotland*, xi, 662–3.

40. *CSP Scotland*, xi, 601.

41. *CSP Scotland*, xi, 626.

42. *CSP Scotland*, xi, pp. 627, 640, 651, 660, 662–3, 678, 679, 681–3; xii, pp. 6, 22, 28–9, 45, 50.

43. Bergeron, *Royal Family*, pp. 54–8, 61–2; Barroll, *Anna of Denmark*, pp. 28–34 and Meikle, 'A Meddlesome Princess', pp. 134–6; Allen B. Hinds *et al.* (eds), *Calendar of State Papers and Manuscripts Relating to English Affairs Existing in the Archives and Collections of Venice*, 38 vols (London, 1864–1940), x, 40.

44. Bergeron, *Royal Family*, pp. 82–3, 89–91.

45. On this topic see David M. Bergeron, *King James and Letters of Homoerotic Desire* (Iowa City, IA, 1999) and Young, *King James*, cited above.

46. John Nichols, *The Progresses, Processions, and Magnificent Festivities of King James the First*, 4 vols (London, 1828), iii, 80–1; Roger Lockyer, *Buckingham: The Life and Political Career of George Villiers, First Duke of Buckingham 1592–1628* (London, 1981), pp. 19–20.

47. This is the central thesis of Leeds Barroll's *Anna of Denmark*. For her adjustment to the changed circumstances in England, see especially pp. 34–5.

48. The definitive study of this subject is W.B. Patterson, *King James VI and I and the Reunion of Christendom* (Cambridge, 1997).

49. There is a multitude of evidence for this cultural war in the tracts and literary works of the period which I discuss in chapters 4 and 5 of *King James*.

50. A work published in 1618 entitled *The Peace-Maker* was endorsed by James and was so similar to his own views about manliness that it has sometimes been wrongly attributed to him. Young, *King James*, p. 86.

51. Raumer, *History*, ii, 206–7.

52. Barroll, *Anna of Denmark*, ch. 3.

53. Young, *King James*, pp. 67–8, 81–4.

54. Barbara Kiefer Lewalski, 'Enacting Opposition: Queen Anna and the Subversions of Masquing', in Lewalski, *Writing Women in Jacobean England* (Cambridge, MA, 1993), pp. 15–43 and 'Anna of Denmark and the Subversions of Masquing', *Criticism* 35 (Summer 1993), pp. 341–55. See also Stephen Orgel, *The Illusion of Power: Political Theatre in the English Renaissance* (Berkeley, CA, 1975), pp. 60–1, 'Jonson and the Amazons', in Elizabeth D. Harvey and Katharine Eisaman Maus (eds), *Soliciting Interpretation: Literary Theory and Seventeenth-Century English Poetry* (Chicago, IL, 1990), pp. 119–39, and 'Marginal Jonson', in David Bevington and Peter Holbrook (eds), *The Politics of the Stuart Court Masque* (Cambridge, 1998), pp. 144–75; Simon Shepherd, *Amazons and Warrior Women: Varieties of Feminism in Seventeenth-Century Drama* (New York, 1981), p. 138; Barroll, *Anna of Denmark*, ch. 4 and 'The Court of the First Stuart Queen', pp. 191–208; and Marion Wynne-Davies, 'The Queen's Masque: Renaissance Women and the Seventeenth-Century Court Masque', in S.P. Cerasno and Marion Wynne-Davies (eds), *Gloriana's Face: Women, Public and Private, in the English Renaissance* (New York, 1992), pp. 79–104.

55. Young, *King James*, pp. 87–9.

56. *CSP Venetian*, xi, 10.

57. Raumer, *History*, ii, 206.

58. Shakespeare's *Henry V* was entered in the Stationers' Register in 1600. The poet Michael Drayton published the 'Ballad of Agincourt', commemorating Henry V's most famous victory, in 1606 and 1619. Richard F. Hardin, *Michael Drayton and the Passing of Elizabethan England* (Lawrence, KS, 1973), pp. 6–7. Malcolm Smuts makes the interesting observation that Prince Henry 'patronized Drayton's epic on the reign of Henry V' – Smuts, 'Cultural Diversity and Cultural Change at the Court of James I', in Peck, *Mental World*, p. 110.

59. Roy Strong, *Henry, Prince of Wales and England's Lost Renaissance* (London, 1986). For Henry's fervent militarism, see pp. 57–72. See also Bergeron, *Royal*

Family, pp. 92–107; Bergeron, *Shakespeare's Romances and the Royal Family* (Lawrence, KS, 1985), pp. 51–9; Shepherd, *Amazons and Warrior Women*, pp. 120–4; and William Hunt, 'Spectral Origins of the English Revolution: Legitimation Crisis in Early Stuart England', in Geoff Eley and William Hunt (eds), *Reviving the English Revolution: Reflections and Elaborations on the Work of Christopher Hill* (London, 1988), pp. 305–32.

60. Orgel, *Illusion of Power*, pp. 66–70.

61. Strong, *Henry, Prince of Wales*, pp. 12, 221.

62. Raumer, *History*, ii, 210.

63. *CSP Venetian*, x, 513–14.

64. Raumer, *History*, ii, 209.

65. *CSP Venetian*, xv, 420.

66. Lyndal Roper, *Oedipus and the Devil: Witchcraft, Sexuality and Religion in Early Modern Europe* (London, 1994). See especially the introduction and chapter 5. Compare Anthony Fletcher, *Gender, Sex and Subordination in England 1500–1800* (New Haven, CT, 1995).

Chapter Eight   Privileges of the soul, pains of the body: Teresa de Jesús, the mystic *beatas* and the Spanish Inquisition after Trent

1. The references to the Inquisitorial investigations are taken from documents belonging to the Archivo de Historia Nacional in Madrid, sub-section on the *Inquisición Española*. The translations are mine.

2. Archivo de Historia Nacional: *Inquisición*, leg. 578, 370.

3. A. Hamilton, *Heresy and Mysticism in Sixteenth-Century Spain: The Alumbrados* (Cambridge, 1992), p. 116.

4. The progressive devaluation of this term in late sixteenth-century Spain, and its use by the Inquisitors has been studied not only by Alastair Hamilton, but also (among several others) by Melquíades Andrés in his article 'El Carácter no Místico de los Alumbrados de Toledo', included in Ángel Alcalá, *Inquisición Española y Mentalidad Inquisitorial* (Madrid, 1984), pp. 420–4; and previously, and at length, by Marcel Bataillon in his *Erasmo y España* (Ciudad de México, 1966).

5. See, for instance, the comprehensive study by Mary Elizabeth Perry, *Gender and Disorder in Early Modern Seville* (New Brunswick, NJ, 1991), pp. 97–8, 111–13.

NOTES

6. H. Kamen *The Spanish Inquisition, an Historical Revision* (London, 1997), pp. 83–102; Alcalá, pp. 426–30.

7. On the work of Jiménez de Cisneros as a humanist and Inquisitor, see the excellent study by Basil Hall in his book *Humanists and Protestants* (Edinburgh, 1990), pp. 9–43; on the change in the policies of the Holy Office after his death and under Fernando de Valdés, see the article by M.-Paz Aspe, 'El Cambio de Rumbo en la Espiritualidad Española a Mediados del siglo XVI', in Alcalá, pp. 424–33.

8. Ribadeneyra 1576, quoted in Alison Weber, *Teresa of Avila and the Rhetoric of Femininity* (Princeton, NJ, 1990), p. 159.

9. Teresa de Jesús, p. 183.

10. Teresa de Jesús, p. 143. There is a good English translation by J.M. Cohen, published in English by Penguin (London, 1957); but I was not completely satisfied with his rendering of the introduction, so I have translated Teresa's texts myself from Dámaso Chicharro (ed.), Teresa de Jesús, *Libro de la Vida* (Madrid, 1997).

11. Teresa de Jesús, pp. 117–18.

12. Alison Weber, *Teresa of Avila and the Rhetoric of Femininity* (Princeton, NJ, 1990), pp. 54–63 has studied in detail the rhetoric of humility in the work of St Teresa. She sees Teresa's insistence on her own worthlessness as a textual strategy that aims to legitimate her mystical experience in the context of Counter-Reformation misogyny; while she proves her point in detail, I think that she does not take sufficient account of the fact that Teresa's main subjective conflict with institutional authority is located not only in the moment of her writing, but also, as I have tried to prove here, in the past, in the conflict between her visions and the attempt to control them on the part of the confessors.

13. Teresa de Jesús, p. 296.

14. Ibid., p. 349.

15. Ibid, pp. 392–3.

16. Archivo de Historia Nacional: *Inquisición*, leg. 2946.

17. Efren de la Madre de Dios and Otger Steggink (ed.), Teresa de Jesús, *Obras Completas* (Madrid, 1986), p. 764.

18. Ibid., pp. 732–4.

19. Ibid., p. 573.

20. In M. Criado de Val, p. 606.

201

Chapter Nine   *'Allarme to England!'*: Gender and militarism in early modern England

1.   Barnabe Rich, *Allarme to England* (London, 1578), sig. H.

2.   John Smythe, *Certain Discourses Military* (London, 1590) p. 119.

3.   Barnabe Rich, *Allarme to England*, sig. Ciii.

4.   Ibid., sig. H.

5.   Glynne Wickham, *The Medieval Theatre* (Cambridge, 1974), p. 155.

6.   For a discussion of the position of these theologians see Simon Barker, '*The Double-Armed Man*: Images of the Medieval in Early Modern Military Idealism', in John Simons (ed.), *From Medieval to Medievalism* (Basingstoke, 1992), pp. 101–21.

7.   Thomas Digges, *Four Paradoxes, or Politique Discourses concering Militarie Discipline* (London, 1604), p. 109.

8.   M.J.D. Cockle, *A Bibliography of English Military Books up to 1642 and of Contemporary Foreign Works* (London, 1900).

9.   See in particular Thomas Kyd, *The Spanish Tragedy* (*c.* 1585).

10.   Thomas Styward, *The Paithwaie to Martiall Discipline* (London, 1588): Geoffrey Gates, *The Defence of Militarie Profession* (London, 1591); Matthew Sutcliffe, *The Practice, Proceedings and Lawes of Armes* (London, 1593); James Achesome, *The Military Garden. Or Instructions For All Young Souldiers* (London, 1629); Richard Bernard, *The Bible-Battels Or The Sacred Art Military. For the Rightly Wageing of Warre According to Holy Writ* (London, 1629).

11.   Peter Whitehorne, *The Art of Warre, Written First in Italia by Niccolo Machiavelli and Set Forthe in English by Peter Whithorne* (Engl. trans. 1560) in Henry Curt (ed.), *Niccolo Machiavelli: 'The Arte of Warre' and 'The Prince'... Englished by P. Whitehorne* (London, 1905), p. 48.

12.   Perry Anderson, *Lineages of the Absolutist State* (London, 1974), p. 125. See also Lawrence Stone, *The Crisis of the Aristocracy, 1556–1641* (London, 1967), pp. 199–270.

13.   François de La Noue, *The Politicke and Militarie Discourses* (London, 1587), p. 124.

14.   Michel Foucault, 'The Subject and Power', in *Critical Inquiry* 8 (1982), pp. 777–95 (p. 779).

15.   Barnabe Rich, *Allarme to England*, sig. H.

16.   Thomas Smith, *The Arte of Gunnerie* (London, 1660), sigs Aii.r–v.

17. Luke Gernon, *A Discourse of Ireland* (London, 1620), p. 15.

18. Edmund Spenser, *A View of the Present State of Ireland* (written *c.* 1596, published 1633).

19. Keith Wrightson, *English Society, 1580–1680* (London, 1982), pp. 150–1.

20. Dekker and Greene's account is reprinted in A.V. Judges, *The Elizabethan Underworld* (London, 1930).

21. See Terry Jones, *Chaucer's Knight* (London, 1980).

22. William Shakespeare, *The Tragedy of Coriolanus* (*c.* 1608), II, iii, 112–30. References to Shakespeare's plays are to Stanley Wells and Gary Taylor (eds), *The Complete Oxford Shakespeare* (Oxford, 1987).

23. William Shakespeare, *The Tragedy of Richard the Third* (*c.* 1592), I, i, 1–13.

24. William Shakespeare, *The Life of Henry the Fifth* (1599), III, iii, 1–41.

25. William Shakespeare, *The Tragedy of Coriolanus*, I, iii, 15–18.

26. Thomas Dekker, *The Shoemaker's Holiday: A Pleasant Comedy of the Gentle Craft* (1599).

27. Francis Beaumont and John Fletcher, *The Knight of the Burning Pestle* (*c.* 1607), V, ii, 44–76.

Chapter Ten   The Guise women: Politics, war and peace

1. Cited by Antonia Fraser, *The Warrior Queens* (London and New York, 1988), p. 326.

2. Lisa Hopkins, *Women who Would be Kings: Female Rulers of the Sixteenth Century* (London and New York, 1991), p. 8.

3. John Taylor's *Memorial of all the English Monarchs* (1622/23), cited in David Cressy, *Bonfires and Bells: National Memory and the Protestant Calendar in Elizabethan and Stuart England* (Berkeley, CA, 1989), p. 133.

4. On the relationship of Louise of Savoy and Francis I, see chapter 5.

5. See Mavis Mate, 'Profit and Productivity on the estates of Isabella de Forz (1260–92)', *Economic History Review* (1980), 326–34; Jessica Munns and Penny Richards, 'Exploiting and Destabilizing Gender Roles: Anne d'Este', *French History* (2) (1992), pp. 206–15; R.J. Kalas, 'The Noble Widow's Place in the Patriarchal Household: The Life and Career of Jeanne de Gontault', *Sixteenth-Century Journal* (1993) 23 (3), pp. 519–39.

6. Kristen B. Neuschel, 'Noblewomen and War in Sixteenth-Century France', in Michael Wolfe (ed.), *Changing Identities in Early Modern France* (Durham, NC and London, 1997), pp. 124, 125. The term 'culture of violence' largely derives from Francis Barker's now classic work of power and its deployment in *The Culture of Violence* (Manchester, 1993). On images of women and war see Ian Maclean, *Woman Triumphant: Feminism in French Literature* (Oxford: 1977), especially chapter VIII; see also J.R. Hale, 'Women and War in the Visual Arts of the Renaissance', in J.R. Mulryne and M. Shewring (eds), *War, Literature and Arts in Sixteenth-Century Europe* (London, 1988), pp. 190–6.

7. Affinity has been defined by Stuart Carroll as 'a motif of concentric circles which denote differing types of bond and strengths of relationship'. Stuart Carroll, *Noble Power During the French Wars of Religion. The Guise Affinity and the Catholic Cause in Normandy* (Cambridge, 1998), p. 7; see also Mark Greengrass's classic essay, 'Noble Affinities in Early Modern France: the Case of Henry I de Montmorency, Constable of France', *European History Quarterly* 16 (3) (1986), pp. 275–312 (278).

8. R.J. Knecht, *The French Civil Wars*, p. xii. See also, R.J. Knecht, *The French Wars of Religion, 1559–1598* (London, 1989); M. Holt, *The French Wars of Religion, 1562–1629* (Cambridge, 1995) and, for a general overview of the sixteenth century, Janine Garrison, *A History of Sixteenth-Century France, 1483–1598*, translated by Richard Rex (London, 1995; Paris, 1991).

9. As cited by R.J. Knecht in *Catherine de' Medici* (London, 1998), p. 73.

10. See Éliane Viennot's biography, *Marguerite de Valois: Histoire d'une femme, histoire d'un mythe* (Paris, 1993; reprinted 1995), see especially chapter 3. The 'myth' can be experienced in Alexandre Dumas's romantic novel, *La Reine Margot* (Paris, 1845), recently made into a lavish film.

11. For example, see Nicola M. Sutherland, *The Massacre of St Bartholomew and the European Conflict 1559–1572* (London, 1973); Denis Crouzet, *Les Guerriers de Dieu: la violence au temps des troubles de religion*, 2 vols (Paris, 1990); B. Diefendorf, 'Prologue to a Massacre: Popular Unrest in Paris, 1557–72', *American Historical Review* 90 (5) (1985), pp.1067–91, and her book, *Beneath the Cross: Catholics and Huguenots in sixteenth-century Paris* (New York and Oxford, 1991); see also R.M. Kingdom, *Myths about St Bartholomew's Day Massacres, 1572–76* (Cambridge, MA., 1988).

12. Nicola M. Sutherland, 'Henry III, The Guise and the Huguenots', in Keith Cameron (ed.), *From Valois to Bourbon, Dynasty, State and Society in Early Modern France* (Exeter, 1989), pp. 21–34 (23).

13. For discussions of the complicated politics of the various Catholic leagues, see R.J. Knecht, *The French Civil Wars*, pp. 218–27, and his biography, *Catherine de' Medici* (London, 1998), particularly, pp. 246–58; Mark Greengrass, *France in the Age of Henry IV* (London, 1984), pp. 39–52; Eliane Viennot, 'Des "Femmes d'Etat" aux XVIᵉ Siècle: Les princesses de la Ligue et l'écriture de l'histoire',

in Danielle Haase-Dubosc and Eliane Viennot (eds), *Femmes et Pouvoirs sous l'Ancien Régime* (Paris, 1991), pp. 77–97 (78). See also J.M. Constant, *Les Guises* (Paris, 1984), chapter 5, as well as *La Ligue* (Paris, 1996).

14. See for instance, R.J. Knecht, *Catherine de' Medici*, pp. 266–7.

15. David Buisseret, *Henry IV* (London, 1984); Mark Greengrass, *France in the Age of Henry IV: The Stuggle for Stability* (London, 1994). On Henry's negotiations (and threats) with the towns, see S. Annette Finley-Croswhite, *Henry IV and the Towns: The Pursuit of Legitimacy in French Urban Society, 1589–1610* (Cambridge, 1999).

16. On the family of Guise, their origins and initial rise to power, see J.M. Constant, *Les Guise*, especially chapter 2; Stuart Carroll, *Noble Power*.

17. G. de Pimodan, *La mère des Guises, Antoinette de Bourbon, 1494–1583* (Paris, 1925).

18. As Rosalind K. Marshall notes, 'in 1520 Claude . . . drew up a document appointing his wife to act as his representative in all his business, and a few months later he had their marriage contract altered, making over to her the castle and lands of Joinville', *Mary of Guise* (London, 1977), p. 26.

19. Stuart Carroll, *Noble Power*, p. 54.

20. For Mary of Guise's fascinating life, see Rosalind K. Marshall's *Mary of Guise*; see also the initial sections of Antonia Fraser's *Mary Queen of Scots* (London, 1969).

21. Marguerite Wood (ed.), *Foreign Correspondence with Marie de Lorraine, Queen of Scotland*, from the originals in the Balcarres Papers, 1547–48, Scottish History Society (Edinburgh, 1925), 3rd series, Letter v.

22. *Foreign Correspondence with Marie de Lorraine*, Letters clxi, lxv, viii, see also Letter lxxx.

23. Mark Greengrass, 'Mary, Dowager Queen of France,' in Michael Lynch (ed.), *Mary Stewart, Queen in Three Kingdoms* (Oxford, 1988), pp. 171–94.

24. Carroll, *Noble Power*, p. 188.

25. See John Bossy, *Under the Molehill: An Elizabethan Spy Story* (New Haven, CT and London, 2001), pp. 188–90; on Henri de Guise's interest in aiding Mary Stuart, see also Carroll, *Noble Power*, pp. 188–9.

26. Carroll, *Noble Power*, p. 150.

27. Ibid., p. 188.

28. *Foreign Correspondence with Marie de Lorraine*, Letter vii.

29. Musée Condé, Chantilly, Série A, Carton 14.

30. Carroll, *Noble Power*, p. 245.

31. G. de Pimodan, *La mère des Guises, Antoinette de Bourbon, 1495–1583* (Paris, 1925), p. 198. See Jessica Munns and Penny Richards, 'Exploiting and Destabilizing Gender Roles', pp. 210–11.

32. For a description of the progress, see Victor E. Graham and W. McAllister Johnson, *The Royal Tour of France of Charles IX and Catherine de' Medici: Festivals and Entries 1564–6* (Toronto, 1979); Jean Boutier, Alain Dewerpe and Daniel Nordman, *Un tour de France royal. Le voyage de Charles IX (1564–1566)* (Paris, 1984).

33. E. Viennot, *Marguerite de Valois*, p. 39.

34. Nicola M. Sutherland, *The Huguenot Struggle*, p. 209; E. Viennot, *Marguerite de Valois*, p. 51. Maurevert, as Carroll has clearly demonstrated, was a Guise servant – *Noble Power*, p. 135.

35. See, for instance, the copious correspondence of Catherine de' Medici.

36. Richard Cooper, 'The Blois Assassinations: Sources in the Vatican', in Keith Cameron (ed.), *From Valois to Bourbon: Dynasty, State, and Society in Early Modern France* (Exeter, 1989), pp. 51–72 (60, 68).

37. Jean-Louis Flandrin (ed.), Pierre de L'Estoile, *Journal d'un Bourgeois de Paris sous Henri III* (Paris, 1966), p. 273.

38. *Le martire des deux freres* (1589), BL 1193.h.27 (1); see also L. Lalanne (ed.), *Oeuvres Complètes de Pierre de Bourdeille, Seigneur de Brantôme, publiées d'après les manuscripts . . .* , (Paris: 1864–82) iv, pp. 186–7.

39. *Remonstrance faicte au Roy par Madame de Nemours, sur la masscre de ses enfants*, BL 1193.h.9 (14) 1588. On the possibility that this is based on a letter from Madame de Nemours to the king, see Richard Cooper, 'The Aftermath of the Blois Assassinations of 1588: Documents in the Vatican', in *French History* 3 (4) (1989), pp. 404–26 (409).

40. *Les Pleurs et soupirs de Madame de Guyse* (1588), BL 1192.e.92.

41. Richard Cooper, 'The Aftermath of the Blois Assassinations of 1588: Documents in the Vatican,' pp. 404–26, 410–13, 422–6.

42. See Barbara B. Diefendorf, 'An Age of Gold?', pp. 171–3.

43. *The Paris of Henry of Navarre as seen by Pierre de L'Estoile*, translated and edited by Nancy Lyman Roelker (Cambridge, MA, 1958), p. 183.

44. Etienne Pasquier, *Écrits Politiques*, edited by D. Thickett (Geneva and Paris, 1966), p. 221. On Pasquier's attitude see also Eliane Viennot, 'Des "Femmes d'Etat" aux XVIIᵉ Siècle: Les Princesses de la Ligue et l'écriture de l'histoire', in *Femmes et Pouvoirs sous L'Ancien Régime* (Paris,1991), pp. 77–97 (90–1).

45. Pierre de L'Estoile, *The Paris of Henry of Navarre*, 183. For further discussion of this event, see Viennot, 'Femmes d'Etat', pp. 82–3; *Marguerite de Valois*, pp. 178–9, 303; Diefendorf, 'An Age of Gold?', p. 172.

46. See Neuschel, 'Noble Women and War in Sixteenth-Century France, in *Changing Identities in Early Modern France*, pp. 124–44; and Diefendorf, 'An Age of Gold?', in the same collection, pp.169–90 (176–83). See also E. Viennot, 'Des "Femmes d'Etat" aux XVIIe Siècle: Les Princesses de la Ligue et l'écriture de l'histoire', pp. 77–97.

47. Claudine Allag, *Chrétienne d'Aguerre, comtesse de Sault* (Paris, 1995).

48. Indeed, Allag suggests they may have worked in concert with each other to effect a peaceful diplomatic solution – *Chrétienne d'Aguerre*, pp. 132–4.

49. Ibid., pp. 133–4, 156.

50. Jean-François Dubost, *La France italienne XVIe-XVIIe* (Paris, 1997), p. 443.

51. L. Lalanne (ed.), Pierre de Bourdeille, Seigneur de Brantôme, *Oeuvres Complètes* (Paris, 1874–78), ix, pp. 360–2.

Works on late medieval and early modern Europe (General)

Christopher Allmand (ed.), *War, Government and Power in Late Medieval France* (Liverpool, 2000).

Alison Brown, *The Renaissance*, 2nd edition (London, 2001).

James A. Brundage, *Law, Sex, and Christian Society in Medieval Europe* (Chicago, IL, 1987).

Stella Fletcher (ed.), *The Longman Companion to Renaissance Europe* (London, forthcoming).

Barbara B. Diefendorf and Carla Hesse (eds), *Culture and Identity in Early Modern Europe* (Ann Arbor, MI, 1993).

Martha Howell, 'Citizenship and Gender: women's political status in northern medieval cities', in M. Erler and M. Kowaleski (eds), *Women and Power in the Middle Ages* (Athens, GA and London, 1988), pp. 37–60.

Olwen Hufton, *The Prospect before Her: A History of Women in Western Europe*, 2 vols (New York, 1995).

Lisa Jardine, *Worldly Goods* (London, 1996).

John Carmi Parsons (ed.), *Medieval Queenship* (New York, 1993).

Myriam Carlier and Tim Soens (eds), *The Household in Late Medieval Cities. Italy and Northwestern Europe Compared* (Leuven–Apeldoorn, 2001).

William G. Naphy and Penny Roberts (eds), *Fear in Early Modern Society* (Manchester, 1997).

Simon Schama, *The Embarrassment of Riches: an interpretation of Dutch culture in the golden age* (New York, 1987).

The Renaissance court

J. Adamson (ed.), *The Princely Courts of Europe, 1500–1750. Ritual, Politics and Culture under the Ancien Régime* (London, 1999).

Yvonne Bellenger (ed.), *Le Mécénat et l'influence des Guises* (Paris, 1997).

Norbert Elias, *The Court Society*, trans. Edmund Jephcott (Oxford, 1969).

J.H. Elliot and L.W.B. Brocliss (eds), *The World of the Favourite* (New Haven, CT, 1999).

R.J. Knecht, *The Rise and Fall of Renaissance France, 1483–1610*, 2nd edition (Oxford, 2001).

David Mateer (ed.), *Courts, Patrons and Poets* (New Haven, CT and London, 2000).

Walter Prevenier, Thérèse de Hemptinne, Marc Boone *et al.*, *Le prince et le peuple. Images de la société du temps des ducs de Bourgogne, 1384–1530* (Anvers, 1998).

David Starkey, *The English court: from the Wars of the Roses to the Civil War* (London and New York, 1987).

R. Mulryne and E. Goldring (eds), *Court Festivals of the European Renaissance: Art, Politics, and Performance* (Aldershot, 2002).

Gender issues

Mary Erler and Maryanne Kowaleski (eds), *Women and Power in the Middle Ages* (Athens, GA, 1988).

Howard Bloch, *Medieval Misogyny and the Invention of Western Romantic Love* (Chicago, IL, 1991).

Marc Boone, 'State power and illicit sexuality: the persecution of sodomy in late medieval Bruges', *Journal of Medieval History* 22 (1996), pp. 135–53.

Kathleen Wilson-Chevalier and Éliane Viennot (eds), *La Royaume de féyminie: pouvoirs, contraintes, espaces de liberté des femmes de la Renaissance à la Fronde* (Paris, 1999).

Walter Prevenier, 'Violence against Women in Fifteenth-Century France and the Burgundian State', in Barbara A. Hanawalt and David Wallace (eds), *Medieval Crime and Social Control* (Minneapolis, MN and London, 1999), pp. 186–203.

Frances E. Dolan, *Whores of Babylon: Catholicism, Gender, and Seventeenth-Century Print Culture* (Ithaca, NY and London, 1999).

Thelma S. Fenster and Clare A. Lees (eds), *Gender in Debate From the Early Middle Ages to the Renaissance* (New York, forthcoming).

Joanne M. Ferraro, *Marriage Wars in Late Renaissance Venice* (Oxford, 2001).

Anthony Fletcher, *Gender, Sex, and Subordination in England, 1500–1800* (New Haven, CT, 1995).

David Herlihy, *Opera muliebria: Women and Work in Medieval Europe* (New York, 1990).

Louis Adrain Montrose, '"Shaping Fantasies": Figurations of Gender and Power in Elizabethan Culture', in Stephen Greenblatt (ed.), *Representing the English Renaissance* (Berkeley, CA, 1988), pp. 31–64.

James G. Turner (ed.), *Sexuality and Gender in Early Modern Europe: Institutions, Texts, Images* (Cambridge, 1993).

Micro-histories

John Bossy, *Giordano Bruno and the Embassy Affair* (New Haven, CT and London, 1991).

John Bossy, *Under the Molehill: An Elizabethan Spy Story* (New Haven, CT and London, 2001).

Judith C. Brown, *Immodest Acts: The Life of a Lesbian Nun in Renaissance Italy* (New York and Oxford, 1986).

Steven Ozment, *Magdalena and Balthasar: An Intimate Portrait of Life in Sixteenth-Century Europe Revealed in the Letters of the Nuremberg Husband and Wife* (New Haven, CT, 1989).

Gene Brucker, *Giovanni and Lusanna: Love and Marriage in Renaissance Florence* (Berkeley, CA, 1986).

Natalie Zemon Davis, *The Return of Martin Guerre* (Cambridge, MA, 1983).

Natalie Zemon Davis, *Women on the Margins: Three Seventeenth-Century Lives* (Cambridge, MA, 1995).

Literature and society

Curtis C. Breight, *Surveillance, Militarism and Drama in the Elizabethan Era* (Basingstoke, 1996).

Kate Chedgzoy, *et al.* (eds), *Voicing Women: Gender and Sexuality in Early Modern Writing* (Keele, 1996).

Richard Courtney, *Shakespeare's World of War* (Quebec, 1994).

Susan Frye and Karen Robertson (eds), *Maids and Mistresses, Cousins and Queens: Women's Alliances in Early Modern England* (New York and Oxford, 1999).

Patricia Fumerton and Simon Hunt (eds), *Renaissance Culture and the Everyday*, (Philadelphia, PA, 1999).

Constance Jordan, *Renaissance Feminism: Literary Texts and Political Models* (Ithaca, 1990).

David Lee Miller, Sharon O'Dair and Harold Weber (eds), *The Production of English Renaissance Culture* (Ithaca, NY, 1999).

Alan Shepard, *Marlowe's Soldiers: Rhetorics of Masculinity in the Age of the Armada* (Aldershot, 2002).

Nina Taunton, *1590s Drama and Militarism: Portrayals of War in Marlowe, Chapman and Shakespeare's* Henry V (Aldershot, 2001).

Bruce R. Smith, *Shakespeare and Masculinity* (Oxford, 2000).

Websites

Renaissance Women Online http://www.wwp.brown.edu/texts/roentry.html

[New] Historians of Early Modern France: Research in Progress http://www.emory.edu/HISTORY/BEIK/expltext.html

The Voice of the Shuttle http://vos.ucsb.edu/

INDEX

Michelet, Jules (*continued*)
 prejudices 73, 88–9
 on women 89
Midsummer Night's Dream, A 18
Milan, duchy of 81, 84, 85
militarism
 and absolutist government 147–8, 151
 Allarme to England 143–5, 149
 Amazons 145
 The Art of Gunnerie 150
 benefits of war 147
 A Bibliography of English Military Books up to 1642 146
 bombing of civilians 141
 Certain Discourses Military 144 (n2)
 Christian theology and 143–4, 146
 civil life *vs.* 156–8
 civil unrest and 147, 148, 151
 civil wars 170
 collective resistance to 152
 demilitarisation 143, 144–5, 147, 148
 A Discourse of Ireland 151
 The Double-armed Man 150–1
 early modern England 142–6, 148–58
 emasculation 143, 144–5, 153–4
 Europe 146, 147–8
 foreign policy 148–9
 Four Paradoxes 146
 gender and warfare 141, 149, 151
 gender identity 143, 145
 gendered subjectivity 140
 historical discourse 141, 142
 ideal soldier 141, 143, 147, 149, 150–1
 ideological debate 142–7
 individuality 140
 Low Countries 142
 martial law 143
 masculinity 154–6
 phoney soldiers 152, 153
 Politicke and Militarie Discourses 148
 practical issues 146–7
 recruitment 149, 152
 sexual orientation 140, 141
 Spain 146
 theatrical representations 142–3, 146, 152–8
 trade and colonialism 149, 151
 twentieth century 141
 women 140, 141, 159, 160–1, 165, 169–70
 writing, military 143–51
 writing, non-military 152
misogyny 28, 43–4, 53, 112
monarchy 96, 105, 107

Montmorency, Anne de, Grand Master 83–5, 88, 89
Montpensier, Catherine, duchesse de 168
More, Sir Thomas 146
More, Treaty of the 77
Mulcaster, Richard 90, 91
mysticism 124
 see also alumbrados; beatas; Teresa de Jesús

names *see* Martinengo of Brescia; onomastics
Navarre 85
 see also Albret, Henri d', King of Navarre; Collège de Navarre; Henry IV
Neade, William 150
Neale, J.E. 100
Nemours, Anne d'Este, Madame de
 arrest of 167
 and assassination of Coligny 166
 after assassination of François 165–6
 after assassination of sons 166–7
 beauty 165, 169
 Catholic League and 167–8
 daughter 168
 and Henry III 167, 168
 and Henry IV 169
 marriage to duc de Nemours 166
 marriage to François, duc de Guise 164, 165
 roles 165
Nemours, Jacques de Savoie, duc de 166
Neuschel, Kristen B. 161
Norfolk, duke of 84, 102
Norton, Thomas 103, 107
Notestein, Wallace 100

onomastics 3, 55, 59, 70
Orgel, Stephen 16
Orléans, duc d' 88
orphans 23, 25, 26, 37–8
outbreading 37

Paget, Sir William 88
Pardoner
 Canterbury Tales 46, 47, 53
 disorderliness 46–7
 Foure PP 40, 44–8, 51, 53, 54
 gender performance 41
 Tale of Beryn 40, 41–2, 46, 47, 53
Parker, Matthew, Archbishop of Canterbury 91
Parlement of Paris 76, 80, 81, 86, 167